# AMERICA'S GAME IN THE WILD-CARD ERA

# AMERICA'S GAME IN THE WILD-CARD ERA

# AMERICA'S GAME IN THE WILD-CARD ERA

## From Strike to Pandemic

## Bryan Soderholm-Difatte

ROWMAN & LITTLEFIELD
Lanham • Boulder • New York • London

Published by Rowman & Littlefield
An imprint of The Rowman & Littlefield Publishing Group, Inc.
4501 Forbes Boulevard, Suite 200, Lanham, Maryland 20706
www.rowman.com

6 Tinworth Street, London SE11 5AL, United Kingdom

British Library Cataloguing in Publication Information Available

**Library of Congress Cataloging-in-Publication Data**

Names: Soderholm-Difatte, Bryan, author.
Title: America's game in the wild-card era : from strike to pandemic / Bryan Soderholm-Difatte.
Description: Lanham : Rowman & Littlefield Publishing Group, 2021. | Includes bibliographical
    references and index. | Summary: "This book examines the competitive landscape of Major
    League Baseball during the wild-card era, including the major storylines for all 30 teams,
    division races, and the state of dynasties in a new age of baseball"—Provided by publisher.
Identifiers: LCCN 2020043419 (print) | LCCN 2020043420 (ebook) | ISBN 9781538145937 (Cloth :
    acid-free paper) | ISBN 9781538145944 (ePub)
Subjects: LCSH: Baseball—United States—History—20th century. | Baseball—United States—His-
    tory—21st century. | Baseball teams—United States—History—20th century. | Baseball teams—
    United States—History—21st century. | Baseball players—Miscellanea. | Major League Base-
    ball (Organization)—History. | Baseball—History—20th century. | Baseball—History—21st
    century.
Classification: LCC GV863.A1 S6876 2021 (print) | LCC GV863.A1 (ebook) | DDC 796.357/
    640973—dc23
LC record available at https://lccn.loc.gov/2020043419
LC ebook record available at https://lccn.loc.gov/2020043420

To Alexandra. Thanks for being you.

# CONTENTS

## IV: PARADIGM SHIFTS                                                         191

# AUTHOR'S NOTE

The 25 years since the end of the 1994–1995 players' strike have been arguably the most dynamic quarter-century in baseball history. Major League Baseball introduced wild-card teams to the postseason and interleague games to the regular season. Bud Selig's consolidation of power, including bringing the administrative functions of both leagues under his office, made him the game's most powerful commissioner since the 1921–1944 reign of Judge Kenesaw Mountain Landis, baseball's first commissioner. The influx of Latin and Asian players changed the shape of baseball's demographics. There was a boom in new stadiums. An analytics revolution reshaped how rosters are constructed, the relationship between managers and the front office, defensive alignments and offensive strategies, how pitching staffs are put together and used, and how players and managers prepare for games. The rise of the power game between pitchers and batters has led to unprecedented strikeout and home-run totals. Major League Baseball as an institution became more profitable than ever. The same is true for the financial value of its franchises.

But there has also been an undercurrent of edginess. The assaults on baseball's hallowed home-run records by Mark McGwire, Sammy Sosa, Barry Bonds, and Alex Rodriguez have been sullied by baseball's repeated steroids scandals. Baseball has had to grapple with significant disparities affecting the competitiveness of small-market clubs relative to much-better-capitalized large-market teams. There has been controversy about competitive integrity because of teams deliberately deciding *not to compete* in their divisions for multiple years in order to build for the future. The owners' unfinished business of trying to rein in player payrolls has been a persistent source of friction with the players union, raising the prospect of another devastating players' strike in 2021 or 2022. The game has also had to grapple with a cheating scandal calling into question the legitimacy of the Houston Astros' 2017 World Series championship. And out of nowhere, just as the 2020 season was about to begin, came a global pandemic that shut down the game for the first time since the 1994–1995 strike before a rump 60-game schedule finally got under way in the late-July dog days of summer.

Together with *The Reshaping of America's Game: Major League Baseball since the Players' Strike*, this book covers the years from baseball's return from the strike to the pandemic. Its focus is on the competitive environment of baseball's new wild-card era. The two books together complete a history of major league baseball that began with *America's Game: A History of Major League Baseball through World War II* (2018), followed up by *Tumultuous Times in America's Game: From Jackie Robinson's Breakthrough to the War over Free Agency* (2019).

# INTRODUCTION

## Back to Baseball: The Wild-Card Paradigm Shift

On April 25, 1995, the Florida Marlins took the field in Miami to take on the Los Angeles Dodgers, officially ending the players' strike that began on August 12 the previous year over Acting Commissioner Bud Selig and the major league owners' hard line in refusing to compromise on demanding that the players agree to a salary cap in the next labor agreement between the league and the players' union. The strike had already cost Major League Baseball the entire 1994 postseason. There was no World Series. Major League Baseball was back in business thanks to a ruling less than four weeks earlier by federal judge Sonia Sotomayor that the owners could not unilaterally impose a salary cap to rein in free agency in the absence of a negotiated new collective bargaining agreement. Her ruling did not itself end the strike, but the owners understood their continuing hard line to limit players' earning potential in free agency would lose in the courts.

Baseball's fans cursed both sides' houses. Players were booed their first games back. So was Selig. Attendance was slow to recover, and in fact would not that year or the next. But Cal Ripken Jr. breaking Lou Gehrig's iconic record for consecutive games played on September 5, 1995, was a grace note that touched on how baseball is sewn into the fabric of America's soul.

Nothing, however, compares with the drama and excitement of a taut pennant race and tense games with everything on the line. And that was what the Seattle Mariners gave baseball in September and October 1995. They overtook the California Angels after trailing them by 12½ games with just 38 left on the schedule to win the AL West in a one-game playoff to decide the division. Then came their compelling takedown of the New York Yankees in their division series—the first year of the prequel to the league championship series occasioned by baseball's 1994 realignment to three divisions and a wild-card team in each league.

The Mariners were on life support in Seattle. One of the American League's 1977 expansion teams, the Mariners had had just two winning seasons in their first 18 years. With a history of front-office mismanagement, including an unwillingness to invest in player development or established players to build and sustain a competitive ballclub, the Mariners had few star players to entice their fan base. And they played in a multi-purpose domed stadium—the Kingdome, built in 1976—that was not aging well; in 1994, falling tiles from the dome forced the Mariners to play what proved to be all of their final 20 games on the road before the strike prematurely ended the season. Playing the familiar build-it-or-we-will-leave card practiced by professional sports teams angling for new stadiums—and given the reluctance of local voters to approve funding for a new ballpark—the Mariners seemed certain to leave Seattle in the near future.

But these were no longer Seattle's same old Mariners. They now had a fiery manager focused on winning in Lou Piniella, whose credentials included playing in four World Series with the Yankees and sweeping Oakland's powerhouse Athletics in the 1990 World Series in his first year managing the Cincinnati Reds. They had one of baseball's most appealing young stars in center fielder Ken Griffey Jr.—"The Kid"—whom the Mariners signed to a four-year $24 million contract in December 1992 as a 23-year-old after just four years in the major leagues, giving him "free-agent money" two years before he could have entered the market. Griffey more than proved his worth by hitting 90 homers and driving in 199 runs in the first two years of his new deal, during the second of which he was deprived of 50 games because of the strike. They had one of baseball's premier hitters in Edgar Martinez, their designated hitter, who won a batting title in 1992. And the Mariners had the "Big Unit"—hard-throwing, fiercely competitive, and menacingly lean and intimidating 6-foot-10 southpaw Randy Johnson, 19–8 in 1993 and 13–6 in 1994 with 512 strikeouts in 427⅓ innings since mastering early-career control difficulties where he walked nearly six batters per nine innings his first four years in Seattle.

Griffey missed three months after breaking his wrist in May crashing into the outfield wall while making a typically terrific Ken Griffey Jr. catch. For the year, Griffey hit only .258 with 17 homers and 42 runs batted in but was scorching hot—4 homers, 12 RBIs, and a .448 batting average—during the Mariners' seven-game winning streak in September that took them from two back of the Angels to three games in front. Martinez, batting fourth behind Griffey, hit .393 with 2 homers and 7 RBIs those seven games on his way to a league-leading .356 batting average. The Angels, after losing 15½ games in the standings over the Mariners in 32 games—they were 7–25 while Seattle went 23–10—since their 12½-game lead on August 20 won all five remaining games, while the Mariners lost three, to force a 163rd-game playoff for the division crown. Johnson threw a three-hit complete game for the win to finish the season 18-2. He led the majors in strikeouts for the fourth straight year and became the first qualifying pitcher in history to average more than 12 K's per nine innings.

The wild-West-winning Mariners had to fly overnight from Seattle to New York for the start of their division series the very next day against the wild-card Yankees—seven games behind Boston in the AL East but with the third-best record in the American League, including better than Seattle. The Mariners were disadvantaged in the new postseason format, in which the first two games of five-game division series were played at the home of the club that made the postseason as the best *second-place* team. Seattle lost the first game at Yankee Stadium, 9–6, despite two home runs by Griffey. The second game was a postseason classic. Paul O'Neill homered for the Yankees in the 7th to tie the score at 4–4. The Kid homered in the 12th to give the Mariners a 5–4 lead. The Yankees tied it in their half of the 12th. The teams played into the 15th inning before a walk and a home run by Jim Leyritz, the Yankees' backup catcher in the starting lineup this night, ended the game. The Mariners were in a "can't lose any of them" situation when the series moved cross-country to the Kingdome for the remaining games.

Johnson, pitching on three days' rest instead of his typical four, threw seven strong innings to lead Seattle to victory in Game Three. Jumping off to a quick 5–0 lead in the third inning in Game Four, it looked like the Yankees were finally on their way to the American League Championship Series for the first time since 1981. But the Mariners scored four in their half of the third, three of them on an Edgar Martinez home run; tied the game in the fifth; and took a 6–5 lead in the sixth on Griffey's fourth homer of the series. After the Yankees tied the game in the eighth, Seattle scored five times in their half of the inning—the first four on a grand-slam by the seemingly-impossible-to-get-out Martinez—and then with-stood two more Yankees runs to win the game, 11–8, evening the series for a decisive fifth game. Martinez was batting .600 in the series.

The fifth game was as dramatic and exciting as any deciding game can be. It not only validated the new postseason three-rounds format as a good idea; it is said to have saved baseball in Seattle and the Pacific Northwest. The Mariners trailed 4–2 when they came to bat in the eighth, down to their last six outs. Yankees ace David Cone was still on the mound, having already thrown 118 pitches. He got the first out, gave up another home run—the fifth in the series—to Griffey, got a second out, then gave up a walk, a single, and another walk to load the bases. Cone had now thrown 141 pitches, 23 in this inning. Rather than bring in rookie reliever Mariano Rivera, still at the "who's he?" beginning of his career, Yankees manager Buck Showalter stayed with dead-tired Cone. Six pitches later, Cone walked his final batter. Jogging home from third to score the tying run was another rookie, 19-year-old Alex Rodriguez, the very first pick in baseball's 1993 amateur draft, who was in the game as a pinch-runner. Rivera got the last out of the eighth on a three-pitch strike-out. The game now tied, Rodriguez stayed in to play shortstop. Sitting on the Yankees' bench, but not on the postseason roster, was another young shortstop of the future, name of Jeter, Derek Jeter.

The drama was just beginning. After the Yankees put runners on sec-ond and third with nobody out in the ninth and three of their best hitters up next, Piniella brought in his own tired ace, Randy Johnson, just two days after he had thrown 117 pitches to win Game Three. He struck out Wade Boggs and retired Bernie Williams and Paul O'Neill on popups. None of them could drive home the go-ahead run from third. Then it was Jack McDowell's turn to play the Randy Johnson role. The Big Unit's opponent in Game Three, McDowell also had just a day of rest when he was called upon in the bottom of the ninth to relieve Rivera with the would-be winning run on second with one out. McDowell got Edgar Martinez to whiff and Alex Rodriguez to ground out. Into extra innings.

Johnson struck out the side in the Yankees' 10th. McDowell navigated around two Mariners singles in the bottom of the inning. The Yankees finally got to the dog-tired Big Unit in the 11th, scoring the go-ahead run on a walk, a sacrifice bunt, and a single. Instead of calling on closer John Wetteland, Showalter allowed McDowell, who pitched 5⅓ innings just two days before, to take the mound for the final three outs. Showalter had his reasons. Wetteland had been awful in the three games he pitched in the series. He had faced 24 Seattle batters, of whom 11 got on base. He gave up seven runs in 4⅓ innings, including Martinez's grand-slam that won Game Four the previous day. Mariners second baseman Joey Cora caught the Yankees' defense flat-footed with a drag-bunt single past the tired McDowell. He advanced to third on a single by Griffey. Edgar Martinez then ripped a one-strike pitch down the left field line, scoring Cora with the tying run. Griffey, never hesitating, raced around third base. Deafening pandemonium enveloped the Kingdome as Griffey slid home ahead of the throw with the winning run.

Martinez batted .571 and drove in 10 runs in the series. Griffey batted .391 with 9 runs and 7 RBIs to go with his 5 home runs. Right fielder Jay Buhner battered Yankees pitching for a .458 batting average, and first baseman Tino Martinez, about to become a Yankee himself, hit .409. Randy Johnson established a reputation for being a reliable go-to winning pitcher whenever he might be called upon in critical postseason games, including in relief, no matter how few days he might have had since his last start. This was a role he would repeat in the World Series six years later, once again at the expense of the New York Yankees.

It didn't matter that the Seattle Mariners lost the ALCS and the American League pennant to the Cleveland Indians in the next round of the postseason. King County voters may have rejected their tax dollars being used to fund a new stadium for Seattle baseball, but six days after the Mariners took down the Yankees in the Kingdome, a special session of the Washington State legislature authorized a funding package for a new stadium that King County executives approved a week later. The Seattle Mariners would not be sold and moved elsewhere. Their new ballpark opened in July 1999.

No less than Cal Ripken's streak seeming to bring a riven Baseball Nation together, Major League Baseball needed the Mariners' compelling narrative to facilitate the quickest possible recovery from the considerable

damage done by the 1994 strike. Very importantly, the drama and excitement of the Yankees-Mariners division series gave validation to baseball's new postseason format of two division series in each league preceding the American and National League Championship Series and the
World Series, the first year of which would have been 1994 but for the
strike.

The animating factor for the new format was the addition of two new
franchises in the National League's 1993 expansion, making for 14 teams
in each league. Both leagues were reorganized in 1994 into Eastern,
Central, and Western Divisions, and the wild card—the second-place
team with the best record—made for four teams in each league now
qualifying for the postseason. It meant, however, that a team that did not
finish first in its division could win the World Series for the first time
since 1897—the last of four years in which the first- and second-place
clubs in the National League (then the only major league) played for the
Temple Cup trophy for championship "bragging rights" after the season.

Critics argued that the additional division-series round extended the
postseason too long or introduced teams into October baseball that really
didn't belong, diminished the importance of the World Series, or reduced
October baseball to survival of the luckiest rather than best-team-wins.
And in a game bound, even straitjacketed, by its fidelity to tradition, a
team having to survive a five-game division series followed by the seven-
game league championship series just to make it to the World Series
risked offending the championship honor of great teams of the past by
allowing for the possibility—indeed, the inevitability—that many would
be the years that either or both pennant-winning teams in the Fall Classic
were not those proven the best by virtue of having their league's best
record over baseball's long 162-game season. The additional round of
postseason series, now including a second-place club, necessarily
changed how we think about great teams and dynasties.

It was, however, a creative and necessary solution to the problem of
seven teams in each division (East and West) in both leagues that was
making the competitive structure of Major League Baseball seem an un-
wieldy, musty leftover from a long time ago in a world very different
from what it was now. And because of the wild-card alternative to finishing first, it was an enervating hybrid of the drama of traditional pennant
races over a long season, where the best teams win out, and the capri-
ciousness of the postseason itself, where the "objectively" best teams may

not. *And* by adding a second wild-card team to the mix in 2012, Major League Baseball raised the stakes exponentially in division races. With a single-elimination wild-card game in each league between the two best-record teams *not winning their division*, now it *really mattered* for a team to finish first in their division—as it did not when the lone wild-card team was guaranteed at least a five-game division series in the postseason and striving to finish first could take a backseat to just getting there. In the past quarter-century, every one of Major League Baseball's 30 teams has played in the postseason. All but eight have played in the World Series at least once.

# I

# Return to Action

# I

# TRIO OF ACES FRONT THE ALWAYS-FIRST BRAVES

**S**omebody could've written a poem, plagiarizing the one penned on Tinker-to-Evers-to-Chance in 1910, about Maddux, Glavine, and Smoltz. For any of the 10 years they were teammates on the Atlanta Braves pitching staff, it would not have been an exaggeration to say that for every other National League team:

> These were the "saddest of possible words."
> Maddux and Glavine and Smoltz.
> Trio of aces, the Braves pitching nerds.
> Making their pitches so good batters struggle.
> Turning offenses into landscapes of rubble.
> "Words that are heavy with nothing but trouble."
> Maddux and Glavine and Smoltz.

Although only Smoltz was there for them all, they were the foundation of the Braves winning 14 straight division titles from 1991 to 2005, not including being second in the NL East when the 1994 season came to its abrupt end because of the strike with no pennant being awarded to any of the first-place teams. Prior to 1991, the Braves franchise since the beginning of the twentieth century had been decidedly mediocre—and often quite bad. They had finished first exactly six times—winning two National League pennants as Boston's Braves in 1914 and 1948; two more in Milwaukee in 1957 and 1958, when all-time greats Hank Aaron, Eddie Mathews, and Warren Spahn were in their prime; and two division titles in 1969 and 1982, after each of which they were swept in the National League Championship Series (NLCS), since moving to Atlanta in 1966.

Left-hander Tom Glavine arrived first. Drafted by the Braves in 1984, Glavine was called up in August three years later and immediately thrown into the starting rotation, where he would be a mainstay for the next 15 years. Then came John Smoltz, signed by the Detroit Tigers in 1985, for whom he never pitched in the majors, and traded to the Braves in the summer of 1987 for veteran Doyle Alexander. It was a trade without which Detroit would not have won the AL's Eastern Division title that year. But it was also a trade that would pay spectacular long-term dividends for Atlanta. Greg Maddux arrived in 1993 as a free agent with 95 wins on his ledger since breaking in with the Cubs in 1986, including having just gone 20–11 to win his first of four consecutive Cy Young Awards. By the time Maddux got to Atlanta, the Braves had already won the first 2 of their 14 straight division titles and been twice to the World Series, losing both times. Glavine, with 20 wins both years, won the Cy Young Award in 1991 and was second to Maddux in 1992. Smoltz had earned a reputation for postseason excellence with a perfect 5–0 record and 2.04 earned run average in 63⅓ innings in nine NLCS and World Series starts.

The Braves already had a third outstanding pitcher when they signed Maddux—lefty Steve Avery, the third pick in the 1988 amateur draft. In 1991, his second year in the majors, Avery's 18–8 record helped the Braves win the NL West. Then he beat Pittsburgh twice without allowing a run in 16⅓ innings in the National League Championship Series to help the Braves win their first pennant since 1958, when they were *Milwaukee*'s Braves.

They were an indominable quartet of aces in 1993. Glavine was 22–6. Maddux, 20–10, had the best earned run average in baseball. Avery won 18 and Smoltz 15. Atlanta's starting pitchers won 45 and lost just 17 in their 84 starts the last three months of the season, during which the Braves—then in the NL West—pulled off a dramatic come-from-behind victory over the San Francisco Giants, fortified that year with their own top-prize free agent, a fellow named Barry Bonds. After Atlanta fell 10 games behind San Francisco on July 22 with 97 games done and only 65 to go, Maddux was 10–2 with a superb 1.76 ERA in his last 14 starts; Glavine 11–2 in 15 starts, including 6–1 down the September stretch; Avery 8–3 in 15 starts; and Smoltz 7–3 in 14 starts.

Because this was the last year when finishing first in the division was the only avenue to the postseason, the race for the top of the NL West in 1993 was baseball's last where winning 100 games did not guarantee playing beyond the 162-game schedule. That had happened just seven times before—three times in each league before divisional alignment in 1969 and in the AL East in 1980. The Braves won 104, the Giants 103. In the immediately forthcoming wild-card era, both teams would have been virtually assured the playoffs as early as September 10, when the Braves finally tied the Giants for first place, since both were 9½ games ahead in what would have been the wild-card standings. They would have spent the rest of the season battling for position rather than a playoff berth, their focus geared more toward lining up their starting pitchers and providing whatever rest was needed for the weary to enhance their prospects in the postseason. But not yet, not in 1993. By failing to win the NL West, the Giants, and their 103 wins and the second-best record in the majors, were going home for the winter.

As indispensable as Maddux, Glavine, Smoltz, *and Avery* were to winning the West, perhaps the most critical factor to that outcome was Atlanta trading three minor-league prospects to San Diego on July 18 for first baseman Fred McGriff, whose multimillion-dollar contract was now too much for the lost-cause Padres. As great as their pitching was, the Braves' offense had failed to gain traction so far in the season. Of the National League's 14 teams, only the Padres and woebegone Florida Marlins, a first-year expansion club, had scored fewer runs. After McGriff was inserted into the cleanup spot between left fielder Ron Gant and right fielder David Justice in the batting order, the Braves' new high-powered offense scored more runs than any other major league team the rest of the way. McGriff hit 19 homers and drove in 55 runs in 68 games for the Braves.

Atlanta's Braves were shifted to the geographically more-sensible Eastern Division in 1994 in the National League's new three-division alignment, and there was no reason to believe they would not continue on the dynastic path manager Bobby Cox had set them on. After holding a two-game lead with the best record in baseball on July 4, 1994, the Braves were just 18-17 the next five weeks, dropping them 6 back of the Montreal Expos in their new division when the strike came. Given their success chasing down the Giants in 1993, it would certainly have been plausible for Atlanta to overcome that modest gap with 48 games still remaining on the schedule had the 1994 season not come to a premature end. While his team was in a funk, Greg Maddux surely wasn't; he won five of his six starts after the All-Star break, during which he allowed just five earned runs in 52 innings. Maddux threw what proved to be the Braves' last pitch of the season when he completed a three-hit shutout against the Rockies in Colorado's thin air on August 11, lowering his major-league-leading ERA to 1.56.

Having won 20 in both 1992 and 1993, Maddux would likely have had four-straight 20-win seasons if not for baseball's shutdown shortchanging the 1994 and 1995 schedules. At 16-6, Maddux would have had at least nine and possibly ten more starts had the full schedule of games been played. And in 1995, the shortened-to-154-games season cost him two starts in a year he finished with a 19-2 record and league-leading 1.63 earned run average. Oakland's Dave Stewart, whose "death stare" at opposing batters had some calling him "Darth Vader," was the last pitcher to win 20 four years in a row, from 1987 to 1990, and he did so without nearly the dominance of "Mad Dog" Maddux, whose own contemplation of batters was more one of studied dissection than hostility but just as unnerving.

By 1998 it seemed the dynamic was set in stone. The Atlanta Braves were always first in the National League's Eastern Division. After winning three-straight division titles since the end of the strike in 1995, the Braves won the division again that year, decisively by 18 games, with 106 wins—still the most in franchise history. Any doubt that the Atlanta Braves were a baseball dynasty, following in the order of the 1921–1964 Yankees (29 pennants in 44 years), 1904–1924 Giants (10 pennants in 21 years), and 1947–1966 Dodgers (10 pennants in 20 years) in years that finishing first automatically meant winning the pennant, was put to rest by the time the twentieth century came to an end.

The team that carried the Braves' dynasty into the new century, however, had undergone a facelift from that which won six division titles and went to three World Series between 1991 and 1997. Bobby Cox was still manager and Maddux, Glavine, and Smoltz provided continuity in an excellent starting rotation, now including right-hander Kevin Millwood, called up in July 1997, to reprise the top-flight foursome the Braves had with Avery in 1993. There had been, however, close to a wholesale turnover of position-regulars. The Braves were now defined as much by Chipper Jones and a dynamic young center fielder from the Caribbean island of Curacao named Andruw Jones as by their trio of stellar aces. In 1996 Chipper began a string of eight straight 100-RBI seasons, during which he batted .314 and smacked 257 homers to establish himself as one of baseball's best-ever all-around third basemen. Andruw reigned as baseball's premier center fielder from his 1997 rookie season to 2007, perhaps the best ever defensively to play the position, and was a potent offensive threat besides, smacking 368 home runs for Atlanta. The two Joneses were the cornerstone position-players that carried the Braves to eight more division titles from 1998 to 2005.

Atlanta's Braves dynasty was winding down, carried now not by superlative pitching but by Chipper and Andruw Jones. In 2003, after leading the majors in fewest runs allowed 11 years in a row, the Braves' team ERA was just ninth in the National League. Glavine left as a free agent in 2003 and Maddux in 2004. Smoltz, the last of the Braves' trio of aces still in Atlanta, became their closer in late 2001 following Tommy John surgery that cost him all of the 2000 season and returned to the starting rotation in 2005. He was 38 years old. Missing hardly a start the next three years, Smoltz won 14 as the Braves claimed their 14th-straight division title in 2005 and led the league with 16 wins in 2006—the year the Braves' dynasty came to an end in third place, four games below .500. The roster stability that prevailed during the 1990s had given way to frequent turnover in the starting rotation and among position-regulars. Besides Smoltz and the two Joneses, shortstop Rafael Furcal and second baseman Marcus Giles were the only core regulars on all five of the Braves' division-winning clubs from 2001 to 2005.

Thanks primarily to Maddux, Glavine, and Smoltz, the Atlanta Braves had the most sustained run of pitching excellence in baseball history. They were at their best between 1993, when Greg Maddux came to town, and 1999—a year that John Smoltz pitched through the pain of a damaged elbow that landed him in Tommy John surgery in 2000. Combining for 342 wins while losing 166, Atlanta's trio of aces won two-thirds of their decisions. Their collective winning percentage (.673) was nearly 50 percentage points better than their team's (.625). And the trio captured five Cy Young Awards when they were in the same rotation. Presiding over the three of them, perhaps most famous for his incessant rocking when sitting on the bench alongside manager Bobby Cox, was Leo Mazzone, whose reputation as the Zen Master of pitching coaches was only enhanced by the work of Maddux, Glavine, Smoltz, and others who helped make Atlanta's the best pitching staff in baseball history. Mazzone himself pitched 10 years in the minors without ever making it to the majors.

Maddux was 128–51 for a .715 winning percentage, won at least 19 four times, and led the majors in earned run average and fewest runners on base four times. Winning the Cy Young Award in each of his first three years in Atlanta gave him the distinction of becoming the first pitcher to win four in a career. From 1994 to 1998, Maddux had an adjusted earned run average—a metric where a pitcher's ERA is normalized for both the context of the time he pitched and his team's home ballpark, with the league average set at 100—twice as good as the league average. The only other starting pitchers in history to do that over a single five-year period were Walter Johnson, from 1911 to 1915, and Pedro Martinez, for seven years from 1997 to 2003. Tom Glavine went 114–56 (.671) between 1993 and 1999, twice won 20, and earned his second Cy Young Award in 1998. Smoltz was 100–59 (.629) those seven years, led the league in winning percentage and innings pitched twice, and won 24 and his own Cy Young Award in 1996.

Unique among the most dominant pitchers in history in that he was neither a power pitcher nor a big strikeout pitcher in the context of his times, Greg Maddux may in fact be *underappreciated* for the dominating pitcher he was. Maddux's mild-mannered appearance on the mound belied his "Mad Dog" competitiveness, as though Clark Kent did his super deeds without bothering to ditch the glasses and change into his Superman tights and cape. Greg Maddux was not a K-man. He did not once lead the league in strikeouts, and his ratio of strikeouts to innings pitched was only marginally better than the league average. Pitching with precision control, averaging 1.3 walks while striking out 6.8 batters per nine innings his first seven years with the Braves, Maddux was arguably an artistic nerd about his craft. Studious, diligent, and observant, Maddux commanded the strike zone not only by exploiting batters' weaknesses and tendencies but also taking advantage of umpires' tendencies by constantly probing what he could get away with *off* the plate to get a strike call.

Maddux may have been the master practitioner, but Glavine and Smoltz were also excellent craftsmen. Glavine, like Maddux, was unprepossessing in stature—both were about six feet and were in the 170-

pound weight class in their prime—and pitched with guile and finesse. He averaged even fewer strikeouts per nine innings than Maddux. Smoltz was a more imposing figure—6-foot-3, more than 200 pounds—and threw much harder, despite which he walked fewer batters than Glavine, probably because Glavine had to work off the edges of the plate to be effective. Smoltz twice led the league in strikeouts, including 276 in 253⅔ innings in 1996, when he went 24–8. It was arguably his averaging more than a strikeout an inning in the 870 innings he threw between 1996 and 1999 that contributed to his blowing out his elbow in spring training the next year. Glavine and Maddux helped ease the Braves' pain of not having Smoltz on the mound in 2000—Glavine with 21 wins (his fifth 20-win season, in all of which he led or tied for the league lead in victories) and Maddux with 19 for the fourth time in eight years.

Few other teams in history can claim a trio of aces together for at least five years who were simultaneously among the elite pitchers in their league. None can claim a trio of such historically prominent pitchers as the 1990s Braves with Maddux, Glavine, and Smoltz. Those were the foundation years for all three making their case for the Hall of Fame. All three were elected in their first year of eligibility. Only two other teams had three Hall of Fame pitchers together in their starting rotation for as many as five years—the Philadelphia Athletics with Rube Waddell, Eddie Plank, and Chief Bender from 1903 to 1907 and the Cleveland Indians with Bob Feller, Bob Lemon, and Early Wynn from 1949 to 1954—but Bender's best years were yet to come, and Feller's best years had come and gone.

Feller was actually the *fourth* best pitcher in Cleveland from 1949 until the sands of time ran out on his career. Mike Garcia was the third man alongside Lemon and Wynn from 1949 to 1954 to give Cleveland arguably the best starting threesome in baseball history . . . until Maddux, Glavine, and Smoltz. Garcia was twice a 20-game winner and twice led the league in earned run average; Wynn won 20 three times and had the AL's best ERA once; and five of Lemon's seven 20-win seasons were during those years. While competitive every one of those seasons, Cleveland won only one pennant—in 1954—because New York's Yankees had an all-around better team *and* their own imposing trio of aces in Allie Reynolds, Vic Raschi, and Eddie Lopat. Raschi won 70 percent of his decisions those years, including three-straight 21-wins seasons, and Reynolds and Lopat both won 68 percent of their decisions in the six years from 1948 to 1953 they were together on the Yankees. None of the Yankees' three are in the Hall of Fame. Neither is Garcia.

In more recent memory, when Maddux, Glavine, and Smoltz were kids, Jim Palmer, Mike Cuellar, and Dave McNally were an impressive threesome of aces helping the Baltimore Orioles to five division titles in six years between 1969 and 1974, including three straight trips to the World Series. Palmer had four consecutive 20-win seasons; Cuellar won 20 four times, including all three pennant-winning seasons; and McNally also won 20 each year the O's won the pennant. Palmer, however, was the only one of Baltimore's vaunted trio to be elected to the Hall of Fame. Like the Maddux, Glavine, and Smoltz Braves of two decades later, the O's were baseball's stingiest team the first five years that Palmer, Cuellar, and McNally pitched off the same rubber in Baltimore.

For five years at the beginning of the new century, the Oakland Athletics could boast of their own trio of aces as a counterpoint to Atlanta's threesome. They were right-hander Tim Hudson and lefties Barry Zito and Mark Mulder. In the five years they pitched together—2000 to 2004—the A's had back-to-back 100-win seasons in 2001 and 2002 and never won fewer than 91 games. Oakland won the AL West three times, was the AL wild card another time, and in 2004 missed out on the division title by one game and the wild card by seven. Hudson, Mulder, and Zito combined for 234 of the A's 483 wins. But those were their best years. Despite their exceptional beginning years, none of the three will make it to Cooperstown. They were more Reynolds, Raschi, and Lopat than Maddux, Glavine, and Smoltz.

Whether viewed as 14 consecutive division titles or, because of the 1994 players' strike, 14 first-place finishes and one premature second-place ending in 15 years, the Atlanta Braves established an unprecedented record of achievement between 1991 and 2005. But they also fashioned a legacy of disappointment that, somehow, they weren't as great as their accomplishments would indicate because they had only five National League pennants, and none since 1999, to show for it and just one World Series triumph. They lost their first World Series in seven games to the 1991 Minnesota Twins, their second in six games to the 1992 Toronto Blue Jays, won their third in six games over the 1995 Cleveland Indians, then lost their fourth and fifth World Series to the end-of-the-twentieth-century Yankees dynasty in six games in 1996 and four in 1999.

In this respect, the Braves' historical legacy is akin to that of the Brooklyn Dodgers for the length of Jackie Robinson's career. The Dodgers were the team to beat in the National League every year, winning six pennants in his 10 seasons and were in the running until their last game two other times. Including Robinson, they had four future Hall of Fame players among their core regulars—Duke Snider, Roy Campanella, and Pee Wee Reese were the others—and two others, Gil Hodges and Don Newcombe, who were borderline candidates considered by the Veterans Committee several times each after they were no longer eligible to be voted in by the baseball writers. But they had only their World Series championship in 1955 to show for their excellence. Atlanta also had four future Hall of Famers—Maddux, Glavine, Smoltz, and Chipper Jones—and a fifth, Andruw Jones, has an objectively strong case for residence in Cooperstown as one of the National League's best players between at least 1998 and 2006. The 1990s Braves, however, were almost the opposite of the late-1940s to mid-1950s Dodgers. While Brooklyn had a dominant offense and decent pitching, Atlanta had superb pitching and a proficient offense.

'Twas their loss to the Yankees in the 1996 World Series that became the Braves' cross to bear as undermining their extraordinary regular-season dynastic accomplishments. When it looked like it might be a World Series romp after they crushed the Yankees 12–1 and 4–0 behind Smoltz and Maddux in the first two games at Yankee Stadium, the celebratory press in Atlanta, and in much of the baseball world, got ahead of itself by proclaiming the Braves on the threshold of a Yankees-like dynasty. Nineteen-year-old Andruw Jones, whose first big-league game was just two months before in August, made quite the impression on baseball's biggest stage in arguably the most prestigious sporting coliseum in the world by hitting home runs in his first two World Series at-bats. (He started all six games and batted .400.) But the Yankees won the third game to avoid a sweep; overcame a 6–0 deficit after five innings the next day to even the series; swept the three middle games in Atlanta when Andy Pettitte outdueled Smoltz, 1–0, in Game Five; and beat Maddux to win the series in six games. That was all the Yankees needed to kick-off their latest variant of the "forever" dynasty.

The defining moment was the three-run home run Jim Leyritz hit off Braves closer Mark Wohlers to tie the score in the eighth inning of Game Four. Wohlers was capable of throwing as hard as any intimidating reliever in the majors. But rather than firing a high-90s fastball, he tried to slip a slider past Leyritz, and instead of a strikeout—or any out—Leyritz powered Wohler's off-speed secondary pitch over the left-field wall to tie the game. That was the last time the Atlanta Braves would have a lead in the World Series.

Whatever the psychological trauma suffered from their 1996 World Series meltdown, the (Maddux, Glavine, and Smoltz) Braves recovered to win more than 100 games each of the next three seasons—the first team to do so since the 1969–1971 (Palmer, Cuellar, and McNally) Baltimore Orioles. While Baltimore beat their rivals in the ALCS all three years to play in the World Series, winning just once, Atlanta lost the NLCS in 6 games in both 1997 and 1998 before making it back to the World Series in 1999, only to run into the Yankees' latest dynastic juggernaut the Braves helped get started three years earlier. The Braves had two more 100-win seasons, back to back, in 2002 and 2003. But they never made it back to the Fall Classic.

If ever a baseball dynasty's legacy of greatness was derailed by the multiple rounds of postseason series in the wild-card era, it was the Atlanta Braves. After being swept by the Yankees in the 1999 World Series, the Braves lost to St. Louis in their division series in 2000; were eliminated in the NLCS by Arizona in 2001; were upended by wild-card San Francisco in their 2002 division series; failed to make it past Chicago in the 2003 division-series round; and were defeated in their division series by wild-card Houston in both 2004 and 2005. The Braves' lack of success in postseason series since Leyritz's home run seems counterintuitive given the year-in and year-out excellence of their pitching staff. But postseason series, particularly the best-of-five league division series are inherently problematic, even for the best of teams, because every team getting there over a grueling 162-game schedule has multiple strengths.

Just as the Braves were not only about their exceptional pitching, the teams they faced in the series they were eliminated in also had good pitching, even if not up to the Braves' standard. It was Atlanta's offense, generally proficient during the season, that sputtered in the crucible of October baseball, perhaps from the pressure of trying to overcome their growing legacy of postseason futility. In the six postseason series totaling 29 games that ended their season between 1997 and 2002—the last year that Maddux, Glavine, and Smoltz (although a closer since 2001) were together—the Braves hit only .229 and averaged 3.4 runs per game, while their opponents averaged 4.7 runs and batted .243. The Braves scored only 9 runs and batted .200 when they were swept by the Yankees in the 1999 World Series.

By 2006 the Atlanta Braves had exhausted their always-first karma. After starting the season slowly, there seemed nothing manager Bobby Cox could do to prevent a horrific month of June in which they were outscored by 43 runs and won only 6 of 27 games to fall far behind the division-leading Mets. Pitching, Atlanta's always-first calling card, had become their biggest weakness. Their starting pitchers' earned run average in June was 4.74 and even higher in July at 6.39, despite which the Braves managed to win 14 of their 24 games that month because they slugged 50 homers and batted .311 as a team. When the season mercifully ended, the Braves had a losing record, 4 games below .500, for the first time since 1990—the year before their string of 14 consecutive division titles began. Atlanta finished third in the NL East, a distant 18 games out, and had only the eighth-best record in the National League. While they finished second in scoring—their 222 home runs led the National League and were second-most in the majors—their pitching staff was tenth in ERA, notwithstanding Smoltz's 16–9 record and 3.49 earned run average in 35 starts.

The Braves were no longer a juggernaut. They were a middle-of-the-pack team. Media mogul Ted Turner, whose cable-broadcasting network allowed him to spend liberally to keep his trio of aces intact and his team competitive, was no longer the franchise owner. The new media conglomerate owning Atlanta's Braves, Time Warner AOL, was less willing to bankroll an always-first philosophy. Most of the Braves' best players were allowed to leave as free agents or traded before they reached their free-agency walk year or became eligible for salary arbitration. Atlanta made no effort to keep Andruw Jones in 2008. Smoltz was released after shoulder surgery sidelined him for most of the 2008 season, having won 210 and saved 154 games in 20 years for Atlanta.

The next time Atlanta was back in the postseason—in 2010, courtesy of the wild card—Chipper Jones was the lone player remaining from the Braves teams whose dominance of the National League now seemed in the distant past. Jones did not play in the postseason because he blew out his knee making a spectacular play at third base in mid-August. At a time when the relationship between players and teams was primarily transactional along the lines of both sides saying, "What have you done for me lately and what will you do for me in the future?" the Braves made sure to keep Chipper Jones in Atlanta for the entirety of his baseball career. Chipper retired two years later with 468 home runs and a .303 batting average, while having reached base in 40 percent of his plate appearances over the course of 2,499 big-league games.

Having returned Atlanta to the postseason after a hiatus of four years, Bobby Cox retired after the 2010 season at the age of 69. Notwithstanding the Braves losing their division series yet again, his legacy is not in the least diminished by his Braves failing to convert their 14 straight division titles from 1991 to 2005 into more than five pennants and one World Series title.

## 2

# RETURN OF THE YANKEES'
# FOREVER DYNASTY

Dr. Bobby Brown might well have cracked a wry smile when Jim Leyritz erased Atlanta's 6–3 lead with a three-run homer off closer Mark Wohlers in the eighth inning of Game Four of the 1996 World Series, saving the Yankees from what might have been a fatal three-games-to-one deficit—and not just because he was two years removed from 10 years as president of the American League. Before that, the 72-year-old Dr. Brown was a cardiologist. But before that, from 1947 until he was drafted for the Korean War in 1952, Bobby Brown was a third baseman for the New York Yankees. Much was made during his playing career about his roommate Yogi Berra reading comic books while he studied medical texts on the road, and the truth was that Brown, a left-handed batter, was platooned at his position and never started more than 86 games in any of the five full seasons he played major-league baseball.

Bobby Brown was not a name people thought about when they thought New York Yankees. They would be teammates Joe DiMaggio, Phil Rizzuto, Tommy Henrich, Berra, Allie Reynolds, Vic Raschi, Eddie Lopat, and even ace reliever Joe Page. But he was a quintessential role-player who came up big in World Series play, helping reinforce the narrative of the Yankees being a relentless, refuse-to-lose team when it mattered most. He had just three at-bats in the 1947 World Series against the Brooklyn Dodgers, all as a pinch-hitter, with two doubles and a single. His pinch-hit double in the fourth inning of Game Seven drove in the tying run and led to the Yankees winning the game and the series. Starting in four of the five games in the 1949 World Series, Brown had 6 hits in 12 at-bats and drove in 5 runs—the most in the series.

One of the heroes of that World Series was aging veteran Johnny Mize, whose ninth-inning two-run pinch-hit single broke open a 1–1 game and gave the Yankees' a two-games-to-one lead on their way to another, seemingly ritual October dismantling of the Dodgers. Mize might also have cracked a wry smile over Leyritz's home run, although from baseball's Mount Olympus. In the Hall of Fame for his excellence as a first baseman with the Cardinals and Giants, the left-handed slugger was a part-time first baseman and frequent pinch-hitter for the Yankees from 1949 to 1953. In 1952 he started in just 23 of the 78 games he played but was again a World Series hero in yet another Yankees beat-down of the Dodgers when he went 6-for-15 in five games with 3 home runs and 6 RBIs.

Like Brown and Mize, Jim Leyritz was an afterthought on an impressive Yankees roster that included former Red Sox star Wade Boggs, outstanding center fielder Bernie Williams, second-year left-hander Andy Pettitte on a pitching staff that also featured David Cone and Jimmy Key, a closer-in-waiting named Mariano Rivera, and 1996 Rookie of the Year shortstop Derek Jeter. The backup to catcher Joe Girardi, Leyritz started 50 games behind the plate during the regular season, three of the nine games the Yankees played in their division and league championship series, and the first game of the World Series. He entered Game Four in the bottom of the sixth after Girardi had been removed for a pinch-hitter. His at-bat in the eighth against Wohlers was his first of the game. Ignited by his game-tying home run, the Yankees went on to win the game, evening the Series, then won the next two to win their first World Series since 1978. He was not one of the stars on a very good Yankees team, and his home run was not the decisive blow in the game, but Jim Leyritz taking Mark Wohlers deep arguably kick-started the return of the New York Yankees as the forever dynasty.

That return was a long time coming, much to the frustration of the Yankees' impatient and tempestuous Boss, owner George Steinbrenner. The last time the Yankees won a World Series was 1978. The last time they had even played in one was 1981. In the intervening years, the Yankees had been a dysfunctional franchise. The Boss persistently upbraided players; interfered with his managers; looked for scapegoats; thought trading for and signing as free agents high-priced, high-profile players was the road to championship success; and fired managers with abandon. None of that earned the Yankees a shot at the World Series after 1981—until Steinbrenner was banished by the commissioner (temporarily, it turned out) in 1990 for paying to dig up dirt on Dave Winfield, one of his star players.

Steinbrenner was still the owner but muzzled. His "baseball people" took advantage of his hiatus to build the foundation for a winning team. Rather than spending big on high-priced stars and trading prospects for established players, they focused on developing a cadre of homegrown players *for* the Yankees, not some other team. And Buck Showalter, having survived a losing record his first year as manager at Yankee Stadium in 1992, by 1995 already had the longest uninterrupted tenure of any Yankees manager in the Steinbrenner era. In 1994, the Yankees had the best record in the American League when the players' strike summarily ended the season. In 1995, the Yankees won the wild card in the AL East but lost the five-game division series to the Seattle Mariners after holding a two-games-to-none lead.

But the Boss, reinstated since 1993, was not pleased by his team's agonizing near miss in 1995. Acting impetuously to make clear who was the Boss, even in the dugout, Steinbrenner's conditions for his continued employment as manager were untenable to Showalter. The Yankees' baseball brain trust recommended Joe Torre as his replacement. In his 14 years as a manager of three National League teams, his teams had lost more games than they won. Torre had not won a pennant. No sooner was Torre hired than Steinbrenner had misgivings, exacerbated in part by the *New York Daily News* calling the Yankees' new manager "Clueless Joe," which the Boss interpreted as a withering indictment of Torre's managerial ability rather than a warning about what it would be like to work for Steinbrenner. In fact, Joe Torre's calm and resolute personality made him a nearly perfect fit for Steinbrenner's Yankees—as long as he won.

By 1996, the Yankees had a talented core of four rising stars in place—center fielder Bernie Williams, lefty starter Andy Pettitte and reliever Mariano Rivera, and shortstop Derek Jeter. And waiting in the wings was a fifth—catcher Jorge Posada. The players they added as free agents or in trades from other teams to add quality depth and experience were more no-nonsense baseball types than flamboyant superstars. They included right fielder Paul O'Neill; right-hander David Cone, who was an elite starter; closer John Wetteland from before Torre came to New York; and Mariners first baseman Tino Martinez, traded for to replace Yankees icon Don Mattingly, following through on his retirement plans because of chronic back trouble after the 1995 season, never having played in a World Series.

The Yankees coasted to the AL Eastern Division title in 1996. Pettitte led the league with 21 wins and Wetteland with 43 saves. In the feel-good story of the season, Cone returned from a life-threatening aneurysm in early May to fire a no-hitter for seven innings before Torre took him out after 85 pitches in his first start since then—exactly four months before—on September 2, in Oakland. Rivera picked up from there and carried the no-hitter into the ninth before surrendering an infield hit with one out. Fielding the ball too deep in the hole at shortstop to have a play on the batter-runner was Derek Jeter.

If it was thought no one could replace Mattingly—"Donny Base-ball"—in the hearts of Yankees fans everywhere, Jeter in his rookie year was already on his way to being the franchise's next matinee idol. No Yankees rookie since Joe DiMaggio in 1936 had such an impact on kick-starting a next generation of the forever dynasty as Derek Jeter did exactly 60 years later. He batted .351 the last three months of the season as the Yankees established their dominance in the AL East. His 8th-inning home run off Baltimore closer Armando Benitez to even the score in the first game of the ALCS, paving the way to an 11-inning win and a five-game takedown of the Orioles, helped establish Jeter's enduring reputation for postseason heroics. Never mind that the home run was deflected into the seats by a 12-year-old kid leaning over the fence on a ball that otherwise might have been caught by Baltimore's right fielder. The Yankees won six pennants and five World Series in the first seven years of DiMaggio's career. In the first seven years of Jeter's career, they won six division titles, a wild card, five pennants, and four World Series and kept going for five more division titles in a row before finally missing out on the postseason in year 13 of his reign as Yankees shortstop and everyday hero.

The Yankees improved from 92 to 96 wins in 1997, but Baltimore's Orioles were the superior team, in first place at the end of every day in the regular season. Mariano Rivera was now the closer, his 130 strikeouts in 107⅔ innings in 61 games in 1996 allowing the Yankees to be fine with Wetteland leaving as a free agent. Signing chunky left-hander David

Wells, whose 16–10 record nicely complemented Pettitte's 18–7 and Cone's 12–6, fortified Torre's starting corps. The wild-card Yankees were four outs from winning their division series against Cleveland in four games until Rivera, protecting a 2–1 lead, gave up a game-tying home run to Sandy Alomar Jr. Even though his closer had pitched just two-thirds of an inning and thrown only nine pitches, Torre replaced Rivera with Ramiro Mendoza in the ninth. That turned out to be a losing proposition; Pettitte lost the next day; and it was Cleveland rather than New York that derailed every-day-in-first Baltimore in the ALCS to advance to the World Series.

Spoiled by the Yankees' return to baseball's ultimate championship in 1996, Steinbrenner was less than pleased by his team having to settle for wild-card status and their ouster in the first round of postseason series in 1997. That was all the more reason, perhaps, that he panicked early and put Torre's job on the line after the Yankees lost four of their first five games in 1998. But the Yankees winning 25 of their next 28 games to take early command of the AL East put an end to that. By the All-Star break, the Yankees were up by 11 games with a 61–20 record, on a pace to win an unfathomable 122 games. They won their 100th game, against only 38 losses, on September 4 and finished the season with 114 wins.

Only the 116–36 Chicago Cubs of 1906 won more regular-season games and 111–43 Cleveland Indians of 1954 had a higher winning percentage in the American League than the 114–48 New York Yankees of 1998. But while those teams went directly to the World Series, which both ironically lost to good but inferior teams (proving the adage that anything can happen in a short series), the 1998 Yankees had to navigate two postseason series just to get to the World Series. After sweeping the Texas Rangers in their division series, the Yankees looked like they might once again fall to the Indians by losing two of the first three games of the league championship series for the pennant. They did not lose again in 1998, sweeping the next three games of the ALCS and wiping out the San Diego Padres four straight in the World Series.

Including the postseason, the 1998 Yankees won 125 of the 175 games they played. They were in the discussion about the greatest single-season team in baseball history with two other Yankee clubs—the 1927 Ruth and Gehrig Yankees that won 110 games and swept the World Series and the 1939 DiMaggio Yankees that won 106 games and swept the World Series. Although Derek Jeter was by now his team's marquee player and most beloved star, he did not have the kind of singularly great season Babe Ruth did with his 60 home runs in 1927 and Joe DiMaggio did with his league-leading .381 batting average in 1939. In fact, no Yankee on the 1998 team had such a season. The AL Most Valuable Player Award went to the Rangers' Juan Gonzalez; Jeter finished third. The Cy Young Award went to the Blue Jays' Roger Clemens; Wells finished third.

The 1927 Yankees with six future Hall of Famers in their prime and the 1939 Yankees with five were both star-studded teams. The 1998 Yankees had only Jeter and Rivera who would be historically great players, and Jeter at the time was widely considered to be only the third-best shortstop in the American League, after Seattle's Alex Rodriguez and Boston's Nomar Garciaparra. In the year that McGwire hit 70 homers and Sosa 66, two other players had at least 50, and nine others hit over 40, Tino Martinez topped the Yankees with 28. Cone tied for the league lead in wins with 20, and David Wells at 18–4 had the best winning percentage among American League pitchers. Only Wells, however, was among the 10 best pitchers in the American League, based on pitching wins above replacement. The Yankees also benefited from 12 wins in 16 decisions by 32-year-old rookie right-hander Orlando Hernandez, fresh off the boat—literally, although descriptions of the "raft" as rickety were an embellishment—as a defector from Cuba, where he had starred on the national team.

What the Yankees had was not a team of outstanding players at most positions, but solid players at every position with an all-for-one and one-for-all ethos in which all that mattered was winning. They included pre-season free-agent acquisition Scott Brosius to play third base. A marginal major-league player his five previous years in Oakland, Brosius found his niche in New York, hitting .300 with 19 homers and 98 runs batted in. In the postseason, he batted .383, including .471 with 2 homers and 6 RBIs in the World Series. Jorge Posada, meanwhile, began easing out Joe Girardi behind the plate.

Going for overkill, early in spring training 1999 the Yankees exchanged starting pitchers with the Toronto Blue Jays, trading David Wells for Roger Clemens, fresh off winning back-to-back Cy Young Awards. With otherwise the same team, the Yankees played comfortably ahead of their Eastern Division rivals for most of the season after the All-Star break, ended up with 98 wins and the best record in the American League, once again swept the Rangers in their division series, needed just five games to dispatch the wild-card Red Sox in the ALCS, and manhandled the Braves four straight in the World Series. After going 21–7 and 20–6 and leading the league in ERA his two previous years in Toronto, Clemens saw his earned run average balloon to 4.60 and his record drop to 14–10 in his first New York season. He did have the honor, however, of winning the Game Four finale of the World Series, Rivera getting the save.

Other than the late-June trade for veteran outfielder David Justice, there were no significant player additions to the Yankees in 2000. With 143 games down and just 19 to go in mid-September, they were coasting to yet another division title when suddenly the apocalypse some sooth-sayers were predicting for Y2K seemed to hit the Yankees with a vengeance. They lost 15 of their last 18 games. Although the Yankees' lead was sufficiently large that their division title was never in jeopardy, they ended up with only 87 wins, just the fifth-best record in the American League, and a host of questions about how they might fare in the postseason. Quite well, it turned out. Joe Torre's Yankees became the first team since Oakland's 1972–1974 Athletics to win three straight World Series, and while Oakland needed to win just the ALCS to get to the Fall Classic, the Yankees had to survive a division series and the league championship series every year.

The 2000 World Series was an all-New York affair—a staple of the Fall Classic between 1947 and 1956 when either the Brooklyn Dodgers or the New York Giants met the Yankees for baseball's championship eight times in ten years. Just for old times' sake, perhaps, as they did in seven of their eight "subway" series back then, the Yankees beat their New York rivals, the Mets, in five games. The Yankees won the opening game on a 12th-inning, two-out, bases-loaded, walk-off single by Jose Vizcaino, but Game One—and the series—ultimately pivoted on an instinctively brilliant play by Derek Jeter to cut down a seemingly certain run at the plate and an interminable 10-pitch at-bat by Paul O'Neill off Mets closer Armando Benitez in which he fouled off numerous pitches before drawing a one-out, nobody-on walk to begin a game-tying rally in the bottom of the 9th.

Showcasing his acute situational awareness, athleticism, and refusal to give up on any play, Jeter's play was, in three words, vintage Derek Jeter. The game was scoreless in the sixth. Timo Perez was the Mets' runner on first. With two outs he was running at the crack of the bat. Jeter noticed, however, that he had slowed to a trot when it appeared the ball would clear the left-field wall. When it hit off the wall instead, Perez was off to the races, but Jeter knew he was not as far along as he could have been had he not assumed a home run. The problem was that the throw from left field to Jeter, the relay man with a direct line to the plate, was far-wide to his left, toward the third base-side grandstand, seeming to preclude any chance for a play at the plate. Except Jeter raced over, caught the throw as though it was a grounder to his backhand in the hole at shortstop and, making the same kind of jump-throw that became his signature play, fired a perfect strike to Posada at the plate that nailed Perez to end the inning, stunning everyone in Yankee Stadium.

For good measure, Jeter batted .409 in the series and was named the World Series MVP for good reason. That play aside, his home run on the first pitch of Game Four at Shea Stadium—also "vintage" Jeter in that he, a right-handed batter, drove the ball to right field—was all but a death sentence on the Mets' chances after they had taken Game Three to end the Yankees' record string of World Series victories at 14 going back to 1996. And in Game Five, his sixth-inning home run tied the game, setting the stage for Luis Sojo to drive in the championship-winning runs in the ninth.

Vizcaino and Sojo, whose hits drove in the winning runs in the first and last games of the 2000 World Series, were just the latest in a line of little-known role-players like Bobby Brown in the late 1940s and Jim Leyritz in 1996 who became Yankees World Series heroes. Neither was even with the Yankees when the season started. Both were acquired in trades—Vizcaino in June, for Leyritz of all players, and Sojo in August— to back up second baseman Chuck Knoblauch, whose suddenly errant throws had undermined his confidence and made him a significant defensive liability. While Knoblauch was the Yankees' designated-hitter for the entirety of the postseason, Sojo played second base during the American League playoffs and Vizcaino started four of the five games— and Sojo the other—in the World Series.

Going for four triumphant World Series in a row—last done when Casey Stengel's Yankees won five straight between 1949 and 1953—the Yankees bolstered their 2001 pitching staff with free agent Mike Mussina, one of baseball's elite right-handers, winner of 147 games and 64.5 percent of his decisions in 10 years with the Orioles. The Yankees once again had the division title well in hand with a 13-game lead when Major

League Baseball—and everyday life in the United States of America—
came to a crashing halt after the September 11 al-Qaeda terrorist attacks
on New York City and Washington, DC. As Americans came together as
a nationwide community with determination and resilience to overcome
the awfulness of that day, and with New York fully engrossed in digging
out and recovering from the calamity, the front-running Yankees, the
forever dynasty baseball fans elsewhere in America loved to hate dating
back to Babe Ruth's days, became the sentimental favorite for many to
run the postseason table.

It looked like it might be an early out for New York when Oakland
took the first two games of their division series at Yankee Stadium. 'Twas
the Yankees' all-American hero, Derek Jeter, who saved the day with the
play that is as iconic as Willie Mays's catch in the 1954 World Series.
Mussina had allowed just two hits through six innings. All he had was a
1–0 lead, courtesy of Jorge Posada's fifth-inning home run. Mussina
retired the first two batters in the seventh. Jeremy Giambi reached on a
cheap single to right field. Terrence Long ripped a double down the right-
field line. Running on contact with two outs, Giambi did not get a good
start off first, just like Timo Perez exactly one week less than a full year
ago. He nonetheless was waved around third. Jeter, in position to relay a
throw to third should Long try for a triple, saw that right fielder Shane
Spencer's throw toward the plate was both too high for first baseman
Tino Martinez to cut off and too far wide, in foul territory off the first
base line, to be snared by the catcher. Whereupon, Jeter raced across the
infield, caught Spencer's off-line throw about 20 feet up the first base
line, and in a single quick, fluid move made a backhand flip of the
baseball to the third base side of home plate for Posada to grab and slap a
tag on Jeremy Giambi, who did not slide.

Again, the play was vintage Derek Jeter. Giambi was much criticized
for trying to score standing up, although to be fair, nobody thought the
Yankees had a play at the plate on a ball thrown off line into what
appeared to be no-man's land—nobody but Jeter. Like his play on Perez,
Jeter's throw to nab Giambi was remarkable and amazing, perhaps mostly
for being so unexpected. Both times the runner seemed certain to score on
the errant throw from the outfield. Ever observant, aware of where all the
relevant actors were on the field and of his own position in time and space
to anticipate what was happening and what might be, both plays showed
Jeter's instinct to always be in the right place at the right time to make

precisely the right play. The A's lost that day, 1–0, and the next two days as well. The Yankees advanced to the ALCS where they faced the Seattle Mariners, whose 116 wins were two more than the 1998 Yankees won in the regular season. The Yankees put an end to Seattle's quest to win 127 games overall by needing just six games to dispatch the Mariners.

It was on to their fourth straight World Series, and fifth in six years, against the Arizona Diamondbacks in just their fourth season. The D-backs won the first two games in Arizona but lost Game Three in New York. They held a two-run lead in the 9th and had the Yankees down to their last out in Game Four before Martinez blasted a two-run homer to send the game into extra innings. Jeter's two-out 10th-inning home run evened the Series. It came moments after the clock passed midnight into the first minutes of November. Let Reggie Jackson have October; Derek Jeter was Mr. November. Game Five replicated Game Four. Once again, the Yankees were down to their last out, trailing by two runs in the 9th. Once again, they got a game-tying home run—this time by Scott Brosius—before going on to win in extra innings.

Heading back to Phoenix for the conclusion of an eventful 2001, the Yankees seemed primed to soon hoist their 27th World Series championship banner. It was not to be. Blown out in Game Six, 15–2, the Yankees took a 2–1 lead into the last of the ninth with Mariano Rivera on the mound to close out a victory. But against the Diamondbacks, even the great Mariano wound up snake-bit. A lead-off single and Rivera's bad throw to second on a poorly executed sacrifice bunt attempt—his error—put runners on first and second for Arizona. The next batter also attempted a sacrifice, poorly. Rivera got the force at third. Third baseman Brosius had a shot at throwing out the batter-runner at first for a double play but did not attempt a throw. A double tied the score, putting runners on second and third. Rivera hit the next batter, loading the bases. Next up was Luis Gonzalez, owner of 57 homers and 142 RBIs while batting .325 during the season. With all bases occupied and just one out, the Yankees infield and outfield had to play in to cut down the would-be winning run at the plate on any ball in play. Gonzalez hit what would ordinarily have been a routine pop-up to the shortstop. This time, playing in, there was nothing Derek Jeter could do about it. New York City, which had been through so much, would not get another Yankees championship.

Gonzalez's weak over-the-infield, walk-off single in Game Seven also signaled the end of a Yankees team defined as much by its "band of brothers" cohesiveness as for its winning accomplishments at a time when the path to the World Series was fraught with the peril of what could happen in a five-game division series and seven-game league championship series just to get there. The Core Five—Jeter, Williams, Posada, Pettitte, and Rivera—were still in pinstripes, but arguably their most indispensable partners in success did not return for 2002. Paul O'Neill, about to turn 39, and Scott Brosius, who turned 35 in August, retired—as they had said they would. Soon to be 34 and at the end of the contract he signed with the Yankees in 1996, Tino Martinez was told by the Yankees he was no longer wanted, despite his team-leading 34 homers and 113 RBIs in 2001, not to mention his dramatic game-changing home run in the fourth game of the World Series. Steinbrenner instead had his eye on 31-year-old free-agent slugger Jason Giambi, older brother of Jeremy, to play first base and anchor the heart of the batting order. All Giambi had done for Oakland the three previous years was club 114 home runs, drive in 380 runs, and bat .330 with an on-base percentage of .458 and a combined on-base plus slugging percentage of 1.075. The American League's MVP in 2000, Giambi had finished second in the voting in 2001, miles ahead of Derek Jeter.

The accomplishments of the 1996–2001 New York Yankees, having to survive three postseason series to win baseball's ultimate championship, rivaled that of the best teams that came before them, including earlier teams in the Yankees' dynastic succession that had but one postseason series to win every year—the World Series. In making it to the World Series five times, they won an incredible 14 of the 16 postseason series they played, a remarkable feat considering the potential for being tripped up in a short series, as the Atlanta Braves could attest with only five pennants and one Fall Classic triumph to show for their 14 straight division titles. Guided by Torre, with Jeter their inspirational never-say-die leader, the Yankees were at their best when the games counted the most in the postseason, even if they did not always have the better team, at least as judged by their regular-season record. Their regular-season .601 winning percentage for those six years was impressive enough. But in 78 postseason games, the Yankees won 56 for a stunning .718 winning percentage, and in their five World Series, Torre's Yankees were even better—a 19–7 record for a .731 winning percentage.

In the pantheon of great Yankee teams, Torre's Yankees most resembled Stengel's 1949–1953 Yankees, then in transition from the Joe DiMaggio to Mickey Mantle era, that won five straight World Series. Neither team had as many outstanding players at multiple positions, or were as dominant relative to their league opponents, as the Ruth and Gehrig Yankees or the DiMaggio Yankees. But both had a tough-to-navigate offense, formidable pitching (a hallmark of most of the great teams in the Yankees' forever dynasty), a deep bench, and a relentless refuse-to-lose baseball work ethic, especially when the stakes were highest in pennant races or postseason series.

What the Yankees were not like in Joe Torre's first six years as manager were the Bronx Bombers of yore. They had no sluggers the likes of Ruth and Gehrig, or DiMaggio, or Mantle and Berra and Maris, or Reggie. Tino Martinez, in 1997 and 2001, was the only Yankee in the American League's top-10 in home runs in any of those six years That did not mean the Yankees weren't very tough on opposing pitchers. Never giving up an at-bat, they were practiced at getting on base, taking advantage of scoring opportunities, and staging comeback rallies. As the Mets and Diamondbacks found out in successive World Series, even though Arizona came out on top in the end, opposing teams could not relax with a late-inning lead until the last Yankees batter made out.

# 3

# CLEVELAND'S RUNAWAY CENTRAL TRAIN

While the AL Eastern Division New York Yankees assumed their historical role of dominance in the American League, and all of major league baseball for that matter, the two other American League divisions were also ruled by a single team in the years between the end of baseball's nearly apocalyptic strike and the beginning of a new millennium. In the Central Division, that team was the Cleveland Indians, winners of five consecutive division titles and two pennants from 1995 to 1999. In the Western Division, that team was the Texas Rangers, winners of three division titles in four years from 1996 to 1999. Texas never made it past the division-series round of the postseason for the chance to play for the privilege of going to the World Series.

The last time Cleveland had a competitive ballclub was in the 1950s. If not for the Yankees, the Indians in the first half of the 1950s would have gone down in history as a great team. Instead, Cleveland finished second to New York six times between 1950 and 1956, beating them for the pennant only by winning an AL-record 111 games in 1954. Little would Cleveland fans have suspected after their 1954 pennant that it would be 41 years before they next finished first. In the first 33 years after baseball's first expansion in 1961, the Indians had a winning record only six times. Upon being transferred to the AL's new Central Division in 1994, the highest they had ever finished in their 25 years in the AL East was fourth. That changed their very first year in their new division. Cleveland was within a game of first place on a pace to win 96 games with 49 remaining on the schedule on the day the players' strike brought an end to their best season since 1955.

The next five years, the AL Central belonged to Cleveland's Indians. The 1995–1999 Indians were the first team since the 1970s Oakland A's to win five straight division titles. No other team in the division came close. In 1995, despite a season reduced to 144 games to give time for spring training after Judge Sotomayor ordered Major League Baseball back into action, Cleveland still won 100 games, their .694 winning percentage the third-highest in American League history to this point after the 1954 Indians and 110-win 1927 Yankees. Cleveland won the division by a colossal 30 games over second-place Kansas City, which had a losing record, then went on to beat Boston in their division series and Seattle in the ALCS to play in their first World Series since 1954. Cleveland lost to Atlanta in six games.

In 1996, the Indians took the division by 14½ games, again with the best record in the major leagues, only to be derailed in the division series in the first round of the postseason. Slumping from 99 to 86 wins in 1997 but still winning their division handily by 6 games, the Indians were hardly the dominating team they were the two previous years. Notwithstanding having only the fourth-best record in their league, the Indians beat the 96-win wild-card Yankees in their division series and the 98-win Orioles in the ALCS to make it back to the World Series—against the 92-win NL wild-card Florida Marlins. They lost the series in seven games on a bases-loaded, walk-off single in the 11th after letting a 2–1 lead slip away in the last of the 9th, two outs away from a championship. The two years following, Cleveland won their division by 9 games and then 21½ games but failed to advance to the World Series either time. Managing the Indians to five-straight division titles was not enough; Mike Hargrove was fired as Cleveland's manager after squandering a two-games-to-none advantage over Boston and an early 5–2 lead in the decisive fifth game of their 1999 division series.

The 1995–1999 Indians were not nearly as dominant as their five blowout division titles suggest because the Central Division was the weakest in the American League. Cleveland had a .596 winning percentage those five years; the rest of the AL Central had a winning percentage of .452—and these were still years of the "balanced schedule" in which AL teams played only one less game against every team outside their division than within their division. Of the four other teams in the AL

Central, only one—Chicago's 1996 White Sox—had a winning record in any of those seasons.

The five-in-a-row Indians were a genuinely very good team only the first two years of their run and the preceding year, 1994, when their bid for the division title was short-circuited by the players' strike. They were an offensive powerhouse. Center fielder Kenny Lofton, batting first in Hargrove's lineup, led the league in stolen bases each of his first five years in Cleveland from 1992 to 1996 while batting .316. Switch-hitting second baseman Carlos Baerga, hitting third, batted .315 for the Indians between 1992 and 1995. Left fielder Albert Belle was devastating in the cleanup slot, smashing 206 home runs, driving in 616 runs, and batting .303 between 1992 and 1996. Belle had a sensational year in 1995, leading the league in runs and runs batted in with 52 doubles and 50 home runs in the shortened 144-game schedule, while batting .317. Sixty percent of Belle's hits were for extra bases, yet somehow he lost out to Boston's Mo Vaughn in a close vote for American League MVP.

All three players were signed to long-term, multimillion-dollar contract extensions in 1993 that took them through their arbitration-eligible years and the first year they could have declared for free agency. Baseball's owners were taking a hard line against free agency in negotiations with the players union, but with a brand-new stadium set to open in 1994 and Cleveland being the only major-league team with a player payroll below $10 million in 1992, general manager John Hart convinced franchise owner Dick Jacobs on the merits of signing talented players like Baerga, Belle, and Lofton to long-term deals to build the foundation for a competitive future in their new home, even though none of the three had more than three years of experience—and Lofton, only one—and there was a risk they would not live up to expectations. All three did, and on June 12, 1995, with Cleveland already in front by 7½ games with a stunning 31–11 record in the year the players' strike ended, the Indians began a string of 455 consecutive home-field sellouts that would not end until April 4, 2001—the day after opening day in the season *after* they failed to finish first following their five-straight division titles. "We came to the conclusion," Hart was quoted in *The Sporting News* in April 1993, that signing promising young players early in their careers "is the only way a small-market club like ours can survive."

None of the three was still there when Cleveland went to the 1997 World Series. Baerga was traded during the 1996 season; Lofton was traded after that season; and Belle, now a free agent, signed with division rival Chicago. Right fielder Manny Ramirez and first baseman Jim Thome, both of whose breakout year was when the Indians won their division by 30 games in 1995, were the new position-player stars in Cleveland. Without Belle batting between Thome and Ramirez in the middle of the lineup, however, the Indians were much less the offensive juggernaut in 1997 and 1998 than they had been the three previous years.

Strengthened by the addition of free-agent second baseman Roberto Alomar, Cleveland was back to being a frighteningly efficient offensive club in 1999, becoming the first team since the 1950 Red Sox to score 1,000 runs in a season. Batting third ahead of Ramirez and Thome, Alomar batted .323, led the league in runs, and established career highs in home runs (24) and runs batted in (120). Five everyday players reached base in over 40 percent of their plate appearances, including Lofton, welcomed back to Cleveland as a free agent in 1998. Omar Vizquel, an outstanding defensive shortstop whose career average in 10 prior big-league seasons was a humble .268, batted .333 to tie Ramirez for the team-lead. Thome hit 33 homers. And Manny burnished his growing superstar credentials with 44 home runs and 165 runs batted in—the most in baseball since Jimmie Foxx's 175 RBIs back in 1938.

The primary difference between the Indians from 1994 to 1996, when they had the best record in baseball, and from 1997 to 1999, when twice they ran away with their division even though winning fewer than 90 games, came down to pitching. In 1995 and 1996 they gave up the fewest runs in the American League; the next three years they were in the middle of AL teams in runs allowed. Right-hander Charles Nagy, their ace, won 83 and lost 43 during Cleveland's five-in-a-row romp of the AL Central and garnered a handful of Cy Young Award votes when he was 16–6 and 17–5 in 1995 and 1996. Nagy was backed up by aging veterans Dennis Martinez from 1994 to 1996 (32–17 those three years) and Orel Hershiser from 1995 to 1997 (45–21), both signed as free agents nearing the end of very distinguished pitching careers, and by Dave Burba and Bartolo Colon the next two years. Burba, acquired from Cincinnati in 1998, was halfway through his career, and Colon, a rookie in 1997, was at the beginning of a 21-year career in which he would pitch for 11 major-league clubs. Colon was Cleveland's best pitcher in 1998 (14–9) and 1999 (18–5).

The Indians fell quickly from contention in 2000 trying to make it six division titles in a row. By the All-Star break they were 10½ games behind the White Sox, just two wins over .500, but had the best record in the American League the rest of the way to wind up with 90 wins. While that was not good enough to salvage their division quest, and despite Manny Ramirez leaving as a free agent after the season for much greater riches in Boston, Cleveland's Indians were still not done. They won the 2001 AL Central by 6 games, only to once again be evicted in their division series. Alomar, batting .336, had his third outstanding season since signing with the Indians; Thome blasted 49 homers; Nagy was ineffective and near the end of his career following elbow surgery the previous year; and 20-year-old rookie southpaw CC Sabathia burst on the scene with a 17–5 record in 33 starts.

By now, Cleveland was in the top tier of American League clubs in player payroll. Escalating player salaries were what motivated Jacobs to sell his team in 2000. Never mind the Indians' sixth division title in seven years in 2001, their new owners were determined to purge payroll. With one year and $8 million left on his contract, Alomar was traded to the Mets before the 2002 season, and Colon, a year away from free agency, was traded to Montreal for prospects Cliff Lee and Grady Sizemore in June after beginning the season with a 10–4 record in 16 starts. Payroll was down from $93 million to $79 million; the 2002 Indians had their first losing season since moving into their new ballpark; and free-agent-to-be Thome crushed 52 home runs to set himself up for a six-year $85 million contract from the Phillies. Jim Thome left Cleveland with 337 home runs on his way to an eventual career total of 612. With Cleveland's player payroll down to $48.6 million in 2003, they lost 94 games.

Cleveland's principal competition in the first years of the AL Central came from Chicago, whose White Sox also had a history of (mostly) failure since the 1950s. Their last pennant was in 1959—their first since the Black Sox disgrace of 1919—and they had done no better than two division titles (in 1983 and 1993) since. But having run away with the AL West in 1993 with a cadre of young stars that included first baseman Frank Thomas—whose power, high batting and on-base averages, and plate discipline reminded many of Ted Williams—and third baseman Robin Ventura, and a strong pitching staff fronted by tall, very slender right-hander Jack McDowell, a 20-game winner in both 1992 and 1993,

Chicago was favored to win the American League's new Central Division in 1994. The White Sox held a slender one-game lead over the resurgent Albert Belle–powered Indians when the players' strike became an abrupt roadblock on their highway to sustained success. In December, even as the players' strike seemed beyond a negotiated resolution and the owners were threatening to use replacement players the next year, Chicago traded McDowell to the Yankees, precisely because he would be eligible for free agency after the 1995 season.

Without McDowell to anchor the starting pitching, the White Sox took a detour into the wilderness of losing teams, even as Thomas and Ventura continued to shine. Every day of the 1995 season ended with them having a losing record. But in 1996, while posing little threat to Cleveland's supremacy, the White Sox found an on-ramp back onto the winning road they had been on before baseball's shutdown. And when Albert Belle entered free agency after the season, his productivity the two previous years—98 homers and 274 RBIs in 301 games—was too much for White Sox owner Jerry Reinsdorf to ignore. Notwithstanding the hard line on limiting free agency he personally was pressing "Acting" Commissioner Selig to take in negotiations with the players union, Reinsdorf signed Cleveland's slugger to a record five-year $55 million contract that included guaranteeing Belle he would remain one of baseball's three best-paid players if the average annual value of his deal was exceeded during its term.

Notionally, signing a player of Belle's magnitude should have simultaneously improved the White Sox while weakening the Indians. The pennant race in the AL Central was closer this time, but even without their former slugger, Cleveland won its third-straight division title, while the White Sox finished second without spending any but the first day of the season in first place. Batting third and fourth in the lineup, Thomas had another Frank Thomas year—35 homers, 125 RBIs, and a .347 batting average and .456 on-base percentage to lead the league in both categories—and Belle slumped to 30 homers, 116 RBIs, and a .274 batting average.

Belle rebounded to hit 49 home runs with a career-high 152 runs batted in while batting .328 in 1998, but Thomas had the first poor season of his career with only 29 homers, 109 RBIs, and a paltry .265 batting average—the first time he had hit below .300. The White Sox finished second to the Indians yet again, with a losing 80–82 record. They did not have a winning record any time after being 2–1 in early April; the last time they were at .500 was 4–4 a week later. As good as he still was, and as potent as he and Frank Thomas were together in the White Sox batting order, Albert Belle had not delivered a pennant, or even a division title, to the south side of Chicago. And while Belle remained among the top three players in annual salary, others had surpassed him on the free-agent marketplace for richest overall contract, and Reinsdorf was not prepared to give his slugger any compensatory raise or contract extension. He did allow Belle to test the market, and Albert left for Baltimore with a new five-year deal worth $65 million beginning in 1999.

Without Belle, Chicago fell to 75–86 in 1999 yet still finished second—21½ games behind Cleveland. The next year, however, the White Sox ended the Indians' string of five straight division titles with the best record in the American League, only to be rolled over in their division series by the wild-card Mariners without winning a game. A bunt single off their closer, Keith Foulke, drove in the winning run in the bottom of the ninth of Game Three in Seattle. Now mostly a designated hitter, Thomas returned to form in 2000 with 43 homers, 143 RBIs, a .328 batting average, and a .436 on-base percentage. Although he would play eight more years, most marred by injury or battling to overcome the effects of injury, that was Frank Thomas's last great season. Albert Belle, meanwhile, in his second year in Baltimore, hit 23 homers and drove in more than 100 runs for the ninth straight year, and then he retired because of chronic pain in his degenerative hip.

Before winning the AL West in 1996, excepting the 1993-expansion four-year-old Florida Marlins and Colorado Rockies, the Texas Rangers were the only major-league team never to have won a division title (and even the Rockies, as a wild card, had already played in the postseason). The Rangers were an expansion team themselves, beginning life as the Washington Senators in 1961 before moving to the Dallas–Fort Worth area in 1972. The assignment of Chicago to the new Central Division in 1994 seemed to open the way for Texas to win the West. The Rangers had finished second to the White Sox in 1993, 8 games out, with the fourth-best record in the American League. Twenty-three-year-old left fielder Juan Gonzalez led the majors in homers for the second year in a row; 24-year-old third baseman Dean Palmer hit 33 homers; and 21-year-old Ivan Rodriguez, in only his third season in 1993, was considered a first-rate catcher. And indeed, the Rangers *were on top* in the AL West in August 1994 when the players went on strike—by just one game and, amazingly, with a losing record, 10 games *below* .500.

Texas won the AL West by 4½ games over Seattle in 1996, by 3 games over Anaheim in 1998 (with a losing record between those division titles), and by 8 over Oakland in 1999. They were decisively beaten in the opening division-series round all three years by superior Yankees teams. All three years, however, 'twas a Texas Ranger, rather than any Yankee, voted the AL's Most Valuable Player—Gonzalez in 1996 (with 47 homers, 144 runs batted in, and a .314 batting average) and 1998 (with 45 homers, 157 RBIs to lead the league, and a .318 average) and Rodriguez in 1999 (35 homers and 113 runs driven in while batting .332). Rodriguez, perhaps best known as "Pudge" (so nicknamed for his squat 5-foot-9, 205-pound build), was now being talked about in the same breath as Johnny Bench as perhaps the best defensive catcher in baseball history, particularly in gunning down base runners. Gonzalez hit 39 home runs in 144 games for Texas in 1999, but leading the team in both homers (with 47) and RBIs (148) was designated hitter Rafael Palmeiro, returning as a free agent to the Rangers, for whom he played from 1989 to 1993, after five years in Baltimore.

Rodriguez, Gonzalez, and Palmeiro would be tarred by Jose Canseco in his 2005 book, *Juiced*, as having injected steroids—Canseco said he personally administered the shots when he played for the Rangers in the early 1990s—at least in the beginning years of their careers. All three players claimed that wasn't true, and Canseco's accusation did not prevent Ivan Rodriguez from being elected into the Hall of Fame in 2017, his first year of eligibility. Palmeiro, however, failed a test for steroids use in 2005. Ordinarily, amassing 3,020 hits and hitting 569 home runs in a career means spending retirement enshrined in Cooperstown. Because of the steroids—and his famously insisting in congressional hearings that he "never used steroids, period!"—Palmeiro dropped off the Hall of Fame ballot after only four years of eligibility.

"Juan Gone" Gonzalez being gone in a trade and Pudge, having the best year of his career (27 homers, 83 RBIs, and a .347 batting average in 91 games), missing most of the second half of the season after breaking his thumb on his follow-through while throwing out a base-runner contributed to the Rangers falling from 95 wins and the division title in 1999 to 91 losses and last place in 2000. That prompted franchise owner Tom

Hicks to make history by signing Seattle Mariners shortstop Alex Rodriguez to a 10-year $252 million free-agent contract that not only set a new record, but blew by the record $160 million over 8 years that Boston had just given Manny Ramirez. Having paid $250 million for the Rangers in 1998, Hicks may have been motivated to invest more than that on a single superstar as much by the desire to compete with the NFL's Dallas Cowboys—"America's Team"—for national "brand" exposure as to return his ballclub to the best in the West and reverse a significant decline in fan attendance since he bought the franchise.

Hicks's A-Rod gambit failed spectacularly. Given that Rodriguez alone accounted for 25 percent of the Rangers' player payroll in 2001, and that nearly another 20 percent went to Pudge and Palmeiro, it was impossible for the Rangers to pay for a "supporting cast" (as Chicago Bulls basketball star Michael Jordan once referred to his teammates) capable of ensuring a competitive ballclub. Unlike in basketball, however, where one superstar the magnitude of Michael Jordan could make all the difference between contending or not—because he could always take control of the game—in baseball, superstar A-Rod was going to come to bat only four or five times a night. Alex Rodriguez was every bit the player Hicks expected. He led the league in home runs each of the next three years with a total of 156 from 2001 to 2003. He drove in 395 runs and scored 382. He batted .305 with an on-base plus slugging percentage of 1.011. He was the 2003 American League MVP. And the Texas Rangers finished last in the AL West all three years, averaging 90 losses a season.

After finishing 31 games behind in the AL West in 2002 while paying his roster over $100 million—the third highest in baseball—Hicks cut payroll. He allowed Ivan Rodriguez to leave as a free agent after 12 years as a Texas Ranger in which he hit .305, belted 215 home runs, and threw out almost exactly half of base-runners attempting a stolen base when the league average was 32 percent of base-runners cut down trying to steal. Pudge helped Florida's Marlins, whose player payroll was less than $50 million, win the World Series in 2003, while the Rangers, still paying their players over $100 million, finished last again. Palmeiro went back to Baltimore as a free agent in 2004.

Alex Rodriguez was desperate to leave a team not likely to get better anytime soon—especially not when the $179 million he was still owed precluded the Rangers from improving the team around him—and Hicks was equally desperate to cut his losses. In February 2004, Hicks traded his superstar shortstop to the Yankees, agreeing to throw in $67 million of his remaining contract. No longer carrying A-Rod and Palmeiro contributed to halving the Rangers' player payroll in 2004. And Texas improved from 91 losses to 89 wins, spent much of July in first place, and ended up just three games behind the division winner.

A-Rod's departure was the third significant body-blow loss Seattle's Mariners had suffered since their surge to the division title and comeback-takedown of the Yankees in their division series in 1995. At the trade deadline in July 1998, the Mariners parted ways with Randy Johnson, their dominating ace, because he was in his free-agency "walk" year. And just as spring training was getting started in 2000, Seattle accommodated Ken Griffey Jr. by trading him to the Cincinnati Reds. In Johnson's case, the Mariners were unwilling to offer the lucrative contract extension he wanted because of concerns about his durability. It didn't matter that the Big Unit had recovered from the back injury that sidelined him after just eight starts (in which he was 5–0) in 1996, almost certainly preventing the Mariners from repeating as division champions, to lead the majors with a 20–4 record in 1997 while striking out 291 batters in 213 innings to help Seattle reclaim the AL Western Division title. In Griffey's case, their star center fielder turned down the Mariners' offer of an eight-year $135 million contract extension and requested he be traded closer to his home on the East Coast.

The Mariners lost not just a supernova when Griffey left Seattle but the face of the franchise. And not just any face of the franchise, but one whose nationwide appeal made him one of the most recognized and beloved baseball players in America and one of the dynamic young stars being marketed by Major League Baseball. Griffey had just led the league in homers for the third straight year in 1999. He was the American League MVP in 1997 when he led the league with 56 home runs and 147 RBIs. In 1998, he hit 56 again and drove in 146. Ken Griffey had 398 career home runs, 1,152 RBIs, and a batting average of .299 in his first 11 big-league seasons in Seattle.

Whereas the two previous years with Griffey batting between A-Rod and DH Edgar Martinez were losing seasons for Seattle, in 2000 without Griffey the Mariners returned to the postseason as a wild card and made it to the ALCS before falling victim to the Yankees. Martinez batted .324

with 37 home runs and led the league with 145 RBIs. Alex Rodriguez had his third-straight 40-homer season with 41, drove in 132 runs, batted .316, and had the best year of his career in terms of wins above replacement. It was the perfect setup, along with accolades about him being already one of baseball's all-time greatest players, for his agent, Scott Boras, to demand an average annual salary of $25 million a year for 10 years for A-Rod's services. And A-Rod had only turned 25 in July.

'Twas thought the loss of A-Rod would be devastating to Seattle's prospects in 2001. While he went to play for a Texas team that won just 73 games, the Mariners—without Alex Rodriguez—won an American League record-setting 116 games, tying Chicago's 1906 Cubs (in 154 games) for the most ever by a major-league team. The Yankees, however, made sure Seattle would not threaten their 1998 record of 125 wins, including the postseason, by handily beating the Mariners in five games in the ALCS. Seattle won 120 on the year. The Mariners had the best pitching in the major leagues in 2001—better even than the Braves. Thirty-eight-year-old southpaw Jamie Moyer was 20–6, including winning 11 of his last 12 decisions. Aaron Sele, a right-hander whose 37–20 record in his two years in Texas helped the Rangers to division titles in 1998 and 1999, had come to Seattle as a free agent in 2000 and was 15–5 in 2001. And Freddy Garcia, one of two highly regarded prospects Seattle got from Houston in return for Randy Johnson, was 18–6 with a league-leading 3.05 earned run average. The other player they got, Carlos Guillen, replaced A-Rod at shortstop.

But it was a pair of free agents in their first year with Seattle that grabbed all the attention—second baseman Bret Boone and right fielder Ichiro Suzuki. Boone had modest credentials at best when he came to Seattle. His career batting average in nine big-league seasons was .255. His career highs in home runs and RBIs were 24 and 95 when he played for Cincinnati in 1998. But in 2001, Boone crashed 37 homers, led the league with 141 runs batted in, and batted .331. He was third in the MVP voting. Suzuki was an eight-year veteran from the Japan Pacific League when he came to Seattle in 2001 for his "rookie" major-league season. Although he left Japan with a .353 career batting average, as the first Japanese position player to be signed by a major-league club to be an everyday player, there was some skepticism as to whether Suzuki would be anywhere near as successful batting against major-league pitchers—and perhaps he might not succeed at all. Universally known by his first name in both countries, Ichiro silenced the skeptics by leading the majors in hits (242) and stolen bases (56) and the AL in batting average (.350). He was voted the AL's Rookie of the Year and Most Valuable Player.

One hundred-sixteen wins might have given the Mariners permission to say they were no longer winless in Seattle, but that was short-lived to one season. Seattle has not been back to the postseason since, not even as a wild-card team. The Mariners were still a very good team the next two years, winning 93 in both 2002 and 2003, but failed to qualify for the postseason either time. Already approaching 40 in 2001, Edgar Martinez was sliding toward the end of his career. Fifteen years after retiring in 2004, Martinez was elected to the Hall of Fame—the first career designated hitter voted in by the baseball writers—on the merits of his .312 career batting average, 309 homers, and 1,261 RBIs. Bret Boone remained an offensive force the next two years, hitting 59 homers and driving in 224 runs. Based on his new sculpted musculature when he came to Seattle in 2001, Canseco suggested in his book that Boone began using steroids when he entered free agency—an allegation Boone denies and that has not been proven. Jaime Moyer, the antithesis of Randy Johnson in that he averaged half the strikeouts per nine innings the Big Unit did, won 21 games for the Mariners in 2003 as a 40-year-old and pitched in the major leagues until he was 49.

Suzuki remained an elite player. In his first 10 major-league seasons, Ichiro collected 2,244 hits, never with fewer than 206, leading the league seven times; had a .331 batting average, hitting over .300 every year, and won two batting titles, his second when he hit .372 in 2004; stole 383 bases in 471 attempts, swiping fewer than 30 only once; and threw out 91 base runners from the outfield. Ichiro was not, however, the kind of impact player that power-hitting shortstop A-Rod was.

# 4

# END OF THE DODGERS' O'MALLEY ERA

It seemed sacrilegious that the Los Angeles Dodgers, the last of baseball's family-owned franchises dating back to before expansion, would be sold to Australian media mogul Rupert Murdoch's Fox Entertainment Group. If Branch Rickey was the architect of the Brooklyn Dodgers' 1950s dynasty, even though he himself left in 1951, Walter O'Malley was the proud paterfamilias. O'Malley's decision to move the franchise to Los Angeles in 1958, after being frustrated in his efforts to build a new ballpark in Brooklyn to replace old, worn-out Ebbets Field, was sad for Brooklyn but ultimately great for both the franchise and Major League Baseball. The Dodgers won four pennants and three World Series in their first nine years in LA. O'Malley passed the torch of running the club's day-to-day operations to his son Peter in 1970. Now in the divisional era, the Dodgers won three NL Western Division titles they turned into three (losing) trips to the World Series before Walter passed away in 1979. Peter O'Malley presided over four additional Dodgers division titles and two World Series championships in the 1980s.

The Dodgers, 3½ games in front of the NL West, were the only team in the division with a winning record and were just 2 games over .500 when the 1994 season came to its abrupt end on August 11. Denied by the strike that year, LA won the division in 1995 by a single game over upstart Colorado, one of the NL's 1993 expansion teams. And in 1996 LA had to settle for the National League wild card after going into their final weekend series against second-place San Diego with a two-game lead, only to lose all three games. The Padres outpaced the Dodgers in the final month in large part on the back of Ken Caminiti's 9 homers, 23 runs batted in, and .375 batting average in September. Six years later, Caminiti would tell *Sports Illustrated* that he owed it all to using steroids that year. For the Dodgers, the 1996 season was perhaps most noteworthy for Tommy Lasorda, in his 20th year as manager, stepping down in late June following a heart procedure. He succeeded Walt Alston, who had managed the Dodgers for 23 years going back to 1954 when they were still playing at Ebbets Field.

The three best players on LA's 1995–1996 Dodgers were NL Rookies of the Year in consecutive seasons—catcher Mike Piazza in 1993, right fielder Raul Mondesi in 1994, and Japanese free-agent right-hander Hideo Nomo in 1995. Beginning with his rookie year in 1993, Piazza in four years had crushed 127 home runs while batting .330 and was already being talked about as the best-hitting catcher in baseball history. Mondesi was an emerging star. And Nomo, only the second player from Japan to ever play in the majors—and the first in 30 years—proved that a top-tier pitcher from the Japanese leagues could excel in major league baseball; in his 1995 rookie season, Nomo had a 13–6 record and 2.54 earned run average while leading the league with 236 strikeouts and 11.1 strikeouts per nine innings.

That the Dodgers were swept in baseball's new opening-round best-of-five division series of the postseason in both 1995 and 1996 made their lack of effort in the free-agent market a source of some frustration for LA's fans. While the Dodgers in the late-1980s and early-1990s invested in such high-profile free agents as outfielders Kirk Gibson (in 1988), Brett Butler (in 1991), and Darryl Strawberry (also 1991) and pitcher Tom Candiotti (in 1992), they signed none in the first years after the players' strike. In January 1997 the Dodgers signed Piazza to a two-year $15 million contract that made him the best-paid player for annual salary in franchise history. Still two years away from free agency, feeling that he deserved a contract comparable to the five-year $55 million deal Albert Belle had just signed with the White Sox, Piazza was not happy with his deal, then went out and had his best year yet in 1997—40 homers, 124 RBIs, and a .362 batting average, tying Bill Dickey (in 1936) for the highest ever by a catcher (since broken by Joe Mauer's .365 average in 2009). The Dodgers ended up second in their division, two games behind their historical rivals in San Francisco.

If the previous year put an end to more than four decades of just two managers (Alston and Lasorda) in Dodger blue, 1997 was the end of nearly a half-century of O'Malley family ownership of the Dodgers when the franchise was put up for sale. There were estate-tax reasons why, but Peter O'Malley was also a disaffected major-league owner. Peter was not the influential power broker in the game's inner councils the way his dad was. The traditional old-boy network that was Walter O'Malley's milieu in the 1950s and 1960s had given way to a new old-boy network. Peter was respected as a baseball legacy owner, but the owners with the greatest influence now were far more wealthy corporate types with different perspectives on the baseball business. O'Malley complained that escalating player salaries made it impossible to stay competitive for even the big-market Dodgers because they did not have the financial depth of corporate owners or the Yankees' enormous broadcast revenues.

The sale of the Dodgers to Fox Entertainment for $311 million—double the assessed value of any major-league franchise at the time—was approved by Major League Baseball in March 1998. The Dodgers got off to a sluggish start. Piazza was traded in May to the Florida Marlins after failing in his bid to get what would have been record-breaking seven-year deal worth over $100 million to stay in LA. Nomo was traded in June. Manager Bill Russell and general manager Fred Claire were fired in June. Claire had been in his position since 1987, and Russell—Lasorda's replacement—had managed the Dodgers for only 322 games—two games fewer than the equivalent of two seasons. Not including interim managers, Russell's tenure was the shortest of any Dodgers manager in 60 years. Clearly, the Dodgers new corporate owners were not committed to honoring the tradition of stability that prevailed during the O'Malley era. The 1998 Dodgers finished third in their first year as part of Murdoch's business empire.

San Diego's Padres, down the freeway from LA, ran away with the NL West in 1998. It was their second division title in three years, both under first-time major-league manager Bruce Bochy, and the third in franchise history. Their 98 wins were by far the most in team history. Veteran 38-year-old outfielder Tony Gwynn, coming off four straight batting championships in which his cumulative average was .371, ran his streak of consecutive years batting over .300 to 16, although with a very modest ninth-best .321 average. Left fielder Greg Vaughn's 50 home runs did not attract the attention they might otherwise because of the Mark McGwire–Sammy Sosa battle to eclipse the Roger Maris record. Elite closer Trevor Hoffman tied the National League record of 53 saves set five years earlier by the Cubs' Randy Myers. Ace right-hander Kevin Brown, whom San Diego got from Florida for virtually nothing because the Marlins were decimating their 1997 World Series–winning team in a massive salary dump, was 18–7 with a 2.38 earned run average. The Padres rolled through their division and league championship series before being obliterated in the World Series four-straight by New York's 114-win 1998 Yankees.

Brown left as a free agent less than two months after the World Series to sign a record-setting contract with the Dodgers. One ace alone, even the magnitude of Kevin Brown, does not a pitching staff make, but without him the Padres' starters ERA jumped from 3.70 in 1998 to 4.40 in 1999 and San Diego began a string of five-straight losing seasons. They returned to the top of their division in 2005. At 82–80, the Padres were the only team in the NL West with a winning record. When they moved into first place to stay at the end of July, the Padres were 3 games *under* .500. After 157 games, with 5 remaining on the schedule, they held a safe 4-game lead and were still a game under .500. It came as little surprise that they were swept by the Cardinals in their division series, never with a lead in any game.

The Padres tied the Dodgers atop the NL West again in 2006, thanks to 12 wins in their final 16 games, but won the division without need of a playoff by virtue of their better record against LA in their season series. The Dodgers had to settle for the wild card. The Padres' September surge was fueled by the offense of first baseman Adrian Gonzalez, playing his first full season in the majors, and veteran outfielders Mike Cameron and Brian Giles. Although only two of their five starting pitchers had winning records, and despite their ace Jake Peavy having a losing record with an earned run average over 4.00 after winning 68 percent of his decisions with an excellent 2.61 ERA the two previous years, the Padres nonetheless had the best team ERA in the National League.

Soon after the Padres' elimination in their division series, Bruce Bochy announced he was leaving San Diego after 12 years to manage in San Francisco. He still had a year remaining on his contract, but despite his back-to-back division titles in 2005 and 2006, to go along with those in 1996 and 1998, the Padres were unwilling to entertain a contract extension. They allowed Bochy to find a better deal. He did. And that turned out great for both the Giants and Bochy personally.

Following the Padres' 1998 trip to the World Series, the dominant team in the NL West straddling the end of the twentieth and beginning of the twenty-first century was the Arizona Diamondbacks—a 1998 expansion team that outdid Colorado and Florida in defying the past trajectory of expansion teams taking years to become competitive. The 1993-expansion Rockies and Marlins both reached the postseason early in their franchise histories by trading with other clubs and using the free-agent market to acquire top-tier players. After losing records their first two years, the Rockies were the National League wild-card team in the strike-shortened, 144-game 1995 season with a 77–67 record. It would not be until 12 years later that the Rockies were back in the postseason. The Marlins didn't have their first winning season until their fifth year in 1997, when they too were the wild-card team, from which they went on to win the World Series. For their part, the D-backs predictably finished last in the NL West their first season with 97 losses, then turned around to win 100 games and the 1999 division title by 14 games.

Arizona took a "win-now" approach from the very beginning. In October 1995, two and a half years before their first game, the newborn franchise jumped quickly to hire Buck Showalter to be their manager after George Steinbrenner pushed him out for the Yankees' failure to get past Seattle in their division series. They jumped quickly *before* Steinbrenner could change his mind, which he did. But Showalter was not persuaded to return to the Boss's den. With no game (or team) to manage until 1998, Showalter focused on developing the D-backs' minor-league system. Before their inaugural season, Arizona traded for Matt Williams to play third base and bat cleanup and signed shortstop Jay Bell and right-hander Andy Benes to front the starting rotation. All three were high-profile veteran players. The next year, they traded for veteran outfielder Luis Gonzalez and second baseman Tony Womack, whom they put in the outfield, and signed center fielder Steve Finley, one of the cornerstones of San Diego's 1996 division title, and Randy Johnson—the most intimidating pitcher in baseball—as free agents.

The results spoke for themselves. Arizona had the 1999 division title wrapped up by the end of August. Johnson fanned 364 batters in 271⅔ innings, was 17–9 in 35 starts, led the league in earned run average, and won his second Cy Young Award, to go with the one he won in Seattle four years earlier. Gonzalez led the league in hits and batted .336. Bell led the team with 38 homers; Williams hit 35 and drove in 142 runs; Finley hit 34; and Womack led the NL in stolen bases for the third year in a row. But New York's Mets clubbed Johnson for 7 runs in 8⅓ innings in the opening game of their division series and went on to defeat the D-backs in four games.

The Diamondbacks spent most of the 2000 season atop the NL West before fading in the final month. But in July, hoping to reinforce their tenuous hold on first place, they traded for Phillies ace Curt Schilling to join Johnson in the starting rotation. The trade did not pay the hoped-for dividends that year, but surely did in 2001 when Arizona won their division, won the pennant, and became the first team to beat Joe Torre's iteration of the New York Yankees' forever dynasty in the World Series. Buck Showalter, however, did not have the pleasure of payback for being summarily dismissed by Steinbrenner. Showalter was let go after the Diamondbacks' sluggish 27–30 record in the final two months of the 2000 season and replaced by first-time manager Bob Brenly. Arizona also signed veteran first baseman Mark Grace and outfielder Reggie Sanders as free agents for 2001.

The 2001 Diamondbacks had a legion of heroes. Gonzalez hit 57 homers, with 142 runs batted in and a .325 batting average, and Sanders had 33 homers to lead the D-backs offensively. But Randy Johnson— "The Big Unit"—and Curt Schilling stood out above all. Schilling was 22–6 and Johnson 21–6, with the pair striking out 665 batters in 506⅓ innings between them in 2001, and then ramped it up in the postseason. Schilling pitched complete-game victories in all three of his division series and league championship series starts; Johnson beat Atlanta twice in the NLCS, including his fifth-game start that sent Arizona to the World Series; and the two pitchers split MVP honors in the World Series for how they handled the Yankees.

The 2001 World Series was played against the backdrop of the 9/11 terrorist attacks on New York City less than two months earlier. Being from the stricken city, the Yankees, for once, were the sentimental favorites. And they brought a three-games-to-two lead with them to Arizona for the sixth and seventh games, thanks to dramatic extra-inning victories in Games Four and Five. Randy Johnson, who shut out the Yankees on three hits in nine innings in Game Two, won the sixth game handily behind his teammates' 15-run, 22-hit assault on Yankees pitching. Schilling, who held the Yankees to just one run on three hits in seven innings in both of his first two starts in the World Series, started Game Seven. Brenly brought on the Big Unit to get the final out of the eighth inning after the Yankees had taken a 2–1 lead. And despite his having thrown 104 pitches the day before, Johnson stayed in to retire the Yankees in order in the top of the ninth.

But the D-backs were still behind, 2–1, and Mariano Rivera—on his way to being the world's greatest closer ever—was on the mound for the would-be series-ending save—except that's not what happened. Grace led off with a single. Rivera made a throwing error to second on a sacrifice-bunt attempt. Two batters later Womack doubled to tie the score. Rivera plunked the next batter to load the bases with one out. And Luis Gonzalez plopped a short fly into shallow left field over the drawn-in infield to give Randy Johnson his third win of the series and the Arizona Diamondbacks a championship in only their fourth year of existence.

Johnson and Schilling reprised their act of domination in 2002. Both made 35 starts. Johnson was 24–5 and struck out 334 in 260 innings, and Schilling 23–7 with 316 K's in 259⅓ innings. The D-backs again won the NL West, giving them three division titles in their first five years, but were swept by St. Louis in their division series. With an 81–27 record and 2.48 ERA from 1999 to 2002, leading the league in winning percentage twice, in earned run average three times, in innings-pitched twice, and all four years in strikeouts, Randy Johnson's first four years in Arizona were as dominant as any pitcher's ever. He struck out 1,417 of the 4,109 batters he faced in 1,030 innings, getting 46 percent of his outs by way of the Almighty K.

Both aces were hurt in 2003, making just 42 starts between them, after which Curt Schilling left as a free agent for Boston, where he would come back in 2004 to torment the Yankees with his bloody sock. The D-backs finished third in 2003 and collapsed to a horrific 51–111 record in 2004, even with the Big Unit going 16–14 and leading the league in strikeouts (with 290) for the fifth time in his six years with the Diamondbacks. He was 40 years old, and with Arizona clearly looking to the future, Randy Johnson left as a free agent for New York and the Yankees.

If Peter O'Malley believed the big-market Dodgers could not afford high-priced players because, as a family-owned franchise, he did not have as vast a financial reservoir to draw upon as big-market franchises owned by wealthy investors, business owners, or corporations, that changed once the Fox Entertainment Group, with Rupert Murdoch's immense fortune behind it, took charge of the franchise. After three years of LA being in the middle of major-league teams in player payroll, in 1999—the first year Fox could set payroll for an upcoming season—the Dodgers vaulted to second in the majors, behind only Steinbrenner's Yankees, in what they paid their players. Over the winter they had signed Padres free agent Kevin Brown, coming off the best year of his career, to baseball's first $100 million contract—seven years for $105 million. LA also inherited the six-year, $61 million deal outfielder Gary Sheffield signed with the Marlins in 1997 when they traded Mike Piazza to get him in 1998. The next year, LA negotiated a six-year, $84 million deal with Shawn Green in order to complete a trade for him with Toronto—an exchange of right fielders, Raul Mondesi for Green.

Brown, when healthy, lived up to his big-salary expectations the five years he pitched for the Dodgers before he and the remainder of his contract, along with his recent injury history, were traded to the Yankees in 2004. Brown was 18–9 his first year in LA in 1999, led the league with a 2.58 ERA in 2000, and came back from two years of injuries to a 14–9 record and 2.39 earned run average in 32 starts in 2003. Sheffield did too, hitting 129 homers—including 43 in 2000 to tie Duke Snider's single-season franchise record set in Brooklyn 44 years earlier—and batting .312 in his three and half years in LA before he was traded to Atlanta in 2002 amid recriminations about the Dodgers not being willing to extend his contract to keep him theirs for the rest of his career. The Snider-Sheffield franchise record for home runs was broken the very next year by Green's 49 in 2001. Green followed that up with 42 homers the next year, including becoming the 14th player in history to hit 4 homers in a game on May 23, 2002. Meanwhile, Eric Gagne—one of their home-grown players, making much less—who the Dodgers converted to closer after two unsuccessful years as a starter, saved 152 games from 2002 to 2004, including a perfect 55 saves in 55 save opportunities in 2003.

By 2003 the Dodgers were back on the market. The widespread criticism provoked by the record-setting contract the Dodgers gave Brown that Fox would use the enormity of its financial resources to buy championships for Los Angeles proved misplaced. In the six years Fox Entertainment Group owned the franchise, the Dodgers never made it to the postseason. Twice, they finished a distant second in the NL West. Murdoch's interest in buying the Dodgers in the first place—and willingness to pay a record-setting amount to get them—was to secure broadcasting rights to their games as the crown jewel of a new regional sports network he was planning for Southern California to compete against a regional sports network planned by Disney/ESPN. As it was, Fox already had local contracts with 21 of Major League Baseball's 30 teams to broadcast their games. It turned out that Disney's ambitions for regional ESPN networks did not come to fruition and hence did not threaten Fox's sports-broadcasting dominance in Southern California (or anywhere else). Owning a baseball team, even a franchise as storied as the Los Angeles Dodgers, was not worth it to Murdoch's business enterprise. Forbes estimated operating losses for the Dodgers under Fox to have been $100 million. In 2004, Fox sold the franchise for $430 million. That turned out to be the beginning of the most scandalous ownership chapter in Dodgers history.

# 5

# THE BOTTOM 25 PERCENT

About a third of major-league teams are in small-revenue markets. Free agency and the vast differences in revenue available to big-market and small-market franchises changed the dynamic of building and keeping intact competitive teams. Even with a core of talented players *not yet eligible* for free agency, small-market teams are disadvantaged by not having the financial resources to add impact players to boost their post-season chances or to keep their best players when free agency looms.

A franchise with a storied history, Pittsburgh's 1990–1992 Pirates—a budding dynasty, winning three NL Eastern Division titles in a row—are perhaps the best team undone by being a small-market club in the free-agency era. With core players that included Barry Bonds, Bobby Bonilla, and Andy Van Slyke in the middle of the line-up and Doug Drabek and John Smiley in the starting rotation, the Pirates were poised to be a power in the National League for many years beyond 1992 and probably would have ruled the NL Central Division, to which Pittsburgh was moved in 1994 when Major League Baseball realigned to three divisions in each league. But their best players were not shy in saying they were underpaid for their skills and accomplishments and that they would prefer to play elsewhere for teams with fewer financial constraints.

Bonilla and Smiley were both gone after the 1991 season. Bonilla left as a free agent and Smiley, despite his league-leading 20–8 record, was traded one year before he was eligible for free agency. After 1992 and a third-straight division title, but with the mission of putting Pittsburgh back into the World Series for the first time since 1979 still unfinished business, both Bonds and Drabek became free agents whose asking price was way beyond what the Pirates could afford. The Pirates plummeted to fifth place and a losing record in 1993. That was the first of 20 consecutive seasons without a winning record—an unprecedented streak of losing futility. They did have some solid players along the way—catcher Jason Kendall (1996–2004); shortstop Jack Wilson (2001–2009); outfielders Brian Giles (1993–2003), one of the best players in baseball, and Jason Bay (2004–2008); and right-hander Jason Schmidt (1997–2001). All were traded while still in their prime before Pittsburgh would lose them to free agency.

Oakland's Athletics, whose powerhouse club went to three straight World Series with the best record in baseball from 1988 to 1990, won a fourth division title in five years in 1992 but did not have a winning season any of the next six seasons. A small-revenue team despite being in the Bay Area, the A's had been on an austerity budget at the direction of new owners since 1996. That caused superstar manager Tony La Russa, who presided over the 1988–1992 A's, to leave Oakland after 10 years rather than be part of an organization with no commitment to spending what it might take to be competitive. Their glory days receded even further in Oakland's living memory when Mark McGwire, their superstar slugger from their championship years and the A's highest-paid player, was traded in July 1997 in a salary dump, no matter his leading the majors in home runs with 34 on his way to 58 for the year—the most since Roger Maris's 61 in '61.

Similarly, Minnesota's Twins went from winning the World Series in 1991—their second championship in five years—to struggling through one losing season after another from 1992 to 2000. Beloved center fielder Kirby Puckett was forced to retire in 1996 because of eye problems; he batted over .300 in eight of his last 10 seasons, including clearing 200 hits five times, and retired with a .318 batting average and 207 home runs. All-star second baseman Chuck Knoblauch was traded to the Yankees in 1998, his 276 stolen bases in his eight years with the Twins the most by any player since the franchise moved to Minnesota. Twins owner Carl Pohlad, one of America's wealthiest persons, was excoriated for cutting payroll rather than invest in building a winning ballclub. Perhaps sensitive to that, he signed their ace—righty Brad Radke, a native of neighboring Wisconsin—to a four-year, $36 million contract in 2000 that was below his likely market value had he opted for free agency at the end of the season.

Much has been made of Montreal's Expos, famously in first place with the best record in baseball when the players went on strike in 1994, being poised to being in the thick of the postseason hunt for many years to come had they avoided the loss of their talented core of young players to free agency or in trades before they became free agents for players of much lesser ability. Outfielders Larry Walker, Marquis Grissom, and Moises Alou; closer John Wetteland; and starting pitchers Ken Hill and Pedro Martinez all helped other teams get to the World Series. The Expos were not quite as hopeless as the Pirates; they had two winning seasons in their next 10 years in Montreal. In 2002, the Expos were first a candidate for contraction should the major leagues downsize to 28 teams, then became wards of Major League Baseball and were given a budget that precluded improvement, while their owners—Major League Baseball— prioritized moving the franchise. In 2005, the Expos moved to Washington, DC, to become the Nationals. Along the way the Expos had a handful of quality players, most notably outfielder Vladimir Guerrero. Before leaving as a free agent after the 2003 season to continue on with his Hall of Fame career, Guerrero belted 234 homers and batted .323 in 1,004 games for Montreal.

Kansas City's Royals, another small-market club, did not so much have a team undone by having to shed no-longer-affordable star players as they were unable to rebuild a competitive team because of budget constraints. A 1969-expansion team the same as the Expos, the Royals were competitive in the AL West most years in the 1970s and 1980s, winning six division titles and going to two World Series—losing in 1980 and winning in 1985—with George Brett their most prominent star. After 1985, they would not make another postseason appearance for 29 years. From 1995 to 2012, the Royals had just one winning season. Criticized by Kansas City fans used to a winning legacy for being unnecessarily chintzy in their unwillingness to spend to improve the roster, the Royals groomed three homegrown stars during those years—outfielder Johnny Damon, called up in 1995; outfielder Carlos Beltran, 1999's AL Rookie of the Year; and right-hander Zack Greinke, who debuted in 2004 and won the Cy Young Award in 2009—all of whom were traded before they would have been lost in free agency. All three played at least five full seasons in Kansas City but only Beltran in 2003 played for a winning Royals team.

And then there was Bud Selig's hometown team—Milwaukee's Brewers, which he owned from their first season in 1970 until handing the ownership reins to his daughter in 1998 to avoid a conflict of interest when he *officially* became commissioner. (Any appearance of a conflict of interest did not seem to matter the six years he was "acting" commissioner.) The Brewers had just one division title in their history—the AL East in 1982, starring shortstop Robin Yount—and went on to lose the only World Series they ever played. As the owner of a small-market team whose local revenue stream was dwarfed by those of big-market clubs, Selig believed there was no hope for his Brewers ever being able to compete unless and until there was revenue-sharing by well-to-do clubs and a competitive balance "luxury" tax on player payrolls exceeding a certain threshold. By 1997, Selig had succeeded in getting both. Not that it helped the Brewers, who went 14 years from 1993 to 2006 without a winning record. Along the way, the franchise was switched from the American to the National League in 1998 to accommodate two expansion franchises—one for each league; opened a new ballpark in 2001; and traded their two best players—third baseman Jeff Cirillo and power-hitting outfielder Jeromy Burnitz—in 2002 before they could enter the free-agent market.

Those six clubs—Montreal, Minnesota, Pittsburgh, Oakland, Kansas City, and Milwaukee—were the bottom 20 percent of major-league franchises in annual local revenue earnings from 1995 to 1999. Montreal, Pittsburgh, Minnesota, and Oakland were also in the bottom 20 percent in average annual player payroll those five years, and Kansas City and Milwaukee in the bottom 25 percent. That data, provided by Major League Baseball, was included in a report on "Baseball Economics" written by four "independent" members appointed to a blue-ribbon panel by Commissioner Selig. The air quotes are mine, given that former senator George Mitchell and former chairman of the Federal Reserve Paul Volcker (both with close ties to owners), Yale University president Richard Levin (who drafted the owners' original salary cap proposal back in 1989), and conservative columnist (and friend of the commissioner) George Will were all appointed by Selig without any input from the players union.

Their report, released in July 2000, reached precisely the conclusions Selig wanted for use as "objective" outside ammunition for Major League Baseball to make its case on the importance of reining in player-payroll costs in upcoming negotiations with the players union for a new collective bargaining agreement. "The size of a club's payroll is the most important factor in determining how competitive the club will be," the blue-ribbon report said. Stating that there was a direct correlation between local revenues and affordable payrolls, the independent members wrote that "a low payroll usually means that a club cannot contend for a post-season berth or a championship" absent "staggering operating losses" to finance a competitive payroll it could not afford. The competitive advantage, they said, was always with the clubs in large-revenue markets that could afford high player payrolls, including bidding against each other for the best available free agents (for whom lots of money was the object).

The report included numerous tables with five years of data from the end of the players' strike in 1995 to 1999 to show that no team in the bottom 25 percent in both local revenue earnings and player payrolls made the postseason, and only one team in the bottom 50 percent did— Houston's 1997 Astros, winning the NL Central with only the fifth-best record in the National League—and they were swept in the division-series round by Atlanta, whose 101 wins were the most in the majors. (Cincinnati's 1999 Reds, eighth from the bottom in local revenue and eleventh from the bottom in payroll, won 96 games but didn't make the postseason after losing a playoff game for the wild card.) As negotiations with the union took on greater urgency with the existing collective bargaining agreement having expired, Major League Baseball released a December 2001 "Update" (although without the involvement of any of the "independent members"), including data from the two most recent seasons to further substantiate the conclusions of the original report. The new data forced Major League Baseball to acknowledge that Oakland— one of the 25 percent—made the postseason in both 2000 and 2001 but added gratuitously that the A's failed to make it past the division series. It was gratuitous because only one other team—Seattle's Mariners, not the Yankees or Braves—won more games those two years than the low-revenue, low-payroll Athletics.

The A's had the fourth-lowest average annual local revenue stream of the 30 major-league teams and operating losses of $45 million from 1995 to 1999, according to the blue-ribbon report published in July 2000. But despite having the majors' fourth-lowest average annual player payroll, the Athletics won three division titles and a wild card from 2000 to 2003, twice with more than 100 wins. In none of those years, however, did they get out of the first round of postseason series. All four years they had a better record than the team they lost to in their division series, notwithstanding their having the lower player payroll.

The secret to Oakland's success, in direct opposition to the dire conclusions of Selig's esteemed blue-ribbon panel, was the counterintuitive strategy A's general manager Billy Beane took to compete against teams with much higher player payrolls. Memorialized by financial journalist Michael Lewis in his book *Moneyball*, Beane and his staff moved baseball into the twenty-first century (as it were), by relying on computer-based, data-driven analytics to identify *affordable* players with particular skill sets—most notably for Beane, on-base percentage—whose value was often unrecognized or underappreciated in the mix of the traditional physical attributes and back-of-bubblegum-card stats used to evaluate players. Beane and his team used Moneyball principles to value-engineer the roster of the Oakland Athletics by signing under-the-radar free agents and trading for players not much in demand.

Beane's cost-effective approach allowed the A's to absorb the free-agency loss of Jason Giambi, their superstar slugger who ably replaced McGwire at first base and in the heart of the Oakland lineup, after he helped power the A's to 102 wins in 2001 with 38 homers and a .342 batting average and leading the league with a .477 on-base percentage. Losing an impact player like Giambi was thought likely to mortally wound Oakland's chances of competing for another shot at the World Series. The $120-million-for-seven-years deal Giambi signed with the Yankees was one more bullet point for Selig's argument that something needed to be done—specifically, putting an end to such exorbitant free-agent contracts—if small-market teams (like Oakland) were to have any chance of competing with free-spending, big-market behemoths like George Steinbrenner's Yankees.

But the A's hardly noticed the absence of Jason Giambi in 2002, winning 103 games (tied for the most in baseball with the Yankees) and their division, followed by 96 wins and another division title in 2003. They still had shortstop Miguel Tejada and third baseman Eric Chavez, both star players not yet eligible for free agency, to provide clout in the middle of the order. And they had a trio of young aces—Tim Hudson,

Mark Mulder, and Barry Zito—that made their starting rotation the best in the American League. Hudson led the league with 20 wins in 2000, Mulder with 21 in 2001, and Zito with 23 in 2002. Inevitably, Oakland's stars became unaffordable for the perennially low-budget Athletics. Tejada left as a free agent in 2004. Mulder was traded after the 2004 season as he was about to enter his free-agent year. Hudson in 2005 and Zito in 2007 were pitching elsewhere, having left Oakland as free agents. Chavez liked Oakland enough that he agreed to a team-friendly, multiyear contract in 2004 to stay with the A's, within three years of which injuries undermined his career.

In 2004, for the first time in five years, Oakland did not make the postseason despite leading their division for most of August and September. They won another division title in 2006, this time won their division series against Minnesota, but were swept by Detroit in the ALCS. Oakland had a losing record four of the next five years as Beane's Moneyball approach no longer had the same impact as before, mostly because it was no longer unique in major league baseball.

Just like Oakland, Minnesota defied the blue-ribbon panel's expectations in 2002 by seizing control of the AL Central by the All-Star break and winning it by 13½ games notwithstanding having the third-lowest payroll in the league, just ahead of the A's. They even beat Oakland in their division series and took the ALCS to the limit before losing to Anaheim, a wild-card team with a better record on its way to a World Series championship. Like Montreal's Expos, the Twins had been on the commissioner's contraction list because of their presumed difficulty competing as a small-market team with limited local revenue streams. Opposition from the players union and a legal challenge from the state of Minnesota kept that from happening in 2002. Having dodged the contraction bullet, and his team unexpectedly running away with the division in 2002 to the delight of its fans, Twins owner Carl Pohlad began investing more in his roster to keep the team competitive and cinch the case for public funding for a new ballpark.

Beginning in 2003, Minnesota moved from the bottom 25 percent of teams in paying their major-league roster to mostly around the middle of the pack for the rest of the decade. Even without spending on costly high-profile free agents, that was enough for the Twins to be the AL Central's most successful team the rest of the decade. In the nine years from 2002 to 2010, Minnesota won the division six times, missing out only in 2005, 2007, and by one game in 2008 when they lost a playoff—their 163rd game—to the White Sox, 1–0, on a seventh-inning home run by Jim Thome off rookie starter Nick Blackburn. In five of their six postseasons, however, Minnesota never made it past their division series. In 2006, as the Twins were on their way to their fourth division title in five years, state authorities finally approved public financing for a new baseball stadium. Target Field opened in downtown Minneapolis in 2010.

Unlike the Oakland A's leveraging Moneyball principles to be one of the best teams, the Minnesota Twins found success the old-fashioned way without relying on esoteric computerized data-sets for player evaluations. Most of Minnesota's core players in the decade—veteran right-hander Brad Radke, center fielder Torii Hunter, third baseman Corey Koskie, catcher A. J. Pierzynski when they won three division titles in a row from 2002 to 2004; catcher Joe Mauer, first baseman Justin Morneau, outfielders Michael Cuddyer and Denard Span (who took over in center after Hunter left as a free agent in 2008), and right-hander Scott Baker after that—were amateur draft picks by the Twins. Joe Mauer, a local St. Paul (Minnesota) native who from 2006 to 2013 was the best catcher in the American League if not all of baseball, became the face of the franchise. Rare for a catcher, Mauer was a high-average hitter who led the league in batting average three times in four years between 2006 and 2009. In 2010, Mauer signed an eight-year, $184 million contract extension that was probably undervalued for the quality player he was to stay with his hometown team.

Minnesota also made astute trades for pitching prospects Eric Milton, Johan Santana, and Francisco Liriano, as well as for reliever Joe Nathan. Left-hander Santana, whom they acquired in 2000 from the Marlins before he ever pitched in the majors, became one of baseball's dominant pitchers. He won the Cy Young Award in 2004 and 2006, leading the league in earned run average both years. Traded to the Mets in 2008 just as he was entering the final year of a four-year, $40 million contract he had signed after winning his first Cy Young, Santana had won 70 percent of his decisions while striking out 1,381 batters in 1,308⅔ innings in his eight Twins years. Nathan averaged 41 saves with a 1.87 ERA in six years as the Twins closer before missing the entire 2010 season recovering from elbow surgery, giving up just 271 hits while striking out 518 batters in 418⅔ innings.

Despite their new stadium and Mauer's big deal, the Twins, averaging 94 losses a year, plummeted to the ranks of the noncompetitive from 2011 to 2016. In the face of the rigorous data analysis now de rigueur in major league baseball, the Twins' reliance on the old-fashioned way to guide decisions involving the amateur draft, trades, and going after free agents was no longer sustainable. Following their freefall from first to last in their division in 2011, the Twins hired Derek Falvey as their chief of baseball operations, who immediately directed the front office to build a robust analytics capability and take advantage of technology to improve player performance.

By 2017 Falvey's approach was paying dividends. Even though Mauer was breaking down rapidly from the rigors of catching and had moved to first base, a bevy of young players beginning to make an impact—shortstop Jorge Polanco, third baseman Miguel Sano, Eddie Rosario in left, Byron Buxton in center, and Jose Berrios in the starting rotation to backstop veterans Ervin Santana and Kyle Gibson—helped the Twins from 103 losses in 2016 to 85 wins and the second wild card in the American League. Two years later in 2019, Minnesota was an American League powerhouse, winning 101 and the AL Central by eight games while blasting a major-league-record 307 home runs. Failing once again to make it out of their division series, for the sixth time in their eight postseasons since 2002, including the 2017 wild-card game, the Twins were eliminated by the Yankees. Their postseason record since 2002? An abysmal 6–25.

Milwaukee, Pittsburgh, and Kansas City—other small-market clubs identified as being in the bottom 20 percent in revenue earnings in 2000 by Selig's blue-ribbon panel on "baseball economics"—followed Oakland and Minnesota in having their competitive say. After more than a decade of losing seasons, their first step was a commitment to winning, including using revenue-sharing funds for the purpose they were intended—on the team roster. Their competitive strategy included raising their player payrolls from the bottom tier into the middle tier (usually the bottom half of the middle tier) leading up and into the years they anticipated being able to compete for the postseason. They understood, however, that their window of opportunity would be limited by the number of years they could sustain success on player salaries at the upper end of their earned local revenues.

Keeping his team "perennially competitive" was in fact Mark Attanasio's cornerstone pledge when he bought Milwaukee's last-in-the-NL-Central Brewers from the Selig family in 2005. He boosted the Brewers' player payroll, the lowest in the majors in 2004, by nearly 50 percent in 2005 and doubled it by 2008. Battling for the wild card that year, the Brewers fired their manager in mid-September after starting the month 3–11, then rallied to win the wild card by a single game. Milwaukee was back in the postseason for the first time since losing the World Series in 1982. Three years later, the 2011 Brewers won a division title for the first time since then with a franchise-record 96 wins.

In Pittsburgh, Neal Huntington took charge as general manager of the worst team in the National League in 2007 and systematically went about building an analytics capability from the ground up to inform the Pirates' player decisions. Six years later, with a player payroll now ranked in the middle of major-league franchises, the 2013 Pirates, finishing 94–68, had their first winning season since the 1992 Barry Bonds Pirates to win one of now-two wild cards in the first year of baseball's new wild-card format. They were a wild-card team each of the next two years as well. In 2013 and 2015, both National League wild-card teams came from the Central Division. In 2015, the three top teams in the NL Central—the Cardinals, Pirates, and Cubs—had the three best records in major league baseball.

In Kansas City, the Royals' once-penurious owner gave new general manager Dayton Moore authorization to spend on improving the club after a third-straight 100-loss season in 2006. Their initial player-payroll boost did not yield competitive dividends, so after losing 95 games in 2010, the Royals cut payroll by more than half to a major-league low of $35.7 million in 2011 and began again. In 2014, now in the top tier of the bottom 50 percent in player salaries, the Royals went to the World Series as a wild-card team and in 2015 won their division *and* the World Series.

The competitive foundation for all three teams was built through developing minor-league prospects, most of whom were their own amateur-draft selections. For the Brewers, they included power-hitting first baseman Prince Fielder, second baseman Rickie Weeks, shortstop J. J. Hardy, outfielders Ryan Braun and Corey Hart, and right-handed ace Yovani Gallardo on Milwaukee's 2011 team. Braun won the MVP Award in 2011 for his 33 homers, 111 runs batted in, and .332 batting average that powered Milwaukee to 96 wins and a division title. Pittsburgh center fielder Andrew McCutchen was the National League's Most Valuable Player when the Pirates resumed their winning ways in 2013. Flanked by Starling Marte in left and Gregory Polanco in right, McCutchen was one of three homegrown stars playing in the Pirates outfield from 2014 to 2017. Right-hander Gerrit Cole, in his third year, was 19–8 for the 98-win Pirates in 2015. First baseman Eric Hosmer, third baseman Mike Moustakas, outfielder Alex Gordon, and catcher Salvador Perez—all originally signed by Kansas City—were the cornerstone players on the Royals' 2014 and 2015 World Series teams.

Once the window of opportunity to challenge for the postseason presented itself, all three of these small-market teams made strategic trades for players and signed *affordable* free agents that could make a difference in getting there. In July 2008, Milwaukee traded with Cleveland for lefty CC Sabathia to anchor their starting rotation for a run at the division title. The Brewers didn't win the division but would not have won the wild card without Sabathia's 11–2 record and 1.65 earned run average in 17 starts. Before the 2010 season Milwaukee signed veteran lefty Randy Wolf and traded for Royals ace Zack Greinke, and before the 2011 season they acquired right-hander Shaun Marcum from Toronto to bolster their starting rotation. Greinke was 16–6 when Milwaukee won the division in 2011, and Wolf and Marcum both won 13. Two of the players the Royals got for Greinke were outfielder Lorenzo Cain and shortstop Alcides Escobar—both instrumental to Kansas City's back-to-back World Series appearances. The 2013 Pirates were helped to their first postseason since 1992 by the veteran leadership of catcher Russell Martin and 16 wins by Francisco Liriano, both signed as free agents before the season.

But they were dancing with the devil. The competitive time-horizon for all three clubs was limited by their being small-market franchises. Sabathia, who perhaps never pitched better than he did in his 17 starts for Milwaukee, signed with the Yankees as a free agent after the 2008 season, prompting Brewers owner Attanasio to complain about the overwhelming financial advantages had by big-market teams, pointing out that the Yankees' infield alone was paid more than his entire team. With Sabathia as their ace, the Yankees won the World Series in 2009. Without Sabathia, the Brewers went from the second-best ERA by starting pitchers in the National League to the worst and were out of contention for even the wild card by mid-August. While Milwaukee did recover after two losing seasons to win the division title in 2011, there followed six pedestrian seasons. Fielder left as a free agent after another strong season in 2011. Braun crashed 41 homers to lead the league in 2012, then crashed on the shoals of a failed test for performance-enhancing drugs he took during the 2011 division series, which he tried to dismiss by alleging that the chain of custody of his blood sample had been compromised. Braun received a 100-game suspension during the 2013 season.

It wasn't until 2018 that the Brewers were back in the postseason. A surprisingly strong second-place finish with the National League's lowest player payroll the previous year caused Milwaukee to eye a new window of competitive opportunity. They signed the Royals' Lorenzo Cain and traded for Miami's Christian Yelich before the season. Trailing by half a game in July, they traded for the Royals' Moustakas. Yelich won the first of two consecutive batting titles and was the NL's Most Valuable Player. The 2018 Brewers' most valuable asset, however, was their trio of hard-throwing relievers—lefty Josh Hader, Jeremy Jeffress, and Corey Knebel—whom manager Craig Counsell used interchangeably in any of the last three innings to secure victories. They took the NLCS to seven games before losing to the Dodgers. The Brewers' chances of winning the division in 2019 were set back by a season-ending injury to Yelich—batting .329 with 44 homers at the time—with 18 games remaining. They won the second wild card but lost a 3–1 eighth-inning lead to Washington in the wild-card game.

Pittsburgh and Kansas City both nose-dived after 2015 and by 2019 were among only eight teams paying their players less than $100 million. After three-straight wild cards, the Pirates' hopes of winning the NL Central in 2016 were upended by McCutchen having the first bad year of his career and neither Cole nor Liriano pitching well. The 2016 Pirates dropped to third with a losing record and haven't recovered since. McCutchen and Cole were traded in 2018, the Pirates' player payroll was back to the lowest in the National League in 2019, and in 2020 they traded Marte. Falling back in the standings to a break-even record in 2016, the year after winning the World Series, and with core players on their championship team becoming or soon to be free agents—Hosmer and Cain left as free agents in 2018, and Kansas City signed Moustakas to an undervalued free-agent deal and traded him in July—the Royals conceded the near term to cut payroll in order to rebuild for the future. That future seemed on the far horizon after back-to-back 100-loss seasons in 2018 and 2019.

Of the teams identified as being in the bottom 20 percent of annual-average local revenue over the preceding five years in the July 2000 report by Selig's "Blue Ribbon Panel on Baseball Economics," only Kansas City has since won a World Series. And they did that only by boosting their player payroll into the middle 50 percent of major league teams in 2013 to take advantage of their perceived competitive window of opportunity. In that regard, while the "independent members" of the blue-ribbon panel may have underestimated the competitive prospects of small-market teams, they *were* largely correct on the broader point about making it to the World Series, let alone winning it. Of the 40 teams that played in the World Series between 2000 and 2019, only eight were in the bottom half of teams in player salaries, four of which were in the bottom 25 percent and just three of them in the bottom 20 percent. The only one of the four teams in the bottom 25 percent to *win* a World Series was Florida's 2003 Marlins, and they were at the top end of the bottom quartile.

The teams with the most success paying their rosters the least in their league were the 2008 Tampa Bay Rays and 2010 Texas Rangers, both advancing to the World Series before losing in five games to a National League club with a substantially higher player payroll but nonetheless in the middle of the major-league pack. The Rangers' 2010 season was an anomaly, however, since Texas had a much higher payroll the years before then and would go back to a much higher payroll almost immediately after.

Both the Rays and the Rangers adapted and improved upon Oakland's Moneyball principles to build competitive teams. Their general managers—Andrew Friedman in Tampa Bay and Jon Daniels in Texas—came from the business world without any prior baseball experience. Friedman brought business strategies from being a Wall Street financier to turn around a Tampa Bay franchise on a limited budget that had never had even a winning record before going from 96 losses and the worst record in baseball in 2007 to 97 wins to win the AL East in 2008 on their way to the World Series. Daniels brought business-management practices to improve a franchise that had been on the edge of competitiveness since, ironically, trading away Alex Rodriguez and his huge contract in 2004 for the purpose of having more payroll flexibility. Both their approaches, like that of the A's, relied on data-based analytics to achieve cost efficiencies in the makeup of their rosters.

It wasn't long before that approach lost most of its comparative advantage. They main reason why? Precisely because of the A's and the Rays' success with it, most major-league teams had developed their own proprietary databases to guide their decision-making processes on roster makeup and player development. "Smaller payroll teams are less disadvantaged in an evidence-based environment," said Minnesota's chief of baseball operations Derek Falvey. But big-market clubs like the Yankees were also using data analytics to their advantage, on top of the overbearing advantage they already had in being able to afford any of the game's best players.

# II

# Wrestling with History

# 6

# WILD-CARD WORLD SERIES

One of baseball's verities is that over six months and 162 games, by the time the postseason arrives the best teams in each league are those with the best record. Another *had been* that finishing with the best record in their division was the singular requirement to play in the postseason. When Major League Baseball restructured its postseason lineup to include a second-place wild-card team in each league, some baseball purists were offended by the sacrilegious notion that a team that clearly was not even first in its division could emerge as World Series champions.

It didn't take long for a wild-card team to make it to the World Series—just two years. And the first wild-card team to do so won the World Series. 'Twas 1997, and that team was the Florida Marlins, one of the 1993-expansion teams in just its fifth year of existence. But the Marlins weren't just *any* wild-card team. True, they finished nine games behind the Atlanta Braves in the NL East and were never in the running for the division title, but their 92–70 record was second-best in the National League—better by two games than San Francisco's NL West–winning Giants and eight games better than Houston's NL Central–winning Astros.

Owner Wayne Huizenga's willingness to spend extravagantly to build a championship-caliber team, motivated in equal parts to pressure the city of Miami to build the Marlins a new baseball stadium so they would no longer have to play in the Miami Dolphins' stadium (he also owned the NFL team) and to boost the value of his franchise (which he was looking to sell), was what brought the World Series to South Florida. No other owner, not even the Yankees' George Steinbrenner, was as active on the free-agent front as Huizenga prior to the 1996 and 1997 seasons. After winning just 67 games in 1995, Florida signed pitchers Al Leiter and Kevin Brown and center fielder Devon White to three-year contracts totaling more than $31 million. The Marlins improved to third with an 80–82 record in 1996. Brown won 17 and led the majors with a 1.89 earned run average. Leiter won 16. Huizenga upped the ante for 1997 by committing $83 million in multiyear contracts to sign White Sox ace Alex Fernandez, Orioles slugger Bobby Bonilla to play third base, and Expos outfielder Moises Alou—all three premier free agents. And just as the 1997 season was getting under way, the Marlins gave their best player, outfielder Gary Sheffield—fresh off 42 homers and a .314 batting average with 142 walks while striking out just 66 times in 677 plate appearances—a contract extension for six years and $61 million beginning in 1998 that was, at the time, the most lucrative contract in baseball history.

Huizenga also made news by signing Jim Leyland in October 1996 to a five-year, $7 million contract to manage in Miami. One of baseball's most well-regarded managers, Leyland had led Pittsburgh to three straight division titles from 1990 to 1992 before his team was decimated by the loss of star players the Pirates could no longer afford. With the third-highest payroll in the National League, the Marlins were in control of the wild-card race the entire summer of 1997 even as they were also-rans, far behind the Braves, in the NL East. While Sheffield had an off-year in part because of injuries, Bonilla led the Marlins with a .297 batting average and drove in 96 runs; Alou led the club with 23 homers and 115 runs batted in; and Fernandez won 17, Brown was 16–8, and Leiter added 11 wins.

But the Marlins' improbable star of the postseason was 22-year-old right-hander Livan Hernandez, one of the first Cuban players to defect for the opportunity to play in the major leagues in the 1990s, whom the Marlins signed for $4.5 million in January 1996. Brought up to Miami in June, Hernandez won his first nine decisions before finally losing in his 13th major-league start in September. Starting the fifth game of the NLCS only because Fernandez had hurt his shoulder pitching in Game Two, Hernandez outdueled Greg Maddux, pitching a three-hit complete-game in which he struck out 15 Atlanta batters to give the Marlins a three-games-to-two edge in the series. His 15 strikeouts were not without controversy, however, in that many called strikes on the outside corner appeared to be so far off the plate as to be unreachable. Hernandez went on to win both his starts in the World Series as the wild-card Marlins beat the Cleveland Indians in seven games. The Marlins overcame a 2–0 deficit to win the deciding game. Bonilla homered in the 7th; Alou singled to lead off the bottom of the 9th and scored the tying run on a sacrifice fly by rookie second baseman Craig Counsell; and 20-year-old shortstop Edgar Renteria, in his second year, smacked a bases-loaded single with two outs in the last of the 11th to walk off a World Series championship for Florida.

Less than three weeks later, the Marlins announced they intended to drastically cut payroll from close to $50 million to below $20 million. "It's not by any means what you're looking forward to doing," their general manager said. "But we have our marching orders." Still determined to sell the franchise, Huizenga claimed the Marlins lost $34 million in 1997; insisted that unless taxpayers were willing to pay for a new stadium for his winning team, there was no way the franchise could turn a profit; and said his team's high player payroll was a disincentive for prospective buyers, never mind that they had just won the World Series and that his spending spree on free agents the two previous years made them likely to compete for championships into the new century, perhaps even supplanting the Braves atop the NL East. That meant a fire sale of all their high-priced players.

Before the 1998 season got under way, Alou, Brown, White, and Leiter were traded. Fernandez might have been too, if not for the shoulder injury that would sideline him for the entire season. Also gone were two original Marlins from 1993—Robb Nen, one of baseball's best closers, and first baseman Jeff Conine. The Marlins lost 11 of their first 12 games. A month later, Sheffield, Bonilla, and highly regarded fourth-year catcher Charles Johnson were sent to the Dodgers in a blockbuster trade that brought slugging catcher Mike Piazza, in the prime of his Hall of Fame career, to Miami. Piazza would play only five games for Florida before being repackaged in a deal with the Mets for minor-league prospects. The Marlins went from World Series champs to Major League Baseball's chumps in 1998 with 108 losses and the game's worst record. As he had done in Pittsburgh when it was clear the Pirates were not going to invest in building a competitive ballclub, Leyland left Florida and the Marlins after that disastrous season to manage in Colorado for the Rockies. In

November 1998, Huizenga sold the franchise to commodities trader John Henry for less than he hoped.

Powered by Piazza and with Leiter their best pitcher, the 2000 New York Mets were the next wild-card team to make it to the World Series. They were a legitimate contender for the NL Eastern Division title, losing out to Atlanta by a single game. They cruised through their division series and the league championship series, only to be swamped by the Yankees in five games in the first all–New York World Series since the Yankees and Brooklyn Dodgers faced off in 1956.

Such an indignity could not befall the wild-card team the next time one appeared in the World Series—because there were two. Neither team in the 2002 World Series won their division, but both were excellent teams. The 99-win Anaheim Angels finished 4 back of Oakland in the AL West, and the 95-win San Francisco Giants finished 2½ games behind Arizona in the NL West. Having gotten through the first two rounds of postseason series, one of those wild cards was going to have to win the World Series. And one did, requiring the full seven games to do so. The Giants had been to just two World Series, in 1962 and 1989, since moving from New York to San Francisco in 1958, losing them both. The Angels, a 1961-expansion team that began with Los Angeles as their city-designator, because that's where they played until 1965 when they moved to nearby Orange County, had yet to appear in a World Series. As the *California* Angels, they had won division titles in 1979, 1982, and 1986 but could not get by the Orioles, Brewers, and Red Sox in the ALCS. Blowing their 11-game lead in 1995 with 44 games remaining, they had not won a division title since, even with one of the best outfields in the game in the late 1990s—Garret Anderson in left, Jim Edmonds in center, and Tim Salmon in right—and even after being rechristened the Anaheim Angels in 1997.

The ground on which the Giants were trying to win their first World Series since moving from New York was seeded in 1993 when Dusty Baker was hired as manager and Barry Bonds came to San Francisco on what was then the most expensive free-agent contract in history. The Giants won 103 games but lost out to the Atlanta Braves for the NL Western Division title and could not take solace in the wild card because the wild-card concept would not come into play until the next year. Trades for Jeff Kent in 1997 and Marlins closer Robb Nen in 1998 helped establish the Giants as an annual contender. In five prior seasons, Kent had yet to hit his stride or even settle in a position. In San Francisco, however, playing second base and batting fourth behind Bonds in the lineup, Kent had six-straight 100-RBI seasons from 1997 to 2002 and was voted the National League MVP in 2000. Bonds and Kent had little use for each other, except hitting back-to-back in Baker's lineup. But they powered the Giants to division titles in 1997 and 2000.

Bonds was already a superstar when he signed with the Giants. Now, his place in history was being considered alongside the likes of his godfather, Willie Mays, and even Babe Ruth. Bonds's 73 home runs in 2001 broke the single-season record set three years earlier by Mark McGwire and gave him 567 for his career. The 46 he hit in 2002 increased that to 613—fourth all-time and just 47 shy of Mays for third—and he was showing no signs of slowing down. So feared was Barry at The Bat, that he walked an astonishing 198 times in 2002, breaking the record of 177 he set the year before; 68 of those walks (more than a third) were intentional. Besides his 46 homers when he wasn't given a free pass to first, Bonds also led the league with a .370 batting average, his .582 on-base percentage eclipsed Ted Williams's 1941 record, and his 1.381 on-base plus slugging percentage edged out Ruth's 1920 record.

The 2002 Angels did not have once-in-a-generation talent on the order of Barry Bonds. But manager Mike Scioscia, the former Dodgers catcher who took over in 2000, did have a productive, well-balanced lineup. Everyone contributed. Second baseman Adam Kennedy led the Angels in batting with a .312 average; scrappy 5-foot-6 overachieving shortstop David Eckstein in runs; third baseman Troy Glaus in home runs; Anderson in RBIs; Salmon in on-base percentage; center fielder Darin Erstad in stolen bases; and Benji Molina, the oldest of the three catching Molina brothers, led the league in gunning down 45 percent of the 77 base runners who dared try stealing on the Angels. Stout defense—the Angels led the majors in making outs on balls in play—contributed to the league's best team ERA. Lefty starter Jarrod Washburn went 18–6 and righty Ramon Ortiz was 15–9. Troy Percival, their closer since 1996, saved 40 of the Angels' 99 wins.

The 2002 World Series between the two wild cards was wild indeed. It went the full seven games. The Giants, taking a 5–0 lead into the seventh inning in the sixth game in Anaheim, were on the verge of winning the series before the Angels scored three in the seventh and three more in the eighth to force a seventh game. Whereupon, John Lackey, 9–4 after being called up in June, became the first rookie to start—and win—a Game Seven in the World Series since Pittsburgh's Babe Adams in 1909. Another rookie, Francisco Rodriguez—a 20-year-old kid called "K-Rod"—did not throw a pitch in the majors until September 18, yet captivated audiences by striking out 13 batters in 8⅔ innings in the four games he pitched in relief against the Giants, which followed his 15 K's in 10 innings over seven games in the division and league championship series. Troy Glaus clubbed 3 homers and drove in 8 runs for the Angels. For the Giants, Barry Bonds, a pitcher's worst nightmare, walked 13 times in his 30 plate appearances. Discretion *was* the better part of valor for Scioscia and his pitching staff, however, because in his 17 at-bats, Bonds had eight hits—four of them home runs.

But for all that, the 2002 World Series was most famous for its optics. The Rally Monkey played big for the Angels on the big screen in center field at Edison Field in Anaheim. Thunder Sticks—inflated balloons designed not to rupture—banged by Angels fans at Edison Field made quite the cacophonous, ear-splitting racket. And as he crossed the plate to score the first of four seventh-inning runs on Kenny Lofton's triple in the Giants' blowout win in Game Five in San Francisco, first baseman J. T. Snow rescued manager Dusty Baker's three-year-old son, a batboy not waiting for the play to end before running out to pick up Lofton's bat, from being steamrollered by the runner barreling in from third on a possible play at the plate. Snow's was arguably the play of the series.

Notwithstanding his just having managed the wild-card Giants to the World Series, Baker's contract was not renewed for 2003. He had been feuding with owner Peter Magowan virtually the entire season about one thing or another, including the tensions between Bonds and Kent—the Giants' two most important players. Kent also did not return, getting away from Barry by signing with Houston as a free agent. Felipe Alou, after 10 years managing the Montreal Expos, took over as manager; Bonds smacked 45 homers; right-hander Jason Schmidt led the league with a 17–5 record and 2.34 ERA; and the Giants won 100 games to run away with the NL West, only to be derailed in their division series by the wild-card Marlins, on their way to another World Series. In 2004, the Giants missed out on winning the West by two games and the wild card by one. Schmidt won a career-high 18 games. Bonds had another 45-homer season, giving him 703 for his career, putting him within 11 of

Ruth's 714 and 52 of Hank Aaron's 755; drew a mind-boggling 232 walks, more than half of which (120) were intentional; led the league in batting with a .362 average, even though opposing teams allowed him only 373 at-bats in his 617 plate appearances; and won his fourth consecutive MVP Award, the seventh of his career.

The beginning of the end of the Giants' Barry Bonds era came in December 2004 when the *San Francisco Chronicle* broke its investigative report about Bonds being administered illegal steroids by Balco—a health-supplements company in the Bay Area—that put into question the legitimacy of at least the 292 homers he had hit for the Giants since 1999. Bonds was said to have turned to steroids wanting the accolades given McGwire and Sammy Sosa in 1998 for their run at Maris's record. His persona widely disliked, if not despised, in baseball circles, Bonds was more toxic than ever. After missing nearly all of 2005 with an injury, he added 59 homers to his career total before retiring after the 2007 season when his contract expired. Bonds finished with 762 home runs—a record without the resonance of the Babe's 714 or Hank's 755.

Although they have not been back to the World Series since, the Angels went on to win five division titles in six years between 2004 and 2009. By 2008, when their 100–62 record was the best in the major leagues, the *Los Angeles* Angels *of Anaheim*, to which they'd changed their name three years prior, had a mostly new core cast of characters. Foremost among them was Hall of Fame–bound Vladimir Guerrero, an elite hitter, signed as a free agent in 2004. The versatile 5-foot-8 Chone Figgins, consistently among the league leaders in stolen bases, had replaced Eckstein as the scrappy overachiever helping his team to victories. Lackey, at 29, was now the old man in the starting rotation, with lefty Joe Saunders and righties Ervin Santana and Jered Weaver rising stars behind him. Francisco Rodriguez lived up to being K-Rod by averaging 12 strikeouts per nine innings since 2004. Leading the league in saves for the third time in four years with 62 in 2008, K-Rod shattered Bobby Thigpen's record of 57 in 1990.

'Twas 2003, the year after the all-wild-card World Series, and the Florida Marlins were back in the World Series—as the National League wild-card team whose 91 wins gave them the third-best record in the league after division-rival Atlanta's 101 and San Francisco's 100. And again, as in 1997, they won the World Series, this time beating the Yankees. And it had been only six years since the 1997 Marlins were torn apart by their owner just weeks after winning baseball's ultimate championship. Wayne Huizenga was long gone as owner.

Also gone was John Henry, to whom Huizenga sold the franchise in November 1998. Henry owned the Marlins through three losing seasons. By 2001, however, they were no longer a dismally bad team. First to third, together as a foursome beginning in 1999, Derrek Lee, Luis Castillo, shortstop Alex Gonzalez, and Mike Lowell gave the Marlins a solid infield. Starters Ryan Dempster, A. J. Burnett, and Brad Penny all had promising futures. But Henry, not having the patience to wait for the Marlins to rise to competitive status, sold the franchise to Jeff Loria in February 2002 so that he could buy a major-league team with much more certain prospects—the baseball team in Boston.

In his first year as owner, Loria cleared the deck by trading away the Marlins' three highest-paid players. The Marlins also traded Dempster but on the same day traded for lesser-paid Carl Pavano to replace him in the starting rotation. For 2003 they added center fielder Juan Pierre and then made headlines by signing free agent Pudge Rodriguez, the best catcher of his generation, to a one-year, $10 million contract. After the Marlins lost seven of their first nine games in May to fall to 16–22, they fired their manager in favor of 72-year-old Jack McKeon, described by Florida's GM as a "resurrection specialist" based on turning around losing clubs in his two previous managerial stints. It didn't matter that McKeon would be the third-oldest manager in major-league history and the oldest ever named to take over a team. The Marlins lost seven of their first ten games under their new old-guy manager, after which "resurrection specialist" McKeon led them to a 72–47 record the rest of the way to win the wild card by a relatively comfortable 4 games. Cast in the role of underdog, the Marlins beat San Francisco's 100-win Giants in their division series, stunned Chicago's Cubs in the NLCS by coming from behind to win Games Six and Seven, and upset New York's powerhouse Yankees in six games to win the World Series.

While Rodriguez's leadership, particularly his handling of a young pitching staff, had the biggest impact on Florida's return to the World Series, it was two rookies that captured the imagination of baseball fans nationwide. In early May, left-hander Dontrelle Willis was promoted to replace Burnett, on his way to Tommy John surgery, in the starting rotation. Willis made 27 starts, finished 14–6, and was voted NL Rookie of the Year. A month later, the Marlins promoted 20-year-old Miguel Cabrera to play left field. Cabrera was a postseason star, going 10-for-30 with 3 homers and 6 RBIs to help Florida beat Chicago in the NLCS, including a three-run shot off Cubs ace Kerry Wood in the first inning of Game Seven. He also hit a two-run first-inning homer off Yankees ace Roger Clemens in Game Four of the World Series. 'Twas, however, the first and last plays that defined the World Series—Juan Pierre, who led the league with 65 stolen bases, dragging a bunt single to start Game One at Yankee Stadium and coming around to score the first run of the series; and Josh Beckett tagging out Jorge Posada after fielding a grounder up the first base line for the final out of the series.

And then, the Marlins did it again. If the teardown of the 1997-champion Marlins was evocative in its immediacy of Connie Mack's 1914 dismantling of his great Philadelphia Athletics team that had just won its fourth pennant in five years, breaking up the 2003-champion Marlins was akin to Mack's slower-roll breakdown of his club that won three straight pennants from 1929 to 1931. Florida ended up third with a modest 83 wins each of the next two years. After the 2005 season, Loria decided everyone must go—except for talented young stars Cabrera, fresh off his second-straight 33-homer season, and Willis, whose 22 wins led the majors, both earning less than $400,000 and still with another year before becoming eligible for salary arbitration. Like Huizenga before him, Loria complained that the failure of state and local government to publicly finance a new baseball stadium in Miami left him no other choice; his franchise could not turn a profit without a new stadium. The best return on investment the Marlins got for purging most of the players on their 2005 roster was the trade that sent Beckett and Lowell to the Red Sox for shortstop Hanley Ramirez and right-hander Anibal Sanchez, considered to be two of baseball's best minor-league prospects.

Florida's payroll went from $60.4 million in 2005 to $14.7 million in 2006—not only the lowest in the majors but more than $20 million below the cross-state Tampa Bay Devil Rays, the team with the next-lowest payroll. The Marlins finished fourth but only six games below .500. Cabrera continued his ascent as a superstar. Ramirez was voted Rookie of the Year. Sanchez was 10–3 with a 2.37 earned run average in 17 starts after being called to Miami in late June. And two other Marlins rookies made an impressive debut—second baseman Dan Uggla and right-hander Josh

Johnson, who worked his way into the starting rotation by May and finished with a 12–7 record and 3.10 ERA.

Even with that future potential, the Marlins would not commit to contending, at least not anytime soon. After the 2007 season, Cabrera and Willis, both two years away from free agency, were traded. Uggla was traded after his fourth 30-homer year in a row for the Marlins in 2010. Ramirez, who won a batting title in 2009, was traded in July 2012, in the year he was about to become a free agent. Johnson, his career ravaged by injuries and surgeries that limited him to only four seasons with more than 14 starts in his seven years in the Marlins' starting rotation, left as a free agent after the 2012 season and was forced to give up his pitching career the next year. His best years were 2009, when he was 15–5 without missing a turn, and 2010 when he was 11–6 and led the league with a 2.30 ERA in 28 starts.

The local city and county governments finally approved a plan in 2008 to fund a new ballpark for the Marlins. Because there was no state funding for the venture, it stood to reason that when the new stadium was ready for baseball in 2012, Florida's Marlins would become Miami's Marlins. The franchise has not had a winning season since. Their best year was 2016. They finished third with a 79–82 record. Former Yankees icon Don Mattingly was their manager. And the Marlins had a trio of exceptional outfielders in Christian Yelich, Marcell Ozuna, and Giancarlo Stanton; a rising star in catcher J. T. Realmuto; and one of baseball's most dynamic young pitchers—Jose Fernandez, 16–8 with 253 strikeouts in 182⅓ innings. The season was nearing its end when Fernandez, who turned 24 just 56 days before, was killed in an early morning, still-dark boating accident.

In November 2017 Loria sold the Marlins to an ownership group including an even greater Yankees icon than Mattingly: none other than recently retired shortstop Derek Jeter. That proved the catalyst for yet another deliberate breakdown of a Marlins team that had the potential for a bright future just ahead, although without ever having made it to the World Series as a wild card as in 1997 and 2003. As the new president and CEO of the franchise, Jeter was determined to cut the Marlins' player payroll to half the $115 million Loria paid his team in 2017 and rebuild from there. Once again, everyone with a big salary had to go, beginning with Stanton, to whom Loria had given a 13-year, $325 million extension in 2014, then the most expensive contract in baseball history.

On December 11, 2017, Stanton was traded to the Yankees, notwithstanding having just been named the National League MVP for his major-league-leading 59 home runs—which some would say is the *real* closest anyone has gotten to Roger Maris's 61 homers because all six times that number was eclipsed were by players using steroids. Four days later, presumed budding superstar Ozuna, having just hit 37 homers with 124 RBIs and a .312 batting average, was traded to St. Louis *before* his stats would have factored into salary-arbitration hearings early in the new year. And in January 2018, superstar-in-waiting Christian Yelich was traded to Milwaukee, where he promptly won two batting titles, an MVP Award in 2018, and was runner-up for MVP in 2019. Without them, the Marlins lost 98 games in 2018. In 2019 it was catcher Realmuto's turn to go—to Philadelphia. The Marlins' 105 losses that year were their most since the 108 they lost in 1998, when Huizenga sold or traded nearly his entire 1997 wild-card World Series–winning team.

In 2004, the Boston Red Sox, now owned by John Henry, became the third wild-card team in a row, and the fourth in seven years, to win the World Series. Theirs, of course, was a miracle. Not because, like the Florida Marlins, they were considered unlikely to compete for a championship—the Red Sox were, in fact, one of baseball's powerhouse teams—but because they had to beat the Yankees to get there. How they did *that* was the miracle. They were the first team in baseball history to overcome a three-games-to-none deficit in a seven-game postseason series—and they did it in the ALCS against those damned Yankees. Sweeping the Cardinals in the World Series to win their first World Series in 86 years was the easy part.

The 2005 World Series was the fourth in a row with a wild-card entry. 'Twas Houston's Astros, with 89 wins, a distant second in the National League's Central Division, 11 games behind St. Louis. It was the first-ever appearance in the Fall Classic for the franchise, which began as a National League expansion team alongside the Mets in 1962. They won NL Western Division titles in 1980 and 1986, only to lose each time in an eventful NLCS. Reassigned to the new NL Central Division, the Astros won their division every year from 1997 to 1999, endured a disastrous 90-loss season, then won the NL Central again in 2001. And failed to make it out of the division-series round in any of those years.

Randy Johnson made a memorable and decisive cameo appearance for the Astros in 1998 with a 10–1 record, a microscopic 1.28 ERA, and 116 strikeouts in 84⅓ innings after being acquired from Seattle at the July trade deadline, even though he was about to enter free agency. Mission accomplished in Houston, Johnson moved to Arizona as a free agent in 1999. The Astros' cornerstone players, however, were first baseman Jeff Bagwell and second baseman Craig Biggio, both consistently excellent year in and year out. Right fielder Derek Bell was not close to their caliber as a ballplayer but dangerous enough at bat to be associated with them as one of Houston's "Killer B's." Bell was no longer with Houston in 2001, but the Astros had a new "Killer B" to complement Bagwell and Biggio—second-year outfielder Lance Berkman, whose breakout season included 55 doubles to lead the majors, 34 homers, 126 RBIs, and a .331 batting average. Shane Reynolds, Jose Lima, and lefty Mike Hampton were the Astros' top starters during their 1997 to 1999 reign over the NL Central, backed up by hard-throwing elite closer Billy Wagner, whose 14.6 strikeouts per nine innings in 186 games those three years belied his modest 5-foot-10, 180-pound frame. In 2001, young risers Wade Miller and rookie Roy Oswalt were the pitching stars for the division-winning Astros.

In 2003, the Astros lost the division race by a single game to Chicago's Cubs, whose distinct advantage was a much deeper starting rotation. Houston moved to correct for that in 2004 by signing Yankees left-handed ace Andy Pettitte and Yankees right-handed ace Roger Clemens, both free agents, to three-year deals. Clemens, notwithstanding he was already 41 years old, won his seventh Cy Young Award with a major-league-best 18–4 record in 33 starts. Pettitte, hampered all year by an elbow injury, made just 15 starts, going 6–4. Oswalt won 20. Brad Lidge, having taken over as closer for traded-away Billy Wagner, had 29 saves, a 1.90 earned run average, and struck out nearly 15 batters per nine innings with 157 K's in 94⅔ innings of work. None of that was enough to come even close to winning their division; the Astros' 92 wins were 13 fewer than the Cardinals' 105, but their major-league-best 23–7 record in the final month allowed them to edge out the Giants for the wild card.

All teams starting with a clean slate in the postseason, it was not necessarily surprising that after polishing off Atlanta in their division series, Houston faced off against their betters in the regular season—division-rival St. Louis—in the NLCS. It went the full seven games. And the baseball world was treated to one of the most stunning displays of postseason power-hitting in the game's history by Cardinals star first baseman Albert Pujols and Astros star outfielder Carlos Beltran. The Astros were able to pick up Beltran in June because 2004 was his free-agency walk year and he was a superstar his team, the Kansas City Royals, could not afford. Against Atlanta in the division series, Beltran smashed 4 home runs, scored 9 runs, had 9 runs batted in, and was 10-for-22 at the plate, while Pujols, in the Cardinals' division series, hit 2 homers, had 5 RBIs, and went 5-for-15. In the NLCS, Beltran was 10-for-24 with 4 more home runs, scoring 12 runs and driving in five. It wasn't enough to beat St. Louis for entry to the Fall Classic, however, because Pujols was 14-for-28 at the plate, scored 10 runs, blasted 4 homers of his own, and had 9 runs batted in. His mission accomplished in Houston, Beltran leveraged his 8 homers, 14 RBIs, 21 runs, and .435 batting average in the 2004 postseason for a big multiyear deal with the Mets.

The setup was much the same but the ending different in 2005. The Cardinals again controlled the narrative in the NL Central, winning 100 and finishing 11 games ahead of the second-place Astros. Houston again had the best record in the league in the final month to secure the National League wild card by a game over Philadelphia. Oswalt again won 20; Clemens was 13–8 and led the league with a 1.87 earned run average; and Pettitte, recovered from elbow surgery, had 17 wins and a 2.39 ERA. The Astros once again beat the Braves in their division series, and once again faced their division-rival first-place Cardinals in the NLCS. This time, however, it was Houston beating St. Louis in six games to advance to the World Series. The Astros' first trip ever to the Fall Classic was over in four games, swept by Chicago's White Sox.

There would not be another World Series in Houston for 12 years. In the meantime, Bagwell retired after his injury-plagued 2005 season with 449 career home runs and a .297 batting average. Clemens and Pettitte both returned to the Yankees as free agents in 2007. Craig Biggio retired after the 2007 season with 3,060 hits and 414 stolen bases in 20 major-league seasons. Like Bagwell, his entire big-league career was in Houston. And Oswalt was traded to Philadelphia in 2010, having won 143 games and 64 percent of his decisions in Houston.

In 2006, Detroit's Tigers made it five-straight World Series with a wild-card team. The last time the Tigers were in the World Series was when they won it all in 1984. The intervening 22 years were not the longest the franchise had gone without winning the American League pennant—there were 25 years between 1909 and 1934 and 23 between 1945 and 1968; both droughts ended with a World Series victory party—but they surely were the worst. Exercising financial austerity, Detroit had not had a winning season since the year before the 1994 strike.

The franchise struggled to regain its footing after longtime manager Sparky Anderson resigned into retirement at the end of the 1995 season. Perhaps not coincidentally, Anderson had been placed on leave without pay following his refusal to manage replacement players in spring training—a gambit franchise owners hoped would force the players' hand as the strike threatened to continue long into baseball's 1995 schedule. Moving into a new stadium in 2000 gave the Tigers only a one-year attendance boost. Just three years later, attendance had dropped by 44 percent, but the 2003 Tigers also lost 119 games. Detroit was spared tying the record of 120 losses by the 1962-expansion Mets (or even exceeding it by one) only by winning the last two games of the season.

But giving a four-year, $40 million free-agent deal in 2004 to Ivan Rodriguez, fresh from being the Marlins best player in their wild-card run to the 2003 World Series championship, signaled the times were changing in Detroit. The next year they signed another high-profile free agent in outfielder Magglio Ordonez, but Ordonez missed half the season with injuries and the Tigers extended their string of 90-plus-loss seasons to five in a row and eight in 10 years. Tired of the losing, the Tigers lured Jim Leyland out of retirement to take charge in the dugout in 2006. Leyland, whose out-of-nowhere wild-card Marlins won the 1997 World Series the year he took over as manager, did it again. Not only did the Tigers compete for the first time since the Sparky Anderson era, they took hold of the AL Central pennant race in May, built a 10-game lead a week into August, and did not drop from the top spot into second place until game 162, done in by a 5-game losing streak to end the season.

'Twas pitching made the difference. After nearly two decades of being consistently in the bottom tier of runs allowed, the 2006 Tigers gave up the fewest runs in the majors. Signing 41-year-old lefty Kenny Rogers as a free agent before the season provided a stabilizing veteran presence for a young starting corps. Rogers led the Tigers with a 17–8 record, and 23-year-old Jeremy Bonderman, after three years of struggling promise, broke through with a 14–8 mark. Making the most significant impact, however, was right-hander Justin Verlander, 17–9 in his rookie (of the year) season. After losing the first game of their division series with the Yankees, running their losing streak to six games, the Tigers won the next three games to advance to the ALCS, where they swept the Athletics to go into the World Series with a seven-game winning streak. The World Series, on the other hand, proved to be a comedy of embarrassing errors as Detroit fell to St. Louis in five games. Eight of the 22 runs the Cardinals scored were unearned. The Tigers made eight errors, five by their pitchers, mostly on errant throws to the bases.

The Colorado Rockies began their trip to the 2007 World Series by winning 13 of their last 14 regular season games to overcome a 4½-game deficit to tie division-rival San Diego in the wild-card race after 162 games, forcing a single-game playoff in Denver to decide the winner. (Both teams finished the regular season a game back of NL West division-winning Arizona.) Tied 5–5 after 9, a Padres rally was snuffed in the 10th and one by the Rockies in the 11th before San Diego took a 7–5 lead in the top of the 13th. In came Padres closer Trevor Hoffman to seal the deal. He had 42 saves, giving him 524 in his career—the most by any reliever in history at the time. Back-to-back doubles and a triple tied the score with nobody out. An intentional walk loaded the bases for a force at the plate, and a sacrifice fly to right drove home the winning run. It was, after the fact, a controversial score because Matt Holliday, tagging from third, did not touch home as he slid past the catcher on the play at the plate. As the catcher was moving to tag Holliday, lying face-down in the dirt some feet beyond home plate, the umpire called him safe. The Padres did not contest the call, but the winning run never actually touched home plate.

For the second time in their 15-year history, the Rockies were the National League wild-card team. The first time was 1995, and Colorado had not had a winning season since 82–80 in 2000. Whereas the 1995 Rockies lost their division series, in 2007 they swept both their division series and league championship series to go into the World Series as the hottest team in baseball, winners of 21 of their last 22 games going back to mid-September. The World Series was also a sweep—by the Boston Red Sox.

The 1993-expansion Colorado Rockies were born into thin air, a mile high in Denver. Oxygen levels in the Mile High City are about 17 percent less than at sea level. As well-conditioned as they were, players not acclimated to the altitude, which meant almost everyone in the major leagues who didn't play for the Rockies, would often be gasping after sudden bursts of speed to run down (or chase after) a fly ball in the gaps at Coors Field, which opened for baseball business in 1995, or trying to score from first on a hit. Pitchers not acclimated would find themselves winded if their pitch count in any inning went too high and get worn out more quickly as the number of pitches thrown in the game mounted with every inning. Air density is about 80 percent of what it is at sea level, air resistance is about 20 percent less, and the air is dry. For pitchers, that means less movement on their pitches, and for batters, balls are hit with greater off-the-bat velocity and travel farther.

That was both a blessing and a curse. The altitude gives the Rockies a unique home field advantage. In the 28 years since Colorado came into the league in 1993, Rockies players have led the National League in batting average 11 times, by far the most of any team—including Larry Walker 3 times in four years from 1997 to 2001—and six Rockies led or tied for the league lead in homers, also more than any other team. On the flip side, however, only 6 of the 10 pitchers who started at least 100 games for the Rockies had an earned run average under 5.00, and just 2— Ubaldo Jimenez, who pitched for Colorado from 2007 to 2011, and Jhou- lys Chacin, a Rockie from 2010 to 2014—had an ERA less than 4.00. The Rockies record in games played in Denver is not only invariably better than their record in other teams' cities, but much better. Only three times in their history has Colorado had a winning record on the road. Only once did the Rockies have a better record on the road than at home, and that was in baseball's pandemic-shortened 60-game season of 2020. The dif- ference in their home versus away winning percentage was equivalent to 25 wins in a 162-game season.

What happened to Darryl Kile and Mike Hampton was a devastating cautionary tale for free-agent pitchers considering offers from Colorado. Possessing a wicked curve, right-hander Kile had just gone 19–7 with a tidy 2.57 earned run average helping Houston win the NL Central in 1997 when he signed a three-year, $24 million contract to pitch for the Rock- ies. His career ERA over seven seasons was 3.79. Kile lasted two years pitching in the Mile High City. His 21–30 record in 1998 and 1999 was worse than the Rockies' winning percentage. In 42 home starts, Kile suffered through a 6.76 earned run average. Kile's altitudinous nightmare came to an end in 2000 when, traded to St. Louis, he was back to the pitcher he aspired to be with a 20–9 record and 3.91 earned run average.

Hampton, a left-handed free agent with a nasty sinker, was signed to a then-record eight-year, $124 million contract in December 2000. A teammate of Kile's in Houston, he led the league with a 22–4 record in 1996, and he had just gone 15–10 and pitched 16 shutout innings in two starts in the NLCS to help the wild-card Mets to the World Series in 2000. In nine big-league seasons, Hampton's career ERA stood at 3.44. Hampton also pitched just two years in Denver, with a 21–28 record and 5.75 earned run average in 62 starts, after which he (and the six years left on his contract) was traded to Atlanta, for whom his ERA dropped to 3.84 in 2003. In 26 starts in Denver as a Rockie, Hampton's home-park earned-run average was 5.73.

Both pitchers' signature pitches were diminished significantly in their effectiveness by the Coors Effect. Curves thrown at that altitude, because they don't break as sharply, have a tendency to hang in the strike zone. Kile had never given up more than 19 homers in any previous year before coming to Colorado; with the Rockies, he surrendered 61 in two years, 37 of them at home. Sinkerball pitchers like Hampton rely on the difference in vertical location of their pitches crossing the plate. In the Mile High City, the rise of four-seam fastballs that sinkerball pitchers use to set up the sinker is not as great as in other ballparks, meaning the relative sink of the sinkerball is perceptually less to the batter's eye, making it far more vulnerable to being identified and clobbered.

Over the years the Rockies have tried different things to mitigate the Coors Effect. In 2002 they began storing baseballs in a humidor so they would retain moisture in the dry Denver air. While that helped pitchers get a better grip on the ball and feel for their pitches, there was nothing that could be done about the lesser air density in Denver's mile-high atmosphere. In 2012 the Rockies experimented with a return to a four-man starting rotation in which each day's starter would be limited to 75 pitches—didn't work and also didn't last long. For all the challenges, several Rockies pitchers have had impressive seasons by any standard—lefty Jeff Francis with a 17–9 record in 2007; Aaron Cook, 16–9 in 2008; Ubaldo Jimenez with a 2.88 ERA and league-leading 19–8 record in 2010; and lefty Kyle Freeland's 17–7 record and 2.85 earned run average in 2018—but such seasons were rarely repeated the next year, and only

Cook had a reasonably successful career (a 72–68 record in 10 Rockie seasons) almost entirely in Denver.

As for batters, the Coors Effect on hitting almost certainly undermined for many years Larry Walker's otherwise impressive Cooperstown-worthy credentials in the Hall of Fame voting. Although Walker was already a bona fide star when he signed as a free agent with Colorado in 1995, it was in the thin air of Denver that he became a superstar. In his 10 years with the Rockies, Walker batted .334 with 258 home runs, including leading the league with 49 in 1997, of which, counterintuitively, 29 were hit on the road. Indicative of batters' splits between Colorado and on the road, Walker's career-high .379 average in 1999 to win the batting title broke down with him batting .461 with 26 homers in 66 home games and only 11 homers and a pedestrian .286 batting average in 61 away games. Not until his final year of eligibility did Walker clear the voting threshold for baseball's Mount Olympus. Similarly, first baseman Todd Helton—a career .316 hitter with 369 home runs whose entire 17-year career from 1997 to 2013 was with the Rockies—had a lifetime .345 batting average in 1,141 games in Coors Field, where he hit 61 percent (227) of his homers, compared to a .287 average in the 1,106 Rockies games he played in other ballparks.

Walker had been traded to St. Louis three years before the Rockies went to the 2007 World Series, and Helton, in his 11th season, had the last of his high-impact seasons that year. Colorado's new stars were left fielder Matt Holliday, whose 137 runs batted in and .340 batting average led the league, and rookie shortstop Troy Tulowitzki. With all due respect to the still-active Derek Jeter, so admired by the Rockies shortstop that he took the field everyday wearing number 2, Tulowitzki quickly became the best at his position in baseball. Holliday, about to enter his free-agent year, was traded after the 2008 season. Whatever questions there might have been about the extent to which his .319 batting average and 128 home runs in five Colorado seasons should be discounted because of the Coors Effect on batting, Holliday went on to have a long and equally productive career after signing with St. Louis as a free agent in 2010.

Tulowitzki's career arc toward the Hall of Fame was derailed by successive injuries that put him on the injured list in five of the eight years following his rookie season. He hit .299 with 188 homers and 657 RBIs and was defensively outstanding in the 1,048 games he played for the Rockies before he was traded in the midst of Colorado's 94-loss season in

2015. By then, the Rockies had a new star—hard-hitting, excellent-defensively third baseman Nolan Arenado—and in 2016 Trevor Story, a power threat at the plate, was in place as Tulowitzki's long-term successor at shortstop. After leading the league three times in home runs and twice in RBIs from 2015 to 2018, the Rockies signed Arenado to a seven-year, $260 million contract a year before he would have been eligible for free agency.

Since making it to the World Series in 2007, the Rockies have been back in the postseason as a wild card team in 2009, 2017, and 2018, when they finished the regular season tied for first in the NL West with the Dodgers but lost the one-game playoff to determine the division winner. Along with the Miami Marlins, the Colorado Rockies remain the only teams in Major League Baseball to have never finished first in their division.

# 7

# CUBS LOSE

## Don't Blame It on Bartman

On October 14, 2003, baseball fans could anticipate the real possibility that two of the game's most beloved losing teams—Chicago's Cubs and Boston's Red Sox—might actually meet in the World Series. It was the first time both teams were in their league's championship series fighting for the pennant since Major League Baseball adopted division alignments in 1969. Granted, the Red Sox lost Game Five of the ALCS that afternoon to their archnemesis, the Yankees, falling behind three-games-to-two, and so were a game away from elimination. The Cubs, playing a night game at home in Wrigley Field, had a three-games-to-two lead over the wild-card Florida Marlins going into Game Six in the NLCS. A win would put them in the World Series.

Their histories were such that, three years earlier, as the new millennium beckoned amid talk of dreaded "Y2K" digital data breakdown scenarios and great concern (by some) over the probable horrific consequences for civilization (and all life) to be visited upon Planet Earth by global warming, if there were baseball zealots in the role of new-millennium Doomsday Prophets, they might have been a Cassandra warning that the Red Sox meeting the Cubs in the World Series would necessarily mean the end of the world as we know it. Because one of them would have to win, and the Universe could not possibly abide *that* happening.

After all, were not both franchises cursed to never again win baseball's ultimate championship? The Cubs, famously, had not won a World

Series since 1908. The Red Sox, equally famously, had not won since 1918—a year, ironically, that they beat the Cubs. It wasn't as though the Red Sox didn't have their chances. They had played in four World Series since then—all since the end of World War II—losing all four in seven games. The Cubs hadn't even been to a World Series since World War II—1945, to be precise, the only one of the five series they had played since 1918 that they were able to extend to seven games before going down in defeat. They had won division titles in 1984 and 1989. That was as close as they got.

With their team ahead, 3–0, in the eighth inning of Game Six and right-handed ace Mark Prior in command, Chicago's fans at Wrigley were primed for an epic celebration for their beloved Cubs about to make it to their first World Series since . . . forever. A fly ball to left, and the Cubs were five outs from the Fall Classic. A double followed, and then a portentous omen. On the 8th pitch of his at-bat, Prior's 113th of the game, Florida's Luis Castillo hit a foul ball toward the grandstands down the third-base line that left fielder Moises Alou had a read on. Two fans with front-row seats saw the ball coming their way and reached out for it—at the same time as Alou. It's unclear whether they reached over the railing into the foul-territory field of play to try to catch a souvenir (which would have been fan interference) or whether Alou reached over the railing into the stands to make the catch (as he was entitled to try). Either way, one of the fans deflected the ball away from Alou's glove. Moises was livid. Prior had to get Castillo out all over again. Castillo walked. A single made the score 3–1. Marlins rookie Miguel Cabrera, with eight hits in 24 at-bats so far in the series, hit a bouncer to shortstop. Perhaps looking too quickly to turn a double-play, Cubs shortstop Alex Gonzalez failed to field the ball cleanly. His error loaded the bases. Anticipating the worst, the fans at Wrigley stood in high anxiety; one fan was shown on the national television broadcast with hands clasped on his head.

The Cubs still had a two-run lead. Prior had now thrown 118 pitches. Derrek Lee, who had homered against Prior in Game Two, was coming up. Manager Dusty Baker had hard-throwing righty Kyle Farnsworth warming up. Despite Farnsworth's year of 92 strikeouts in 76⅓ innings, Baker stayed with his tired ace. Lee doubled. The game was tied. Now Baker replaced Prior with Farnsworth. And the worst was yet to come. The Marlins scored five more runs before a second reliever finally got the final out of a nightmarish eighth. Crowd shots on the television broadcast showed the fans at Wrigley standing in dejected, stunned silence. Mark Prior was seen sitting in the dugout, wiping away tears. The Marlins had tied the series. All was not lost—yet. The Cubs still had Kerry Wood, their other ace, ready for Game Seven.

As the disastrous top-of-the-eighth was coming to an end, play-by-play broadcaster Joe Buck expressed some concern for the fan whose hand deflected from Alou's glove what could—likely should—have been the second out of the inning. Buck proved to be prescient. The fan's name was Steven Bartman. And when the Marlins overcame a 5–3 deficit to win Game Seven and advance to the World Series, the play that wasn't made that was most remembered—and which lived on in Chicago infamy until 2016—was not the Gonzalez error that opened floodgates for seven more runs, but the catch Moises Alou did not make because Bartman deflected the baseball. For their long-suffering fans, it was not just 95 years since they had last won a World Series; it was 58 years and still counting since the Cubs had last even appeared in one. It was easier to blame Bartman.

But it was only 44 years since the last time a World Series *was* played in Chicago. And while 1908 was the year the Cubs last won one, the city of Chicago got to celebrate a World Series championship as recently as 1917, when Woodrow Wilson was president and America was sending troops "over there" in Europe to fight in World War I. That World Series was won by the now oft-forgotten-about (because of the city's affection for the Cubs and the baseball world's fixation on the Cubs' century-long championship drought) *other* team that played in the Windy City—Chicago's White Sox. That Chicago ballclub was a dynasty in the making, starring Shoeless Joe Jackson. Two years later he and seven teammates brought shame to America's game by conspiring with high-stakes gamblers to lose the 1919 World Series they were widely expected to win.

The stigma of the Black Sox scandal was an enduring taint on the franchise, no matter that the White Sox had long since moved on from that wretched stink. Forty years in the wilderness was their penance before returning to the World Series in 1959. And then another 46 years, during which they won just three division titles, most recently in 2000, before the White Sox finally made it back to the Fall Classic. And it was they, and not the seemingly forever cursed but beloved Cubs, that brought a World Series championship back to Chicago in 2005. The 2005 White

Sox were in command of the AL Central by the All-Star break, their 99 wins were the most in the American League, and they lost only once in the three rounds of postseason series, capped off by a sweep of Houston's Astros in the World Series. The 1999 (not the 1998) Yankees are the only other team to have had such a dominating romp through the postseason since the division-series era began in 1995.

Mark Buehrle (16–8), Jon Garland (18–10), Jose Contreras (15–7), and Freddy Garcia (14–8) all started at least 32 games and pitched more than 200 innings. First baseman Paul Konerko hit 40 homers and drove in 100 runs. Catcher A. J. Pierzynski, signed as a free agent in January, made headlines for his scrappiness and leadership and his ability to annoy opposing players. After 507 at-bats in 129 regular-season games, lead-off batter Scott Podsednik did not hit his first home run of the year until the White Sox' opening-game blowout of the Red Sox in their division series. His second came in the bottom of the ninth to win Game Two of the World Series off Astros' closer Brad Lidge.

Unable to play in the World Series, and in the last of his 16 years in Chicago as one of the greatest players in franchise history, Frank Thomas, primarily a designated-hitter since 1998, began the season on the injured list and hobbled through 34 games on a bad ankle before being sidelined in July for the rest of the year. Leaving as a free agent after the season, Thomas holds still-standing franchise records for home runs (448), RBIs (1,465), runs (1,327), on-base percentage (.427), and slugging percentage (.568), and his .307 batting average is the highest of any White Sox player whose career began after World War II.

For north-side Chicago, however, their Cubs not making it to the 2003 World Series was a bitter pill to swallow, especially given how close they came and how they lost. The Cubs had generally been a mediocrity since being moved from the NL East to the newly formed National League Central Division in 1994. Chicago made the postseason just once—in 1998 after winning a one-game playoff for the wild card—thanks to Sammy Sosa's breakthrough as a superstar and Kerry Wood's sensational rookie season. That was the year Sosa, acquired in a trade from south-side Chicago's White Sox in 1992, dueled with Mark McGwire to be first to break Roger Maris's single-season home-run record. Slammin' Sammy blew by Maris to hit 66 but lost the duel and finished second to Big Mac's 70. Wood, 13–6 in 26 starts, struck out a third of all batters he faced—

233 in 166⅔ innings—including 20 in a one-hit complete-game shutout against Houston in only the fifth start of his big-league career. Chicago's postseason sojourn was over quickly in a three-game sweep by Atlanta in their division series. Smoltz, Glavine, and Maddux smothered the Cubs, surrendering just four runs. The Cubs' only home run was *not* hit by Sosa. Wood lost the deciding third game to Maddux, allowing just one run in five innings; Maddux doubled, went to third, and scored on a two-out passed ball.

A pair of last-place endings followed that disappointment. Sosa proved his Maris chase was no anomaly by smashing 63 home runs in 1999, once again second to McGwire, and a league-leading 50 in 2000. Wood missed the 1999 season recovering from Tommy John surgery and struggled to an 8–7 record in 23 starts with fewer strikeouts than innings pitched when he returned the year after. After tying for the worst record in the major leagues in 2000, the Cubs were in the running for the division title in 2001 until an 8–15 stretch in August proved them more pretenders than contenders. Wood returned to form with a 12–6 record in 28 starts and was back to blowing away batters with 217 K's in 174⅓ innings. Sosa cracked the 60-homer barrier for the third time in four years with 64—once again a runner-up, this time to Barry Bonds's 73. In 2002 the Cubs were back to being one of the worst teams in the National League, losing 95 times despite Sosa leading the league with 49 homers. Mark Prior, making his debut in May 2002, struck out 147 in 116⅔ innings.

It took a strong 19–8 September finish for the Cubs to prevail by one game in a tight three-team race for the 2003 division title. Sosa had 40 homers but for the first time in six years was neither first or second in the league in home runs. Prior led the Cubs with an 18–6 record and 2.43 earned run average, including a 5–1 record in the final month. Wood, 14–11 for the year with a 3.20 ERA, led the majors in strikeouts with 266 (in 211 innings), and Prior was second with 245 (in 211⅓ innings). Carlos Zambrano, in his second year with the Cubs, led the staff with 214 innings in 32 starts, winning 13. The Cubs won the division by one game and knocked out the 101-win Braves in their division series. Their 88 wins for the season were three fewer than wild-card Florida had in the NL East, and the Cubs were not necessarily favored when the two clubs met in the NLCS. They were, however, the overwhelming favorite after winning three of the first four games—only to be shut out on two hits in

Game Five. Then came the blame-it-on-Bartman sixth game and their failure to hold onto a 5–3 lead in the fifth inning of Game Seven.

Still on their World Series quest, in 2004 the Cubs brought Greg Maddux back as a free agent to join Prior, Wood, Zambrano, and Matt Clement in what was thought *could* be the best starting rotation in baseball. Maddux and Zambrano both won 16. Wood and Prior both spent two months on the injured list. The Cubs not only ended up third in their division, despite improving their record to 89 wins, but lost their wildcard bid by losing seven of their next eight games after holding a 2½-game lead with nine left on the schedule. It was the beginning of a long good-bye to Dusty Baker's managerial tenure in Chicago.

Not in the lineup on the final day—the Cubs having already been eliminated from the postseason hunt—Sammy Sosa left the clubhouse just 13 minutes into the game, then lied about sneaking out early, never to return. The player who had cultivated an Ernie Banks–type, ever-smiling, always happy personality turned out to have been deeply resented and widely despised in the Cubs' clubhouse, even in the years he was their superstar slugger. Sosa routinely arrived late for spring training. The salsa music that helped define his endearing personality did not endear him to his teammates because he cranked the volume on his boombox to drown out everything else in the clubhouse. He was self-centered, insisting on his entitlement to various indulgences not allowed other players. He disrespected his managers. All of this was tolerated by Cubs management because of his prodigious productivity—332 home runs from 1998 to 2003—and the cult of personality Sosa promoted for himself.

But as the Cubs struggled in 2004, it all came undone for Sammy Sosa. He was ejected for using a corked bat in a game. His once adoring fans were now booing him. His teammates were fed up with him. And that was even without his fans or his teammates knowing he had tested positive for using steroids in Major League Baseball's anonymous survey of players in 2003—a fact that would not be revealed for another nine years. The Cubs were sufficiently desperate to be rid of him that when they traded him to Baltimore just before spring training in 2005, it was along with $16 million of the $25 million he was still owed on the four-year contract he signed in 2001.

Dusty Baker, as close as five outs away from becoming baseball's first manager to go to back-to-back World Series with two different teams (he was there with the Giants in 2002), was fired after the Cubs finished last in 2006. Baker left Chicago widely criticized for overusing his starting pitchers. He was accused of ruining Prior's and Wood's careers; Mark Prior's was over at the age of 25, derailed by injuries, and Kerry Wood's was undone in 2006 by shoulder problems. In 2003 and 2004, the Cubs were the only National League team whose starting pitchers worked more than 1,000 innings. Baker was also criticized for his bullpen management—for example, leaving Prior in the game, having already thrown 118 pitches, rather than bringing in Farnsworth after the Bartman incident *and after* the untimely error that loaded the bases in that ill-fated Game Six of the 2003 NLCS—but he also had a relief corps whose collective ERA was in the middle of NL teams both those years. Carlos Zambrano, however, despite throwing more than 200 innings and averaging nearly 110 pitches a start in the four years he worked for Baker, stayed healthy and was 16–7 for the last-place, NL's worst-record 2006 Cubs.

Perhaps it *was* the manager. The very next year under Lou Piniella, another experienced manager, the Cubs reclaimed the top of the NL Central, albeit with a pedestrian 85 wins that gave them only the sixth-best record in the National League. And in 2008 Piniella's Cubs won the division again with 97 wins and the best record in the league. By 2008 Wood, trying to revive his injury-plagued career, was the Cubs' closer, saving 34 games while striking out 84 in 66⅓ innings. Ryan Dempster, their closer the three previous years, excelled as a starting pitcher, going 17–6. Neither year did the Cubs get beyond their division series. Come 2009, not only did the Cubs fall from contention, but they and their storied ballpark were sold to billionaire Tom Ricketts for a then record $845 million. It was now 101 years since the Cubs had won a World Series and 64 since they had won a pennant.

Dusty Baker was back as manager of the Cincinnati Reds in 2008. Notwithstanding Cincinnati's historical standing as home of baseball's first proclaimed professional team in 1869 and a National League team since 1890, the city had celebrated only nine pennants and five World Series championships. Cincinnati baseball was at its best when Sparky Anderson managed the "Big Red Machine"—Pete Rose, Johnny Bench, Joe Morgan, and Tony Perez their most prominent stars—to five NL Western Division titles, four pennants, and two world championships between 1970 and 1976. The last time the Reds were in the World Series, in 1990, they surprised the baseball world by sweeping the heavily favored Oakland Athletics in the World Series. Piniella was their manager.

The Reds, a small-market franchise, had suffered through seven straight losing seasons when Baker took over. Their only division title since being removed from the NL West in 1994 to be placed in the new NL Central was in 1995. Four years later they won 96 games, their most since the 1976 Reds, but ended up a game back of Houston in the division and lost a 163rd game playoff for the wild card to the Mets. Hall of Fame shortstop Barry Larkin, the Reds' last link to their 1990 championship, retired after the 2004 season, having spent his entire 19-year career playing for his hometown team. Ken Griffey Jr., whose own Hall of Fame career was made in Seattle before he came to Cincinnati in 2000, specifically to play for the team his dad did in its Big Red Machine iteration, was in his late 30s and nearing the end of his career. After his fifth-straight 40-homer season in his first year with the Reds, Griffey's career was undermined by injuries. Only twice in his nine years in Cincinnati did he play in more than 130 games. At the trade deadline in 2008, Griffey was traded to the White Sox, who were in a battle for first place in the AL Central. His 608 career home runs when he left Cincinnati were fifth on the all-time list. Ken Griffey Jr. retired in 2010 with 632.

The string of losing seasons ran to nine in Baker's first two years in Cincinnati, the longest since the Reds went 11 years without a winning record in the immediate aftermath of World War II. He did, however, inherit the makings of a competitive team that included consistently reliable second baseman Brandon Phillips and durable right-handed starting pitcher Bronson Arroyo. But it was the Reds' rookie class of 2008 in Baker's first year as manager—first baseman Joey Votto and right fielder Jay Bruce, both left-handed power threats, and right-hander Johnny Cueto—that soon returned postseason baseball to the Queen City. Two years later, the Reds won the division by five games, and Votto was the NL's 2010 MVP. In 2012, Cincinnati commanded the NL Central narrative with 97 wins; Cueto was 19–9 and Cuban defector Aroldis Chapman saved 38 games with a 1.51 ERA while striking out 122 batters in 71⅔ innings in his first year as closer. And in 2013, with Bruce leading the team in homers and RBIs, they were the second wild card in a year when the top three teams in the Central Division all made the postseason. In none of the three years did Cincinnati advance to the NLCS.

The Dusty Baker era came to an end in 2013. He was fired for his team's stumbles in the final week of the season, similar to what happened to his 2004 Cubs. With five games remaining on the schedule, Cincinnati was tied with Pittsburgh, both in the NL Central, in the wild-card race. In the second year of two wild cards, both teams were already guaranteed to play in the wild-card game. The only question was which team would get home-field advantage. The Reds lost all five, including three to the Pirates on the final weekend of the season, and then lost to the Pirates again in the wild-card game.

The next year, without Baker in charge, was the first of six straight losing seasons for Cincinnati's Reds. Cueto, whose 2013 season was limited to 11 starts because of injuries, won 20 and led the league in starts, innings, strikeouts, and fewest hits per nine innings. He was traded in 2015; Chapman and Bruce followed in 2016. Joey Votto, meanwhile, was a worthy successor to Albert Pujols as the best first baseman in the game. From 2009 to 2018, Votto hit 241 homers while batting .312 and reaching base in 43 percent of his plate appearances. He led the league five times in walks and seven times in on-base percentage.

Dusty Baker resurfaced in 2016 as manager of the Washington Nationals, leading them to back-to-back division titles in the NL East, again failing to take his team beyond the division series, and again finding himself without a job. Baker managed four teams a total of 24 years in the major leagues, winning division titles with each of them. In only eight of those seasons did his team have a losing record. He won 1,863 games as manager against 1,636 losses. All that was after his 19 years as a major-league outfielder that included playing in three World Series. He managed in one. Dusty Baker's only championship ring was as the Dodgers left fielder in 1981. And just when it was thought he was waiting for a Cooperstown verdict, Baker was brought back in 2020 to straighten out the Houston Astros, whose 2017 World Series championship was irrevocably tainted by the revelation in November 2019 that their players implemented a sophisticated electronic sign-stealing scheme to advantage their at-bats. The reviews of Baker as a game manager may have been mixed, but his integrity was unassailable.

# 8

# YANKEES "APOCALYPSE NOW" BECOMES RED SOX RESURRECTION

The Yankees–Red Sox rivalry is the most famous in American sports, and all the more intense because it has been so one-sided in favor of New York. The seeds of the rivalry were laid in the waning days of December 1919 when the Red Sox sold baseball's power-hitting revolutionary, a fellow named Babe Ruth, to the Yankees. That deal fundamentally changed the fortunes of two franchises. The Yankees became the forever dynasty. The Red Sox, after winning all five they had played in between 1903 and 1918, seemed cursed to never again win the World Series. From the end of World War I to the end of the century, the Red Sox played in only four World Series and lost them all in seven games.

The truly high-stakes competitive rivalry of the two franchises fighting each other for first place, however, really traces back only to the immediate postwar years. The Red Sox won a blowout pennant in 1946, the Yankees in 1947. In 1948, 'twas the Red Sox eliminating the Yankees from contention on the final weekend of the season. In 1949, 'twas the Yankees, down a game in the standings, winning their final two games of the season against the Red Sox to eke out the pennant. Between 1946 and 1950, the Red Sox and Yankees faced off in 110 games. Both teams won exactly half. The Red Sox went to the World Series just once and lost; the Yankees went three times and won all three.

The rivalry lost its edge in the 1950s and 1960s, mostly because the Red Sox took a competitive hiatus, only to be reinvigorated in the mid-1970s when both franchises reemerged as contenders and unheralded

Bucky Dent capped the Yankees' comeback from a 14-game deficit in mid-July with a home run over the Green Monster—Fenway Park's 37-foot-high left-field wall—to win a playoff for the 1978 AL Eastern Division title. By now, Yankees fans were delighted to remind Boston fans how many years it had been since the Red Sox had last won a World Series. The answer: 1918, way back when the United States was fighting the *First* World War.

Notwithstanding the Red Sox seeming to be "cursed" while the Yankees had an impressive history to fall back on, Boston's fifth division title in 1995 matched New York exactly for the number of times winning the AL East since divisional alignment in 1969. The Yankees, finishing second to the Red Sox in 1995, were the AL's first wild-card team. Neither club made it past their respective division series. Of Boston's two biggest stars of the 1980s, Wade Boggs was now playing for the Yankees, and Roger Clemens, despite his 10–5 record in 23 starts, pitched like he might be nearing the end of his career. Starring instead for Boston were fourth-year shortstop John Valentin, whose 8.3 wins above replacement made him the best position player in the American League; first baseman Mo Vaughn, whose 39 homers and league-leading 126 runs batted in earned him the Most Valuable Player Award; and knuckleball-throwing right-hander Tim Wakefield, Pittsburgh's rookie sensation just four years before, restarting his flagging career in Boston with a 16–8 record and 2.95 ERA in 27 starts after struggling with his command the two previous seasons in the Pirates' organization.

It wasn't until 1998 that the Yankees and Red Sox began a tango that ended with Boston finishing runner-up to New York in the AL East every one of the next eight years. Averaging 92 wins a year, the Red Sox were good enough to win the wild card five times. In three of those wild-card years, they met the Yankees in the ALCS. Clemens was no longer a Red Sox, spurning the low-ball contract he was offered and leaving Boston following their third-place 1996 season. The Red Sox finished fourth without him in 1997 but did introduce shortstop Nomar Garciaparra to the baseball world as Boston's answer to New York's shortstop, Derek Jeter. And in 1998, Boston traded two minor-league prospects to Montreal for Pedro Martinez, a hard-throwing right-hander whose 17–8 record, league-leading 13 complete games and 1.90 ERA, and 305 strikeouts in 241⅓ innings earned him the National League's Cy Young Award. The Red

Sox were the beneficiary of the cash-strapped Expos disposing of top-tier talent on the cusp of becoming unaffordable.

Garciaparra quickly became a superstar—and the best all-around shortstop in baseball after Alex Rodriguez, better even than Derek Jeter. He was 1997 Rookie of the Year and won back-to-back batting titles in 1999 and 2000 with .357 and .372 averages. In Garciaparra's first seven years as Boston's shortstop, including 2001 when he played in only 21 games because of a wrist injury, only Rodriguez had a higher position-player value, based on wins above replacement, and Nomar was a better defensive shortstop than either Jeter or A-Rod.

The whippet-thin Martinez was a power pitcher with a devastating array of pitches he could throw from multiple arm angles with uncanny precision. As if his first year in Boston in 1998—a 19–7 record, 2.89 earned run average, and 251 strikeouts in 233⅓ innings—wasn't impressive enough, the next five years, 1999 to 2003, Martinez won 82 games and nearly 80 percent of his decisions, with an earned run average of 2.10, and averaged 11.6 K's while walking only 1.7 batters for every nine innings pitched. He led the majors in winning percentage three times and ERA four times. When a shoulder injury limited him to just 18 starts in 2001, his ERA was still the lowest of the 131 major-league pitchers starting that many games. In 1999, Martinez struck out 313 batters in 213⅓ innings to become the first qualifying pitcher in history to average more than 13 strikeouts per nine innings. Only Randy Johnson in 2001 and Gerrit Cole in 2019 have done that since.

Those five years were the best by any American League pitcher—and arguably any pitcher in baseball, including Sandy Koufax and Greg Maddux—since Lefty Grove between 1929 and 1933. Grove also won nearly 80 percent of his decisions and led the league in ERA four times. What made both pitchers' achievements so remarkable is that they occurred in the peak years of a hitters' era. Given that his ERA adjusted for context from 1999 to 2003 was more than twice as good as the league-average pitcher four of those five years—a level of superiority no other pitcher has ever reached—it would not be unfair to say Pedro Martinez had the best five years of any pitcher ever.

Mo Vaughn had another outstanding season in 1998 with 40 homers, 115 RBIs, and a .337 batting average, which he followed up by batting .412 with 2 homers and 7 RBIs in Boston's four-game loss to Cleveland in their division series. Over the four previous years, he had smashed 158 home runs, had three 100-RBI seasons including 143 in 1996, and had run his string of consecutive .300 batting averages to five years. The Red Sox front office, however, was unwilling to match, let alone exceed, the six-year, $72 million offer the Angels presented him as their opening bid when Vaughn became a free agent after the 1998 season. Like Clemens two years earlier, Vaughn, a fan favorite, left Boston feeling unappreciated and bitter, not helped by Red Sox officials taking to Boston media to call attention to Vaughn's 240 pounds and assert that, as one baseball columnist put it, their star first baseman just wanted "Mo Money."

The Red Sox front office, however, was committed to competing with the Yankees. In 2001 they brought outfielder Manny Ramirez to Boston as a free agent, his 127 home runs, 432 runs batted in, .324 batting average, and 1.072 on-base plus slugging percentage his prior three years in Cleveland making him an attractive slugger. The next year they brought on board coveted free agent Johnny Damon to play center field and bat lead-off. And in January 2003, in an under-the-radar signing, Boston offered a modest $1.25 million, one-year deal to David Ortiz, Minnesota's left-handed designated hitter against right-handed pitchers, whom the Twins released after the 2002 season. All three would be fundamentally important to Boston's continuing success as a viable rival to New York's powerhouse Yankees in the years ahead. So too would the decision to move closer Derek Lowe, whose 42 saves led the league in 2000, into the starting rotation in 2002. His 21–8 record that year, coupled with Pedro Martinez's 20–4, helped the Red Sox to 93 wins—10 fewer than the Yankees won and not enough to capture the wild card.

In New York, meanwhile, while their homegrown Core Five—Jeter, center fielder Bernie Williams, catcher Jorge Posada, lefty starter Andy Pettitte, and closer Mariano Rivera—remained the Yankees' cornerstone players, owner George Steinbrenner was reverting to his old ways of spending big on high-priced stars to keep his dynasty on a role after winning five pennants and four World Series between 1996 and 2001. In 1999, he traded with Toronto for former Red Sox ace Roger Clemens. In 2001, he added Mike Mussina, Baltimore's ace for virtually the entire 1990s, and in 2002 the Boss brought back David Wells and signed Jason Giambi, a quality hitter and slugger of the Manny Ramirez mold. In 2003, Steinbrenner set the Yankees' sights and money on foreign stars: Japanese outfielder Hideki Matsui, playfully called Godzilla for his power, and Cuban defector Jose Contreras, whose defection from the national team in Mexico made him eligible to sign with any major-league team, as long as he did not come to the United States first. The Red Sox also aggressively pursued Contreras, holed up in Nicaragua, aggressively. They made an offer he seemed eager to accept—until the Yankees came calling with an even better deal. All of which prompted Red Sox team president Larry Lucchino to channel *Star Wars* imagery by calling out the Yankees as "the evil empire."

Their rivalry had become so compelling that the drama and stakes of the World Series seemed to pale in comparison whenever the Yankees, as the division winner, and Red Sox, as the wild card, met in the ALCS for the American League pennant. The first time was in 1999—the year after the Yankees' historic 125-win season, including the postseason. Pedro Martinez's masterful six innings of no-hits-allowed relief to win and finish off the decisive fifth game of Boston's division series with Cleveland, after having to leave his Game One start after just four innings because of back spasms, sent the Red Sox into the ALCS. The Yankees beat them with relative ease in five games. Boston did have the satisfaction, however, of clobbering Clemens for five runs in just two innings in his postseason Fenway Park debut as a Yankee in Game Three, in which Martinez gave up just two hits in seven innings for the Red Sox' only win of the series.

It wasn't until four years later in 2003 that the ALCS again headlined a Yankees–Red Sox showdown for the pennant. Boston had finished six back in the AL East and were 9–10 in their season series against New York. The series came down to a decisive win-or-go-home seventh game at Yankee Stadium, Clemens against Martinez. Clemens had beaten Martinez in Game Three at Fenway, the highlight of which was a baseball brawl. The Yankees heckled Martinez unmercifully as he gave up a 2–0 lead in the fourth. Pedro appeared to retaliate by hitting a Yankees batter. Two innings later, Clemens nearly hit Ramirez, which the Red Sox slugger, perhaps not unreasonably, interpreted as being intentional. Manny charged the mound. The dugouts emptied. And in the dustup on the field, Joe Torre's 72-year-old bench coach, Don Zimmer, made a beeline for Pedro Martinez, standing outside the Boston dugout, only to find himself tossed to the ground as the Red Sox ace sidestepped the charging Zimmer and pushed him away.

In the series finale, Clemens was knocked out in the fourth and replaced by current Yankees ace Mike Mussina, who had himself been roughed up by Boston in his two starts in the series, giving up seven runs and 14 hits in 12⅓ innings. But this time, Mussina shut down the Red Sox, pitching three innings in relief without allowing a Boston score. David Ortiz homered off Wells to give the Red Sox a 5–2 lead in the eighth. Rather than go to his bullpen for the final six outs, manager Grady Little stuck with Martinez, notwithstanding his having already thrown more than 100 pitches. He got one out. A double by Jeter and a single by Bernie Williams made the score 5–3 and still no relief for Pedro. A ground-rule double by Matsui put the tying runs in scoring position. Everyone in Red Sox Nation, sensing imminent disaster as they were wont to do, was imploring Little to take Martinez, clearly fatigued and now ineffective, out of the game. The manager did not—not until *after* Jorge Posada's double tied the score.

The game went on. Mariano Rivera pitched three scoreless innings to bring the game to the last of the 11th. Little called on Tim Wakefield, whose reliance on the knuckleball promised he could go quite some number of innings if needed. Wakefield's dancer had stymied Yankees batters for Red Sox wins in both his ALCS starts, and the Yankees had hit just .217 in the 25 innings he pitched in his four starts against them in the regular season. Of the 106 Yankee batters Wakefield faced during the season, just one—Jason Giambi, paid to do what he did—hit a home run off him. Leading off the bottom of the 11th was Aaron Boone, who had entered the game as a pinch-runner in the 8th. This was his first at-bat of the night. Boone was not only not a Giambi power threat, he was struggling at the plate. Boone had only five hits in 31 at-bats so far in the postseason and was only 2-for-16 in the ALCS.

Aaron Boone is now in the annals of Yankees bit players coming up big in the postseason, joining the likes of Bobby Brown, Billy Martin, Buck Dent, Jim Leyritz, Jose Vizcaino, and Luis Sojo. He drove Wakefield's first pitch of the game over the left-field fence, making Steinbrenner happy by returning the Yankees to the World Series. The Florida Marlins' six-game victory over the Yankees in the 2003 World Series was itself dramatic and quite the story to tell. But nothing compared to the 2003 ALCS showdown between the Yankees and Red Sox. All winter long, Boston players were condemned to hearing chants of "1918! 1918!" by Yankees fans in their heads.

One hundred and sixty-five games later—the 2004 regular season, in which Boston's 98 wins were second-most in the American League after the Yankees' 101 and their three-game sweep of the Angels in their division series—the Red Sox once against faced off as the wild card against the indomitable Yankees in the ALCS. It appeared the Red Sox were still hungover from their mismanaged and demoralizing defeat the year before because they were thoroughly outplayed by the Yankees in the first three games of the series. The Yankees had seemed to nail the Red Sox' coffin shut in a Game Three 19–8 drubbing at Fenway. They had four chances to win the one that would bury the Sox for good—or at least until baseball's annual resurrection of every team the next spring.

Coming back from a three-games-to-one deficit in seven-game postseason series was rare enough. No team had *ever* come back from a three-games-to-none deficit by winning the next four. But a steal, Big Papi's last words, a bloody sock, the slap heard 'round the world, and a band of idiots changed all that. But before we get to that, here's a look at an eventful off-season for both franchises.

The day after the Yankees lost to the Marlins in the 2003 World Series, it was no surprise that Boston manager Grady Little paid the price for staying too long with Pedro Martinez. A month later, the Red Sox made big news by negotiating a trade with Arizona for their right-handed ace, just-turned-37 Curt Schilling, who had pitched so brilliantly for the D-Backs *against the Yankees* in the 2001 World Series. Because Schilling was still under contract and had a no-trade clause, the Red Sox needed to make him a new offer he could not refuse to supersede his existing contract to get him to Boston, which they did, in his home, over Thanksgiving. With his blessing, the trade with Arizona for his services was consummated. In December, Terry Francona became Boston's latest to try his hand at becoming the first manager since Ed Barrow in 1918 to lead the Red Sox to baseball nirvana. Francona had four years of prior managerial experience in Philadelphia. None of his teams had a winning record. The Phillies won just 44 percent of the 648 games he managed. And in January the Red Sox signed free-agent closer Keith Foulke to shore up a bullpen that had the major leagues' third-worst ERA in 2003, which Little was afraid to rely on in the ALCS.

Baseball's "hot stove" conversation that winter, however, was consumed by both the Red Sox and Yankees unexpectedly angling for the services of the highest-paid player in baseball. That would be Texas Rangers shortstop Alex Rodriguez, whose record-smashing 10-year, $252 million free-agent contract in 2001 became an albatross around his new team's neck and left him unhappy in a losing situation, while his short-stop rivals Jeter and Garciaparra, neither as talented as he, were playing for winning teams and winning the affection of fans nationwide. Since his rookie year in 1995, Rodriguez had hit 345 home runs with a .309 career batting average. He had led the American League in home runs all three years since signing his $25 million-a-year deal with Texas. But taking up more than one-fifth of the Rangers' 2003 player payroll, Rodriguez left 91-loss Texas with precious few dollars to improve a team that finished last all three years he was there.

A-Rod was so desperate to play for a winning ballclub, he was willing to agree to a reduction in the remaining seven years of his contract. The Rangers were desperate to get rid of his contract. A deal was worked out to send him to Boston in exchange for Manny Ramirez. With the Com-missioner's Office favorably disposed to the deal, the Red Sox were prepared to make room for the Rangers' superstar shortstop by trading Garciaparra to the White Sox for star outfielder Magglio Ordonez to be Manny's replacement. All that was needed was for the players union to give its approval to a reduction in A-Rod's contractually obligated future earnings. Well aware that allowing the terms of lucrative contracts to be renegotiated down for the benefit of the team would set a bad precedent, the players union objected. That killed the deal. It also further alienated Garciaparra, already sorely disaffected by the Red Sox offering a contract extension before the 2003 season substantially less than the $189 million over 10 years the Yankees gave Jeter in 2001.

While Boston's complicated tango with the Rangers and the players union over an A-Rod deal was playing out, the Yankees bolstered their lineup by signing free-agent outfielder Gary Sheffield. Since signing a six-year, $61 million contract extension with the Marlins in 1997, Shef-field had been one of the most productive and dangerous hitters in base-ball—even more so after he was traded to the Dodgers and then the Braves. And now, the Yankees had an opportunity to bolster their offense even more. Just when Rodriguez thought he would be stuck in Texas, a recreational basketball injury ended Aaron Boone's 2004 season even before it started. The Yankees needed a third baseman. The whole base-ball world knew about the Red Sox trying to get A-Rod. To fortify their club for the years ahead, and probably also taking pleasure at twisting the knife in the back of Red Sox Nation, the "evil empire" worked out a deal whereby they traded Alfonso Soriano, their second baseman and lead-off hitter whose 77 home runs in 2002 and 2003 were second on the club only to Giambi and with 76 stolen bases besides, to Texas for Rodriguez.

Unlike the Red Sox with Nomar, the Yankees never gave any thought to moving Jeter to another position (and certainly not to another team) to make room for Rodriguez. A-Rod came to New York with the certain knowledge that he was not going to play shortstop. It didn't matter that he was much better defensively at the position. And there was no love lost between Jeter and his new teammate, notwithstanding they once were friends. Insecure perhaps in his own greatness, jealous of Jeter's leadership on a winning team, and probably envious of Jeter's celebrity—unalloyed celebrity was something A-Rod craved—Rodriguez in the past had said things intended to diminish the Yankee shortstop's greatness on the diamond, especially relative to himself. Jeter never said anything negative about Rodriguez but also was not one to forgive and forget.

The Red Sox got off to a good start despite Garciaparra starting the season on the disabled list with a strained Achilles tendon and feeling disrespected by the front office, which was unwilling to negotiate any substantial increase in salary for their star shortstop even though the A-Rod deal fell through. That lasted until June, when the Yankees pushed into first place to stay. They led by as many as 10½ games in mid-August before coasting to an ultimate 3-game margin of victory that was not as close as it appeared. Garciaparra was back in action by early June, but at the end of July was traded to Chicago after all—to the Cubs—in a three-team transaction that brought Expos shortstop Orlando Cabrera to Boston. Although his tender Achilles had substantially reduced Garciaparra's range and agility at a defensive position that required both, he had been on a hot streak at the plate since the beginning of July. Nomar Garciaparra's .386 batting average in his last 21 games for Boston was the highest by a Red Sox regular that month.

The first three games of 2004's ALCS left the Red Sox reeling, not only because they suffered the kiss of death by losing them all. Boston's spirit seemed totally crushed after they came from behind to tie the score at 6–6 in the third inning of Game Three at Fenway Park, only to be outscored 13–2 the next six innings. In Game Four, it was 2–0 Yankees after three, 3–2 Red Sox after five, and 4–3 Yankees after six. That was the score when Mariano Rivera, about to begin his second inning of work, took the

mound for the ninth inning. He needed three outs for the Yankees to head
to another World Series

## The Steal

Rivera uncharacteristically walked the first batter, for whom Terry Francona sent Dave Roberts in as a pinch-runner. The Red Sox had traded for
him in July to add depth and speed to their bench. In 422 games in his
career, Roberts had 135 stolen bases in 167 attempts—an 81 percent
success rate. After three pick-off attempts by Rivera on a very cold night,
the now-warmed-up Roberts stole second on Mariano's first pitch to Bill
Mueller. It was close, but Roberts was safe and in scoring position.
Mueller singled up the middle, tying the game.

## Big Papi's Last Words

The game went into extra innings. The Yankees squandered a bases-
loaded, two-outs opportunity in the 11th. In the last of the 12th, as the
game passed the five-hour mark, David Ortiz, a left-handed power-hitter
affectionately known as "Big Papi," stepped to the plate against right-
hander Paul Quantrill with a runner on first and nobody out. Ortiz had
turned out to be quite the free-agent bargain with 31 homers his first year
in Boston in 2003, meriting a much better contract, which he more than
earned by hitting 41 homers and driving in 139 runs in 2004. He was 13-
for-27 so far in the postseason, 6-for-16 against the Yankees. On Quantrill's fourth pitch, Ortiz drove the ball deep into the right-field seats at
Fenway. At the very least, Boston would not be swept.

Big Papi had the last word in Game Five as well, and for the second
day in a row Mariano Rivera surrendered a lead that would have sent the
Yankees to the World Series. The Yankees were ahead 4–2 in the 8th, and
the Red Sox down to their last six outs, when Ortiz crashed a home run
off reliever Tom Gordon. A walk and a single, putting runners on first
and third, caused Torre to bring on Rivera, whose challenge was to get all
three outs in the inning without allowing the tying run to score from third
base. He did retire all three batters he faced in the 8th, but the first of
those outs was a fly ball to center field deep enough to score the tying
run. The game stayed tied at 4–4 until, with runners on first and second
and two outs in the bottom of the 14th inning in a game that was approaching six hours, Ortiz came to bat against Esteban Loaiza—a bust
since the Yankees traded Contreras to get him from the White Sox (for

whom he was 21–9 and second in the Cy Young voting the previous year) at the trade deadline—making just his first appearance in the series. Ortiz lined a single to center. The game won, the ALCS returned to Yankee Stadium. The Yankees still had a three-games-to-two edge. The Red Sox had the momentum—and a problem.

### The Bloody Sock

The Red Sox were certainly grateful for Thanksgiving 2003. Adding to Pedro Martinez's 16–9 record, Curt Schilling, 21–6 in 32 starts his first year in Boston, couldn't have made Red Sox Nation happier. But in the opening game of their division series against the Angels, pitching with a big lead, Schilling tore the tendon sheath in his right ankle fielding a dribbler near the mound. Gamely taking the mound for the opening game of the ALCS, Schilling lasted just three innings pitching on a wobbly ankle held in place by a brace. He left trailing 6–0. The Yankees' rout of the Red Sox had begun. As a right-hander, Schilling's delivery began with his weight on his right foot pushing off the pitching rubber. In his follow-through, he was careful to put minimal pressure as his foot touched down.

Once the Red Sox forced a series return to Yankee Stadium, it was an open question whether Schilling could take his turn on the mound. But take the mound he did for Game Six, his torn tendon sheath stapled to his ankle to provide stability in a procedure that was first tested on a cadaver to see if it would work. There was some thought among the Yankees that he wasn't as hurt as the Red Sox made out—"I don't believe this whole injury aspect of it," Torre told his team—but the blood seeping through his sock from where the sutures were leaking was visible for all on national television to see. Especially given the circumstances, Schilling pitched seven outstanding innings on 99 pitches giving up just four hits. He struck out the last batter he faced, leaving with a 4–1 lead.

### The Slap Heard 'Round the World

The Yankees took advantage of Schilling's departure to pounce on Boston reliever Bronson Arroyo in the eighth. A one-out double and a Jeter single made the score 4–2 with Alex Rodriguez up as the tying run. Until Game Four, A-Rod was having an outstanding postseason, batting .424 with 2 homers and 6 RBIs overall. Batting second in the order after Jeter, A-Rod was 8-for-19 in the Yankees' four-game ouster of the Minnesota

Twins in their division series and 6-for-14 in the ALCS. That followed a year in which he hit 36 home runs, drove in 106 runs, and batted .286 while mastering his new position in his first year in pinstripes. After hitting a two-run homer in the third inning of Game Four, A-Rod went hitless in his next three at-bats with one walk. He was hitless in four at-bats with two walks in Game Five. And in this game, he had gone 1 for 3 against Schilling.

Arroyo was 9–8 in 29 starts for the Red Sox during the regular season. He was the winning pitcher in the final game of Boston's sweep of Anaheim in their division series but was bombarded by the Yankees for six runs in two innings in his Game Three ALCS start. Rodriguez doubled and homered off him in that game, but this time A-Rod hit a weak dribbler up the first base line that Arroyo fielded, his momentum carrying him toward tagging Rodriguez out as he ran to first. Had Arroyo tried to slap his glove across A-Rod's chest, Rodriguez could have run hard through his outstretched glove, perhaps causing him to drop the ball. Instead, Rodriguez reached over to slap Arroyo's glove, causing the ball to fall out. In the fire drill that followed, the Red Sox chased after the ball; Jeter came around to score; and Rodriguez wound up on second base—a hero to Yankee fans everywhere for his base-running savvy. After some confusion, he was called out and Jeter was returned to first base. A-Rod's slap was not only against the rules; it made him look like a petulant child. He went from momentary hero to looking ridiculous. Jeter did not score. The Yankees put the tying runs on base in the ninth but again did not score. Improbably, the ALCS that the Yankees had once been so in command of was now tied for another Game Seven showdown at Yankee Stadium. Despite playing in their own ballpark, having lost three games in a row, now it was the Yankees feeling all the pressure.

The Yankees sure could have used Andy Pettitte . . . or Roger Clemens . . . or David Wells. All three notched victories against the Red Sox in the 2003 ALCS. None of the three were Yankees in 2004. Clemens announced he would call it a career after 310 regular-season victories once the 2003 season was over. And the Yankees opted not to re-sign 40-year-old Wells, notwithstanding his 34–14 record in 61 starts in 2002 and 2003—his second stint in pinstripes. Their biggest mistake, however, was failing to give Pettitte a contract extension worthy of what he had meant to the Yankees the nine previous years, in every one of which his team played in the postseason.

Pettitte did not have the gravitas of fellow staff mates David Cone or Clemens, but he was the anchor of the Yankees pitching staff. In the mold of Eddie Lopat on the 1949–1953 Yankees, Pettitte was a southpaw who was consistently dependable and durable, rarely missing a start, with 149 wins and a .656 winning percentage from his 1995 rookie season to 2003. The Yankees had also won 20 of his 30 postseason starts, in which he personally was 13–8. Yet, because Pettitte wasn't an elite pitcher, Steinbrenner often thought of him as expendable trade bait. Whether they expected their 31-year-old lefty to sign below his market value to stay in New York or were not interested in keeping him in pinstripes, it wasn't until *after* he was successfully wooed by Houston's Astros, his hometown team, that the Yankees tried to change his mind with a far more generous offer. He declined and went to Houston. A month later, Clemens walked back his retirement and also signed as a free agent with the Astros, *his* hometown team too. The Yankees were forced to rebuild the starting rotation for 2004 around their one remaining ace—Mike Mussina.

The Yankees' two most reliable starting pitchers—Mussina and Jon Lieber—had started Games Five and Six. Loaiza had thrown 59 pitches in Game Five, and Torre had lost confidence in him anyway. He had also lost confidence in Javier Vazquez, whom the Yankees acquired from the impoverished Expos before the season. That left him no choice but to count on Kevin Brown for the seventh game finale. Brown, one of the finest pitchers of his generation, was also a preseason trade pickup, at the cost of taking over the last two years of the $105 million, seven-year deal he signed with the Dodgers in 1999. But the temperamental Brown missed more than a month because of back problems and three weeks in September after breaking his hand punching a concrete wall in anger about being taken out of a game. Brown had pitched poorly in Game Three at Fenway, giving up four runs in two innings before the Yankees blew the game open, but Kevin Brown it was for the seventh game.

## The Idiots

Johnny Damon called himself and his teammates "idiots" on the eve of the Red Sox sweeping their division series against the Angels. By this he meant they were too stupid to know, as everyone else did, they were supposed to have no chance—zero!—against the 2004 Yankees juggernaut in the ALCS. That certainly seemed true when the Red Sox faced an impossible 3–0 deficit against the Yankees going into Game Four. But "we have something to prove," he elaborated before Boston finished off Anaheim. "We want to be known as the team that rewrites the history book."

Rewrite the history book they did. David Ortiz hit a two-run home run off Brown in the first, and after Torre replaced Brown with the bases loaded in the second, Damon greeted new pitcher Vazquez by driving the first pitch he threw into the right-field seats—where the Babe used to hit 'em in the House That Ruth Built—for a grand slam and a 6–0 Boston lead. It was 8–1 after four innings, and the Red Sox cruised to a 10–3 victory to make them the first team ever to come back from a 3–0 deficit to win a seven-game series. Making it all the more sweet was that Boston's archrival the New York Yankees—a franchise that won 26 World Series in the 86 years since the Red Sox last won in 1918—were the ones to suffer the most ignominious postseason defeat in baseball history. Perhaps sweeter still was that it was done in front of *their* crowd, silencing forever their "1918! 1918!" mocking of the Boston Red Sox.

Of course, it was still incumbent for the Red Sox to win the World Series—which they did in an impressive four-game sweep of the St. Louis Cardinals, the team whose 105–57 record was the best in baseball since the newly A-Rod-less Mariners won 116 in 2001. Schilling pitched six strong innings on his injured ankle to win Game Two, and Martinez pitched seven shutout innings to win Game Three. But it was Boston's unprecedented stunning takedown of the New York Yankees in the ALCS that continues to be what Red Sox Nation, Yankees fans, and baseball fans around the world most remember. And maybe the Babe, too, up on baseball's Mount Olympus. The Curse of the Bambino was swept into the dustbin. The world as we know it did not come to an end.

Since the 2004 ALCS exorcism that finally ended Babe Ruth's haunting of his original team, the Red Sox have been to three World Series and won them all, and the Yankees to just one, which they also won. But there was no dramatic turn in their fortunes relative to each other. The next year, in 2005, the Red Sox and Yankees finished with the same record, but because the Yankees won their season series, Boston for the eighth year in a row had to settle for runner-up in the AL East to New York. Neither team made it past their division series. Pedro Martinez had left for New York—the Mets—as a free agent, and Curt Schilling made only 11 starts and pitched 21 games out of the bullpen because of the residual effects of his ankle injury. Helping to pick up the slack was 42-year-old David Wells, one-third of whose 15 wins came in starts against his former teammates in New York.

Trying to fix their starting pitching around Mike Mussina for 2005, the Yankees sent Vazquez to Arizona in a trade for 42-year-old Randy Johnson, after agreeing to give him a $32 million contract extension. They also committed $51 million in multiyear deals to sign free-agent right-handers Jaret Wright, 15–8 with Atlanta in 2004, and Carl Pavano, 18–8 with Florida. Pavano's one-run, eight-inning gem against the Yankees in Game Four of the 2003 World Series was surely remembered by Team Steinbrenner. The Big Unit won 34 games in his two years with the Yankees but was never comfortable in the Big Apple and often confrontational with the New York sports media. Wright and Pavano proved to be costly free-agent busts because of injuries and questionable attitudes that alienated their teammates.

In 2006 the Yankees won their ninth-straight division title by a comfortable 10-game margin over Toronto. Boston was third, 11 games back. Taiwan-born right-hander Chien-Ming Wang went 19–6 as the Yankees' best starting pitcher. Striking out only 76 batters in his 218 innings-pitched, Wang's success was stunning given his strikeout ratio was half the average of 6.2 K's per nine innings by major-league starting pitchers. Derek Jeter was second in the league in batting with a .343 average. Second baseman Robinson Cano, in only his second big-league season, was right behind Jeter with a .342 average. Jason Giambi crushed 37 home runs, and A-Rod hit 35. And with Bernie Williams being phased into retirement, now playing center field for New York's Yankees was . . . Johnny Damon, committing the unpardonable sin in Boston of signing with the enemy Yankees as a free agent.

They kept finishing first, but owed in large part to Alex Rodriguez's eternal quest for attention, the Yankees were sorely lacking the clubhouse cohesion of their 1996–2001 club that won five pennants, a wild card, and four World Series in six years. Derek Jeter himself said it just wasn't the same. The Yankees band-of-brothers striving for championships had become something more like a cohort of talented individuals that did not exhibit much of an all-for-one and one-for-all ethos.

The Red Sox finally beat out the Yankees in the AL East in 2007. On July 4, New York was two games below .500 at 40–42, and Boston's lead was 11½ games. New York was 9½ games better than Boston the rest of the way but could do nothing to prevent the Red Sox from (mostly) coasting to the finish, even if their final margin of victory was only 2 games. For the third year in a row the Yankees went down in defeat in their division series, this time as the American League's wild-card team. That defeat cost Joe Torre his job, never mind that his Yankees played beyond 162 games all 12 years he was their manager. The Red Sox went on to win their second World Series in four years—a four-game sweep of the Colorado Rockies.

Torre wasn't exactly fired. His contract had expired. But he also wasn't told the Yankees no longer wanted him. Instead, with George Steinbrenner ailing and no longer dominating front-office decision-making, Torre was told by his son Hal that the Yankees would like him to return in 2008 on a one-year contract for $5 million, one-third less than he was paid in 2007, *but* with "incentive" bonuses of $1 million for bringing the Yankees a 13th-straight postseason under his leadership, for winning the division series, and for winning the league championship series to make into the World Series. The idea Torre needed "incentives" was a humiliating putdown by Yankees executives to maneuver their popular manager into deciding to leave of his own accord without them having to tell him he was no longer wanted.

They wanted a different kind of manager: someone more open to intrusive data-based advice from the front office and someone more intense than the laid-back baseball professional—"Corporate Joe," some players called him derisively—that was Joe Torre. That someone would be Joe Girardi, the starting catcher for Torre's 1996 and 1997 Yankees, whose only managerial experience in charge of the Marlins in 2006 ended with his being fired for not being "a good fit"—a month after which he was voted the NL's Manager of the Year.

# 9

# METS MELTDOWNS

New York's Mets—not the Yankees—were the domineering bad guys of Major League Baseball in the middle to late 1980s. Led by a pair of seemingly Hall of Fame–bound young stars, outfielder Darryl Strawberry and pitcher Doc Gooden, the 1984–1988 Mets were unquestionably the best team of the 1980s even though they won only two division titles and just one pennant and World Series. They won at least 90 games all five years, including 108 in 1986, when they won their division by 21½ games and went on to dramatically snatch a World Series victory over the Red Sox, and 100 in 1988, when they won the NL East by 15 games but lost to the Dodgers in the NLCS. The Mets' fall from a should-have-been dynasty was precipitated by the immaturity of both their young stars and more than a few of their teammates, whose celebrity lifestyles too often got the better of them. Strawberry and Gooden sabotaged their careers, squandering their Hall of Fame potential, by falling prey to recreational drug and alcohol abuse.

In an embarrassing coda to the powerhouse team they recently were, the Mets plummeted from a dynasty-in-the-making to a mortifying caricature of dysfunction through the first half of the 1990s. It wasn't that the Mets entered the 1990s with a weak foundation and did nothing to improve the quality of their roster. Third baseman Howard Johnson was one of the National League's elite sluggers until injuries in 1992 short-circuited his career. In 1991 the Mets added speed to the top of their lineup by signing free-agent outfielder Vince Coleman and his 549 stolen bases for St. Louis the six previous years. The next year they brought on Pirates free agent Bobby Bonilla as a power-bat to replace Strawberry, whose own free-agency departure after his 37 home runs in 1990 contributed to the Mets dropping from the highest-scoring team in the major leagues to just eighth in the National League. Gooden was still the staff ace, but David Cone was arguably the better pitcher. Trying to maintain a top-tier starting rotation, the Mets traded for Twins ace Frank Viola in 1989 and, after Viola left as a free agent, Royals ace Bret Saberhagen in 1992. They also traded for Reds closer John Franco prior to the 1990 season.

The defining moments of the Mets' disrepair came in the summer of 1993. On their way to a major-league-most 103 losses, the bad press of dangerous immature pranks by would-be team leaders eclipsed the bad press of mediocre baseball. Saberhagen, just given a lucrative contract extension, set off firecrackers and sprayed bleach at reporters in separate incidents as a "practical joke," he said. "If the reporters can't take it, forget them." Coleman, whose first two years in New York had been marred by injuries, had his own fun with firecrackers in the parking lot at Dodger Stadium after a loss, setting a big one off that injured a young woman and two children. Both players were suspended by the Mets for their explosive pranks. These Mets were definitely not the endearing, lovably "Amazing" Mets that captured the hearts and imagination of their fans despite playing often atrociously laughable baseball in the first six years of their existence in the 1960s. These Mets were just losers—and nasty ones at that.

By 1996, however, the Mets appeared poised for a comeback. If Atlanta's Braves were dominating the National League with a trio of aces—Greg Maddux, Tom Glavine, and John Smoltz—New York's Mets were expecting three of their own to emerge as top-tier aces, perhaps that very season, to challenge the Braves for supremacy in the NL East. They were southpaw Bill Pulsipher, a second-round pick in baseball's 1991 amateur draft; right-hander Jason Isringhausen, also drafted in 1991; and right-hander Paul Wilson, the first pick in baseball's 1994 amateur draft. After excelling in the minor leagues, Isringhausen and Pulsipher were both called up and took their place in the Mets' starting rotation in the summer of 1995. Wilson was promoted at the beginning of the 1996 season. The three were featured on the cover of the 1996 preseason baseball issue of *The Sporting News*. They were hyped as "Generation K" in a nod to the impending turn of the century. Mets general manager Joe McIlvaine was quoted later by *Newsday* as saying he had told "somebody" that "one of them is going to be really good, one of them is going to get hurt, and one of them is going to underachieve."

As it happened, none of the three came close to meeting the Mets' great expectations. All three endured injuries early in their careers that required Tommy John surgery, which was not yet as routinely effective at restoring a pitcher's career as it would soon become. Isringhausen had the most career success, not as a starting ace and not with the Mets, but as a closer for the Oakland A's and St. Louis Cardinals, racking up 300 saves in 13 years as a reliever. Once recovered from his surgeries, Wilson was four years a starting pitcher for Tampa Bay and Cincinnati in the first years of the new century, finishing his career with 40 wins—just five with the Mets, for whom he pitched only one year before injuries betrayed him. Pulsipher went from spring training hype in 1996 to missing the entire season because of his torn ligament. He never fully recovered and wound up winning just 13 games in parts of six big-league seasons. Only 5 of his wins were as a Met.

Despite not having their own presumed trio of aces to throw at opposing batters, the Mets by the close of the 1990s had re-emerged as a bona fide contender—although one unable to dethrone Atlanta in the NL East. The Mets were the beneficiaries of Marlins owner Wayne Huizenga deciding to break up the team that had, improbably, just won the 1997 World Series because his player payroll was more than he was willing to bear. Huizenga's decision to shed the Marlins' high-priced stars led to veteran lefty Al Leiter being traded for three minor leaguers to the Mets in February 1998, and third baseman Bobby Bonilla, who had left the Mets in 1995, outfielder Gary Sheffield, and catcher Charles Johnson being sent to Los Angeles in mid-May 1998 for Mike Piazza. Given that Piazza's 177 career home runs and .331 batting average in seven years with the Dodgers had him already regarded as the best-hitting catcher in baseball history and that he was being paid $8 million for the season, it was a foregone conclusion that his time in Miami would be transitional. A week later he and his contract were traded to the Mets for three minor-league prospects. Piazza picked up his career in New York where he had left off in Los Angeles, becoming the power fulcrum of the Mets' offense, his 23 homers and .348 batting average the rest of the season helping his new team to 88 wins and second place in the NL East.

But it wasn't just Piazza giving the Mets a new look and the Shea Stadium faithful a reason to hope. On September 6, 1999, with the Mets boasting the second-best record in the National League after division top dog Atlanta, *Sports Illustrated*'s cover story proclaimed, "The Best Infield Ever? Four Amazing Mets"—an attention-grabbing overstatement to be sure, but nonetheless indicative of how good the Mets had become. *SI* was talking about veteran first baseman and former Blue Jays star John Olerud, second baseman Edgardo Alfonzo, shortstop Rey Ordonez, and veteran third baseman and former White Sox star Robin Ventura. Olerud, in his third year as a Met, batted a robust .354 in 1998, coming within six hits of becoming the first player since 1901 to win batting titles in both leagues; he had led the American League with a .363 batting average five years before. Venezuelan-born Alfonzo and Cuban-born defector Ordonez were both originally signed by the Mets. Ordonez was exceptional defensively. Alfonzo could play anywhere in the infield and had a breakout season at bat in 1999. Ventura, signed as a free agent over the winter, belted 32 homers, drove in 120 runs, and had arguably the best year of his already distinguished career in 1999. Piazza blasted 40 home runs and had 124 RBIs, matching his career highs with LA in 1997.

Add in the ageless Rickey Henderson's .315 batting average, .423 on-base percentage, and 37 steals in his first (and only) full season with the Mets after signing as a free agent, and the 1999 Mets had an offense rivaling the Braves. Their 96 wins were seven fewer than always-first Atlanta, begging the what-if question of whether Isringhausen, Pulsipher, and Wilson would have made a difference in the outcome of the NL East had they been healthy and lived up to their hype as the Mets' answer to Maddux, Glavine, and Smoltz. The Mets tied with Cincinnati for the best record among the National League's second-place clubs, forcing a one-game playoff for the wild card. Leiter pitched a complete-game shutout for his team-leading 13th win to give the Mets their wild-card ticket to the postseason, where they beat the 100-win Arizona Diamondbacks in their division series, then lost to Atlanta in the NLCS.

The Mets finally got ahead of Atlanta in the Year 2000, but only in the postseason because once again, they were second to the Braves in the NL East. Their final one-game deficit masked the fact that they were five games behind with just six remaining. It was they, however, as the wild-card team, and not the Atlanta Braves, that went to the World Series. 'Twas probably a good thing that the Braves were knocked off in their division series, precluding the Mets from having to play them in the NLCS. The Mets had fortified their starting rotation by trading for Astros ace Mike Hampton, whose 22–4 record in 1999 made him unaffordable and ultimately expendable, as far as Houston was concerned, especially since he was about to enter his free-agency year. Hampton won 15, Leiter won 16, Piazza hit 38 homers while batting .324, and while Alfonzo had a career-year with 25 homers, 94 RBIs, and a .324 batting average, Ordonez missed most of the season with a broken arm. The Mets' championship dreams died in five games at the hands of New York's more imposing team—the Yankees. The die was cast when closer Armando Benitez, having assumed the role mid-season in 1999 because of an injury to Franco, failed to protect a one-run ninth-inning lead in the series opener at Yankee Stadium.

The Braves were indisputably the team against which the Mets—and their fans—measured themselves, fueling a bitter rivalry that was ameliorated only after Atlanta's string of 11 consecutive Eastern Division titles ran its course in 2005. The intensity of Mets fans' feelings about the Braves was inflamed by Atlanta closer John Rocker acting like "a one-man psycho circus" at Shea Stadium, to quote *Sports Illustrated* in an article on him in December 1999. Commenting for the article on the verbal abuse he got from the Shea faithful for his gratuitous and sometimes obscene acts of disrespect, Rocker was nothing if not racist and homophobic in his words about Mets fans traveling to the Stadium on the Number 7 subway line and about New York City's multicultural diversity in general.

Even after Rocker was long gone from the Braves, disgraced by his deliberately impolitic remarks, and even as the Mets ceased to be a challenger in the NL East beginning the year after playing in the 2000 World Series, Atlanta's Braves remained the opposing team Mets fans most loved to hate. Chipper Jones will always remember Mets fans mockingly serenading him by his given name—"Larry . . . Larry"—whenever he came to bat at Shea Stadium. His answer? "Larry" was at his best on the road at Shea—19 home runs, 63 runs, 55 RBIs, and a .313 batting average in the 88 games he played there.

Somebody besides the Atlanta Braves finally won the NL East in 2006. 'Twas New York's Mets! Tied with the New York team that played in the Bronx for the best record in baseball! The Mets had a very good team, to be sure. Shortstop Jose Reyes and third baseman David Wright, both 23, were young stars unfazed by the pressures of playing in New

York. Reyes, whose rookie year was 2003, was a throwback to 1960s shortstops like Luis Aparicio and Maury Wills—lead-off batters with excellent speed who did not draw many walks but were very proficient at stealing bases and defensively deft—except that Reyes was a more dangerous hitter. Since being called up in July 2004, Wright was the Mets' answer to Derek Jeter—a model of consistency who hit with power, hit for average, and was the team leader. He was the Mets' biggest position-player star since Strawberry, but without the baggage of surly behavior.

Veteran center fielder Carlos Beltran, signed as a free agent in January 2005 just months after his extraordinary display of hitting prowess and power for Houston in the division and league championship series the previous October, had a monster year for the Mets in 2006 with career highs in homers (41), RBIs (116), and runs scored (127). By the metric of offensive wins above replacement, he was the best hitter in the National League, a shade better than Albert Pujols and Miguel Cabrera. The Mets had also added, by way of pre-season trades with the stingy, cash-strapped Marlins, first baseman Carlos Delgado and catcher Paul Lo Duca. Delgado came to New York with 369 career home runs (all but 33 for Toronto), to which he added 38 more his first year with the Mets. Lo Duca, whose path to New York was the same as Mike Piazza's, both having started their careers with the Dodgers before being traded to the Marlins as an interim step to the Mets, led the team with a .318 batting average.

And now pitching for the Mets were a pair of aces in the waning years of their careers, still capable of excellence—Tom Glavine, who left Maddux and Smoltz in 2003 to sign as a free agent in New York, and Red Sox ace Pedro Martinez, signed as a free agent before the 2005 season. Glavine had his first winning season since leaving Atlanta with a 15–7 record. Martinez, 15–8 in his first season with the Mets the year before, won his first five starts before a litany of injuries to his hip, calf, toe, and shoulder limited his effectiveness. Closer Billy Wagner, free-agent pick-up over the winter, was uniformly excellent, saving 40 games, allowing runs in only 12 of the 70 games he pitched, and striking out 94 batters in 72⅓ innings.

Glavine won on opening day, the Mets lost their next game, and Martinez won their third game of the year to put the Mets half a game up in the standings—with 159 left to go. At the end of every game thereafter, win or lose, the Mets were never anywhere other than first. They won the division by a 12-game margin—their 97 wins nine more any other National League club. Then they swept their division series only to be upended in the NLCS by 83-win St. Louis. The seventh game at Shea Stadium was one for the ages. With the score tied 1–1 and a Cardinals runner on first with one out in the sixth, Mets left fielder Endy Chavez robbed Scott Rolen of a home run with a leaping catch at the wall and turned it into a double play, shades of Brooklyn's Sandy Amoros robbing Yogi Berra in the 1955 World Series and doubling up the runner at first. St. Louis went ahead on Yadier Molina's two-run homer in the top of the ninth. Then the Mets loaded the bases against rookie reliever Adam Wainwright, promoted to the role of closer for the postseason. There were two outs. To the plate came Carlos Beltran, with three homers in the series. And Wainwright froze him at the plate on an 0–2 curveball that had as nasty a break as Beltran had ever seen. That didn't stop Mets fans from wondering how he could take that pitch, ending the Mets' season with the bases loaded.

That was just the start of what seemed destined to be an annual ritual of Mets competitive meltdowns. Given their 2006 dominance of the NL East and the National League, they expected to do the same in 2007. Most of the summer, the Mets were in command of their division. After winning 10 of their first 12 games in September, New York's 7-game lead on September 12 seemed unassailable with 145 down and just 17 to go. Next up, the second-place Phillies were coming to town for three games knowing they really needed to sweep at Shea Stadium to have any shot at engineering a reverse outcome from 1964 when, with 145 down and just 17 to go, they held a six-game lead, and lost. The Mets lost all three and their next two in Washington to the lowly Nationals to see their lead cut to a mere game-and-a-half with 12 remaining.

Seeming to recover, the Mets won four of their next five and returned home for their final seven games with a 2½-game lead—whereupon they were swept by Washington and lost to St. Louis and then to Florida to find themselves enmeshed in a five-game losing streak and a game *behind* the Phillies with just two games to go. A 13–0 mauling of the Marlins and a Phillies defeat brought both contenders to game 162 tied for first. But while the Phillies easily defeated the 73-win Nationals, Glavine was only able to get one out as the 70-win Marlins scored seven runs in the first inning to crush the Mets' spirit and send them into the off-season with an epic September collapse of their own. That was the last game Tom Glavine pitched for the Mets before returning to Atlanta the next year as a free agent, where he finished his career with 305 major-league victories.

Glavine's spot in the rotation was taken by another left-hander seeming destined for Cooperstown when the Mets traded with the Minnesota Twins for Johan Santana and promptly signed him to a six-year, $137 million contract. Santana did not let them down, going 16–7 in 34 starts and leading the league in innings and earned run average. Undefeated in his last 17 starts—the entire months of July, August, and September in which he won eight and his team went on to win five of his other games—Santana bore no blame for another Mets' September meltdown in 2008. The Mets began the month with a one-game lead over the Phillies and finished with a mediocre 13–12 record, including losing six of their last nine, that condemned them to another second-place ending, three games behind. While Santana went 4–0 in six September starts with a 1.83 ERA, the rest of the Mets starters were 3–7 with a 5.76 earned run average in 19 starts.

On September 15, 2008, with the Mets holding a one-game lead on the Phillies pending the outcome of their game that Monday night in Washington, the U.S. government announced it would not be bailing out Lehman Brothers from the weight of some $60 billion in mortgage debt it was holding, forcing the investment bank into a bankruptcy that precipitated a hugely dramatic drop in the stock market. The subsequent meltdown of the American and world economies was of infinitely greater consequence than any Mets meltdown, but the fallout had a direct effect on the fortunes of the Mets franchise when countless clients of supposed investment guru Bernie Madoff, concerned about their financial futures, wanted to cash out their portfolios. Problem was the man to whom they had entrusted their money with visions of high returns had been perpetrating a massive fraud that counted on there *not* ever being such a large-scale demand for payouts that would expose his Ponzi scheme of investments by overwhelming his capacity to make good on his side of the transaction. Among Madoff's high-profile clients were Mets' owner Fred Wilpon, his son and owner heir-apparent Jeff, and team president Saul Katz. Wilpon and Katz were close personal friends of Madoff.

The Mets' ownership group reportedly lost up to $500 million when Madoff's Ponzi scheme collapsed of its own weight in November and

December 2008. It couldn't have come at a worse time for the Mets. Befitting a team playing in New York City that had been one of the best in baseball the three previous seasons, notwithstanding the devastating endings to all three, the Mets had by far the largest player payroll in the National League, dwarfed only by that of New York's more famous team in the Bronx. And they would open the 2009 season in a brand-new stadium financed in large part with public money. The financial fallout for the Mets from the Madoff scandal was immediate. In addition to using his Madoff investments as collateral to secure loans for the Mets' part in constructing the new ballpark, Wilpon had entrusted to Madoff players' annuities, deferred payments for long-term player contracts where the team got to keep any returns over the agreed interest rate in the player's contract, and money paid by team sponsors. The Mets were suddenly in financial straits.

As if that was not bad enough, Wilpon and the Mets found themselves entangled in the blame for the Madoff affair. The judge-appointed trustee seeking restitution for Madoff's victims was suing Wilpon and Katz for hundreds of millions in financial claims. Their fault was encouraging others to invest with Madoff when, according to the trustee, their financial involvement with Madoff was so extensive they must have known, or at least should have known, that their good friend Madoff was perpetrating a fraud on his clients. Moreover, Wilpon and Katz (and arguably the Mets franchise) had benefited from the Ponzi scheme by withdrawing more money—other people's money, hence profits they had not earned—from their Madoff accounts than they had put in. And now was payback time. Although arguing that they had been duped by Madoff, close friend though he be, and had no way of knowing about his illegal scheme, Wilpon and Katz eventually agreed to avoid trial by paying back $162 million of their "fictitious profits." A deal brokered in 2012 ultimately reduced that by more than $100 million, saving Wilpon from having to sell the team.

The Mets' inadvertent involvement in the Madoff affair plunged the team's finances into disarray. Wilpon owed between $400 and $500 million in debt on the team and was struggling to fund its baseball operations. As spring training 2011 beckoned with Wilpon facing the possibility of having to pay hundreds of millions to the victims of Madoff's scam, Major League Baseball stepped in to provide the Mets a $25 million loan to keep the franchise functional and to help secure a bridge loan from a major New York bank until the Mets' financial situation stabilized. It wasn't until after three straight losing seasons since missing out on the 2008 division title by three games, and a spending deficit of $120 million in 2010 and 2011, that Wilpon and Katz finally agreed to settle with the trustee for Madoff's victims.

# 10

# PHILLIES FLIP THE '64 SCRIPT

The history of dramatic comebacks from big deficits to overtake a team seeming certain to finish first is not as sparse as it might seem. Those pennant races are almost all remembered for the team, or defining moments by players on that team, that surged to their improbable victory atop the standings. There were, for example, 1914's Boston "Miracle" Braves and 1969's New York "Miracle" Mets. And there were Bobby Thomson's home run that capped off the 1951 New York Giants' "Miracle of Coogan's Bluff" and Bucky "F-word" (as far as Red Sox Nation was concerned) Dent's home run that capped off the 1978 Yankees' operatic drive to the American League's Eastern Division title—both of which came in playoff games to decide the regular-season standings.

The 1964 National League pennant race, which the Cardinals won after trailing by 11 games with one week to go in August and just 39 games remaining on their schedule, is remembered less for their scintillating 28–11 surge to overtake *three* teams ahead of them than for the epic collapse of the Philadelphia Phillies in the last two weeks of the season. Not expected to contend to begin with, the Phillies held a comfortable 6½-game lead with just 12 left to play, only to lose 10 in a row and, with them, the chance to play in the World Series that the City of Brotherly Love assumed in mid-September to be their destiny. With such a big lead and so few games still to play, that horrific ending scarred a generation of Phillies fans and became a stigma on the franchise that even three consecutive division titles in the mid-1970s and a World Series championship in 1980 (finally!—the first in the franchise's 97-year history) with lefty

Steve Carlton and best-ever third baseman Mike Schmidt, and two subsequent (losing) trips to the World Series in 1983 and 1993, could not erase.

Erased from history, certainly not, but the '64 Phillies flop was finally exorcized 43 years later in 2007 when Philadelphia was the beneficiary of another team's epic collapse in the final weeks of the season to lose a seemingly certain trip to the postseason. That team was the New York Mets, cruising to a second-straight division title with a 7-game lead and just 17 games to go. Losing 12 of those games, the Mets did not displace the '64 Phillies in the realm of worst late-season collapses but nudged them aside. Same as the National League's 1964 pennant race, the legacy of the 2007 NL East division race was defined more by the Mets' collapse than by the Phillies winning 13 of their final 17 games to win the division title.

Philadelphia had not seriously contended since Toronto's Joe Carter ended the 1993 World Series with a Game Six three-run walk-off homer off Phillies' closer Mitch Williams. The 1993 Phillies were a rabble-rousing hard-scrabble team of overachievers. First baseman John Kruk was irreverent, sloppy in appearance (shaggy and overweight), but effective—particularly at bat—endearing him to working-class fans. Center fielder Lenny Dykstra, a star on the Mets' exceptionally talented and hard-partying 1986 championship team, brought his obnoxiously aggressive "tough as nails" persona cultivated in New York to Philadelphia when the Mets traded him to their division rival in 1989. Catcher Darren Daulton was the hard-driving, all-business team leader. Right-hander Curt Schilling, a fierce competitor, had his breakout season with a 16–7 record for a team nobody expected to contend that year—not after finishing last in the division the year before.

The 1993 season turned out to be the Phillies' last in the twentieth century with a winning record. It didn't help that Atlanta's far-better Braves were assigned to the NL East in the National League's 1994 realignment, or that Montreal's Expos, finishing three games back of Philadelphia in 1993, had emerged as a top-tier team in its own right. Kruk, Daulton, and Dykstra all saw their careers prematurely ended by injuries, and Dykstra later admitted—even bragged about—bulking up with steroids to become a much better player in Philadelphia than he was in New York. Schilling's path forward was to become an elite pitcher. His 619 strikeouts (in 523 innings) in 1997 and 1998 were just one less than Randy Johnson's total (in 457⅓ innings) for those two years. Destined for last place in their division with the worst record in the National League in 2000, Philadelphia traded Schilling to Arizona in July.

In 2001 the Phillies had a near-repeat of their 1993 division championship, getting off to a fast start, leading the NL East virtually all of the first three months and hanging close the rest of the way before losing out by two games. Their offense was powered by right fielder Bobby Abreu, third baseman Scott Rolen, and left fielder Pat Burrell batting third, fourth, and fifth. At the top of the order was rookie shortstop Jimmy Rollins, whose 46 steals led the league. Rollins and Burrell were foundation players for the Phillies becoming the National League's dominant team from 2007 to 2011. Neither Rolen nor Abreu made it that far. Unhappy in Philadelphia and about to become a free agent, Rolen was sent to St. Louis at the trade deadline in 2002. Happy, extraordinarily productive, and a model of consistency in Philadelphia, Abreu was traded to the Yankees at the trade deadline in 2006 for minor-league prospects, none of whom panned out. Both were among the best players in baseball when they were traded. The Abreu trade was motivated in part by front-office dismay that the Phillies, after finishing just two games behind Atlanta in 2005, dropped out of contention early in 2006 with a horrendous 9–18 month in June.

Entering the final month of the 2007 season only 2 games back of the Mets in the East and 2 back in the wild-card standings, the Phillies lost seven of their first 11 games in September to seemingly fall out of contention, 7 games back of the Mets on September 12 with 145 done and 17 to go. After beating Colorado the next day, while the Mets were idle, to narrow their deficit to 6½ games—a familiar number in Philadelphia's baseball history—the Phillies traveled to Shea Stadium for a three-game weekend series. Realistically, they knew they needed a sweep to have any shot at doing to the Mets what was done to them in 1964. Winning all three would narrow the Mets' lead to a tough but manageable 3½ games; losing just one would have left the Phillies with a more daunting challenge—5½ back with just 13 games remaining.

In the series opener, the Phillies had only two hits off Mets ace Tom Glavine and trailed 2–0 going into the 6th. A walk and a home run by Chase Utley tied the score. The Phillies escaped a bases-loaded jam in the 8th and went on to win on a sacrifice fly in the 10th inning. The Mets carried a 3–1 lead into the seventh inning in the second game, which the

Phillies cut to a run with an unearned run. A home run by Aaron Rowand and two-run triple by Jimmy Rollins in the eighth gave Philadelphia another critical win. They now trailed by 4½ games. In the series finale—and the last game in which the two clubs would face each other in 2007—the Phillies broke open a 5–5 tie with a five-run sixth inning highlighted by pinch-hitter Greg Dobbs belting a grand slam for Philadelphia's only hit of the inning. Three walks and an error got the Mets into more trouble than they could handle even before Dobbs came to bat. Dobbs would hit 46 career home runs in 2,097 major-league at-bats; it was his only grand slam.

Taking two of three in St. Louis, three of four in Washington, and two of three at home against Atlanta, the Phillies pulled even with the Mets going into the final weekend. Both teams were closing out the season at home against terrible teams. The 87-loss Nationals were at Citizens Bank Park in Philadelphia; the 90-loss Marlins at Shea Stadium in New York. A win and a loss later for both teams brought the 2007 NL East race down to game 162. In New York, the Marlins battered Glavine for seven runs before the Mets even came to bat. In Philadelphia, the Phillies had a 1–0 lead after one, led 3–0 after three, and won by a 6–1 score while the Mets went down in an 8–1 loss. The Phillies' bid to make it to their sixth World Series in franchise history foundered in Denver when they were swept by the wild-card Colorado Rockies in their division series.

A similar narrative played out in 2008. After 146 games with 16 to go, the Phillies trailed the Mets by 3½ games. Since they had completed their season series with New York and could not gain any ground directly against them, the Phillies would have to rely on other teams to beat the Mets, while doing their best to catch up. The Phillies won 13; the Mets lost 10 of their last 17; and Philadelphia won the division by 3 games. This time Philadelphia soared through the postseason, losing just once in their division series, just once in the NLCS, and just once in the World Series against the Tampa Bay Rays. The deciding fifth game began in cold conditions. Winterish weather was expected. By the middle innings, the game was being played in impossible conditions. With players having to navigate massive puddles on the mound and in the infield amidst driving, freezing rain, the game was finally suspended in the middle of the sixth *after* the Rays tied the score. A miserable time was being had by all.

In *not* one of baseball's finest moments, especially it being the Fall Classic, the game was suspended to be continued another day. But Commissioner Selig, six years after being forced to suspend the All-Star Game—and roundly mocked for doing so—because both teams had run out of players, was in a bind. With the Phillies unable to bat in their half of the sixth because conditions were dangerously awful, the score ordinarily would have reverted to the Philadelphia's 2–1 lead after five—an official game. To do that, however, would have stripped the Rays of their game-tying run and made the Phillies World Series champions in a game that did not go nine innings. And so, the suspended game resumed two days later, after the horrid weather finally cleared. The Phillies immediately broke the tie in their half of the sixth and went on to win the game, 4–3, and only the second World Series in franchise history.

Somewhere on baseball's Mount Olympus, Hall of Famers Walter Johnson, Goose Goslin, and Kiki Cuyler, and their Washington Senators and Pittsburgh Pirates teammates, must have smiled in recognition and even sympathy. They played Game Seven of the 1925 World Series in similarly cold and wet conditions. Commissioner Kenesaw Mountain Landis was in a similar bind as Selig would be 83 years later. That game was also played in a downpour. With Washington ahead, 6–4, after five innings, Landis was reluctant to call it an official game, not the final game of the World Series. He could, however, have called the game after Pittsburgh tied the score in the bottom of the seventh, in which case the seventh game would have been replayed from scratch. Instead, Landis insisted the game go on in impossible conditions. Cold and drenched, Johnson was victimized by sloppy defense behind him on a messy field. The game finally turned on Cuyler's two-run double into the rain and fog with two outs in the eighth, breaking a 7–7 tie, that left fielder Goslin insisted was foul and stuck in the mud.

Philadelphia was back in the World Series in 2009. They won their division handily, hit little trouble in the first two rounds of the postseason, then lost to the Yankees in six games. In 2010 they again won the NL East by a comfortable margin, but this time were upended in the league championship series. And they won a fifth-straight division title in 2011 by 13 games with the major league's best record, only to lose in their division series. After becoming the third team to win five division titles in a row—after the Braves' 14 straight during Bobby Cox's reign and the

Yankees' nine in a row under Joe Torre—the Phillies fell out of contention in 2012.

The Phillies' surges in 2007 and 2008 to overtake the Mets in the final weeks of both seasons established them as imposing, resilient, and the most formidable team in the National League. Under manager Charlie Manuel's direction, the Phillies improved their record every year from 2007 to 2011. Philadelphia's leading men for the entirety of this run were lefty Cole Hamels, slugging left-handed-batting first baseman Ryan Howard, second baseman Chase Utley, and shortstop Jimmy Rollins. Catcher Carlos Ruiz, center fielder Shane Victorino, and eighth-inning setup reliever Ryan Madson all five years; left fielder Pat Burrell for their first two division titles; right fielder Jayson Werth for their first four division titles; and closer Brad Lidge in the middle three years (2008 to 2010) were impactful costars.

Batting lead-off, Rollins had a year for the ages in 2007. His 139 runs led the league. His 212 hits included 38 doubles, a major-league-leading 20 triples, and 30 home runs. He swiped 41 bases in 47 attempts. Rollins was the catalyst for Philadelphia's first division title since 1993, for which he was voted the National League's Most Valuable Player. Usually batting second, Victorino had the best year of his career in 2011, leading the league in triples for the second time in three years. Utley, Howard, Burrell in 2007 and 2008, and Werth ensured that the middle of the Phillies' batting order was hard for opposing pitchers to get through. The Phillies led the league in home runs both years they went to the World Series. Howard powered the Phillies with 204 home runs during their five-in-a-row streak of division titles.

Chase Utley was one of the best, most complete ballplayers of his generation. From 2005 to 2009, he had three seasons with more than 30 home runs, four consecutive years driving in more than 100 runs, and was either the second- or third-best position player in the National League every year, based on the wins-above-replacement metric for player value, and in 2010 he was in the top ten. Albert Pujols, the best player in the National League all six years, was the only position player whose player value exceeded Utley's 45.5 wins above replacement between 2005 and 2010. Utley's career-defining moment was probably the 2009 World Series in which he blasted Yankees pitchers for 5 home runs, matching Reggie Jackson's record for the Fall Classic, and drove in 8 runs.

Ryan Howard's destiny, on the other hand, was as a cautionary "lesson learned" tale for all of major league baseball. After four years in the Phillies' minor-league system, Howard's big break came in 2005 when slugging first baseman Jim Thome, who hit 89 home runs the two previous years after signing with Philadelphia as a free agent, was injured in late June and out for the rest of the season. Howard won Rookie of the Year honors; Thome, nine years older and now expendable, was traded in November. There were no regrets in Philadelphia. Ryan Howard in 2006 led the majors in both home runs with 58 and RBIs with 149 to dominate the MVP voting.

Having hit all 58 of his homers by the Phillies' 153rd game, Howard was not going to top Barry Bonds's single-season 73 in the nine games remaining. But given that all three players who exceeded 61 home runs—Bonds, McGwire, and Sosa—were suspected of having most likely used steroids, there was some sentiment that should the untainted Howard hit just four more in those nine games, then he should be considered—on merit, because he could not be statistically—the rightful successor to Roger Maris. Howard went 10-for-31 the rest of the way and walked 11 times. Six times he was intentionally walked. Only 2 of his 10 hits were for extra bases—both doubles.

After Howard hit 47 homers the next year and led the majors again in both home runs (48) and runs batted in (146) in 2008, plus hitting 3 more and driving in 6 runs in Philadelphia's World Series triumph over Tampa Bay, the Phillies rewarded him with a three-year, $54 million contract during spring training in 2009. He returned the favor by hitting 45 homers and leading the majors again in RBIs with 141 to help power the Phillies to their third-straight division title. That motivated the Phillies to add a five-year, $125 million extension to cover the 2012 to 2016 seasons. At the time he signed in April 2010, the $25 million in guaranteed salary he was due each of the last three years of the contract was exceeded only by A-Rod's 2007 contract for average annual salary.

Notwithstanding his having just hit 198 home runs in four years, it did not go unnoticed that Howard was approaching 30 years old, that he was overweight, that he was a one-dimensional player, and that he was being paid vastly more than Utley, indisputably the Phillies' best and most valuable player, whose average annual salary through 2016 was only $15 million. Howard emphasized his committing to a rigorous fitness regimen to stay in shape. He hit 31 and 33 home runs in 2010 and 2011 while driving in 108 and 116 runs. And then fate intervened to condemn his contract to becoming a financial albatross for the Philadelphia Phillies.

Ryan Howard made the last out in the Phillies' five-game loss to the Cardinals in their 2011 division series. 'Twas a pitching duel at Citizens Bank Park between Philadelphia ace Roy Halladay, who surrendered just one run, and St. Louis ace Chris Carpenter, who threw a three-hit complete-game shutout. Howard grounded out to second but barely got out of the batter's box—not because there was no point in running it out but because he collapsed in a heap with a torn left Achilles tendon. The juxtaposition of the Cardinals celebrating a series win while Howard lay in agony on the baseline was a poignant moment—conquering heroes paying no heed to their vanquished enemy laying grievously wounded on the diamond battlefield. The Cardinals were on their way to a World Series championship, it turned out; Howard was carried off the field of baseball battle.

Celebrating his 32th birthday the next month and carrying a heavy build, Howard never fully recovered from that injury. He missed the first half of the 2012 season in recovery and the second half of the next season with an injured knee that needed repair. In the five years his contract extension covered, Howard played in only 545 games, after six seasons of rarely missing a game; his power declined precipitously—Howard hit only 96 home runs; and both his batting average and on-base percentage plummeted as he became increasingly less disciplined in his at-bats while pitchers picked apart his weaknesses. The huge contract the Phillies gave him limited the team's options regarding other players and came to be regarded around baseball as a telling example of free agency run amok— in Ryan Howard's case, giving him a lucrative contract extension to keep him in Philadelphia rather than risk losing him as a free agent on the open market, and him coming up an extraordinarily expensive bust. It was a mistake that, by the time the Phillies were able to shed themselves of his contract following the 2016 season, most other franchises were determined not to make—especially not for a player in his 30s who was seen as one-dimensional.

Pitching was perhaps the most compelling story line of the best five-year stretch in Phillies franchise history. In only his second year, Cole Hamels emerged as Philadelphia's ace in 2007 with a 15–5 record in 28 starts. The next year was the first of nine straight years the southpaw started at least 30 games, barely missing a turn. He was 4–0 with a 1.80 earned run average, holding opposing hitters to a .190 batting average, in five starts in the 2008 postseason. Pitching in impossibly cold and muddy conditions in freezing rain in a game that should have been stopped before he took the mound in the top of the sixth inning of his Game Five start in the World Series, Hamels gave up the tying run before the umpires finally suspended the game to continue another day. Due to lead off in the last of the sixth, Hamels was removed for a pinch-hitter when the game resumed two days later, who doubled and scored the tie-breaking run. He would not be the winning pitcher, however, since Tampa Bay tied the score again the very next inning before Philadelphia went on to win. The win went to reliever J. C. Romero and the save to Brad Lidge.

Lidge had the closer's equivalent of a perfect season in 2008—41 saves and 2 wins in 72 games, without a loss or a blown save in the regular season, and 7 saves in 7 chances (and no losses) in nine postseason games. Even discounting the postseason, no closer had ever before had a perfect season of no blown saves and no losses, not even Mariano Rivera. When the Dodgers' Eric Gagne made history with 55 saves in 55 save opportunities in 2003, he also lost 3 games he was called into with the score tied (and so were not "save opportunities") in the ninth inning or later. There have been no perfect-closer seasons since.

Philadelphia traded with Houston for Lidge and his fearsome fastball before the season specifically to address the franchise's long-standing problem of lacking a consistent shutdown closer. In his five previous years with the Astros, Lidge averaged 1.4 strikeouts an inning but with mixed results—a 22–20 record and 27 blown saves to go along with his 123 saves in 372 games. The same would be true of his time in Philadelphia. The year after his perfect-closer season, Lidge lost eight games without a win and had 11 blown saves, nearly offsetting the 31 games he did save. By 2011, Ryan Madson had replaced Lidge in the closer's role.

As they were cruising to their third-straight division title in 2009, the Phillies added star power to back up Hamels in their starting rotation. One was a fading star, the other one of baseball's best pitchers. The fading star was Pedro Martinez, whose injury-plagued 2007 and 2008 seasons with the Mets left him unwanted on the free-agent market until the Phillies signed him during the summer of 2009. He was 5–1 in nine starts for the Phillies. Cleveland's Cliff Lee, a southpaw like Hamels, was coming off a superb 22–3 record and American League–leading ERA in 2008 and was available at the trade deadline because the Indians had collapsed and were heading toward rebuilding for a down-the-line future. He finished the year 7–4 for the Phillies and was 4–0 in the postseason, including winning both his starts in the 2009 World Series—the only two wins Philadelphia managed against the Yankees. Martinez pitched seven innings of shutout ball against the Dodgers in his NLCS start but lost twice to the Yankees in the World Series. His Game Six loss that sent the Phillies home for the winter to try again in 2010 was his last game. Pedro Martinez won 219 against only 100 losses while averaging 10 strikeouts an inning since throwing his first pitch for the Dodgers in September 1992.

Aiming for four division titles in a row, and hoping for a third-straight trip to the Fall Classic in 2010, the Phillies boldly traded for Toronto Blue Jays ace Roy Halladay, unquestionably the American League's best pitcher the first decade of the new century. They gave him a high-priced contract extension. Because franchise executives believed they could not afford both Lee and Halladay, Lee was traded to Seattle. Halladay had arguably the most dominant season in his then 13-year career with a 21–10 record his first year in Philadelphia, leading the league in complete games, shutouts, and innings pitched. At the end of July, trailing Atlanta's Braves by 3½ games, Philadelphia traded for Houston's longtime ace, right-hander Roy Oswalt, to make up for the departure of Lee. Oswalt was 7–1 in 12 starts for the Phillies; Hamels was 5–1 in his last seven starts of the season; Halladay won all five of his September starts; and the Phillies' 19–5 run to end the season allowed them to overtake Atlanta.

In his last start of the regular season, Halladay shut out Washington's Nationals on two hits. In the first game of the Phillies' division series against Cincinnati's Reds, Halladay pitched another shutout, this time allowing *no* hits—a fifth-inning walk his only blemish. It was not a perfect game, and it did not come in the World Series. But Roy Halladay's no-hitter was the first in any postseason series since Don Larsen's perfect game against Brooklyn's Dodgers in the 1956 World Series. There have been none since. His, and the Phillies', luck ran out in the NLCS, which they lost in six games to San Francisco's Giants. Halladay and Oswalt were both 1–1 against the Giants; Hamels lost his only start.

For 2011, the Phillies front office concluded they could indeed afford Cliff Lee *and* Ray Halladay *and* Roy Oswalt *and* Cole Hamels. When Lee signed as a free agent with the Phillies, their fans could be forgiven for salivating about having notionally the best starting foursome since Maddux, Glavine, Smoltz, and Avery 18 years before. Except for one day in late April, when a loss dropped them half a game out of first, the 2011 Phillies led the NL East from start to finish, ending up with a 13-game advantage over the second-place Braves and with the best record in baseball for the second year in a row. Halladay (19–6 with a 2.35 ERA), Lee (17–8 and 2.40), and Hamels (14–9, 2.79) lived up to their Maddux, Glavine, and Smoltz hype. Oswalt missed a month and a half in the middle of the season because of a bad back and ended up 9–10 in 23 starts. Philadelphia's 102 wins were the most in franchise history, after which they lost their division series to St. Louis.

As surely as Ryan Howard went down, seriously injured, making the final out of Philadelphia's 2011 division series loss, the Phillies' NL East dominance came to an end. Both Howard and Chase Utley missed the first half of the 2012 season. Shoulder problems caused Halladay to miss nearly two months from May to July. By the time they returned, the Phillies were already out of the division race. The franchise, however, was still thinking big; in July Hamels signed a six-year, $144 million deal intended to keep him in Philadelphia, presumably for the rest of his career, with the expectation that he, Halladay, and Lee would give the Phillies baseball's most formidable starting top-three for another two or three years.

It didn't turn out that way. With Halladay able to make only 13 starts in 2013 because of persistent back problems, the Phillies endured their first losing season in 14 years. Halladay retired in December. Lee retired the next year, unable to pitch effectively because of chronic elbow pain. Finally, wanting to shed high-cost players to focus on rebuilding, the Phillies traded Rollins after the 2014 season and both Hamels—in the middle of his new deal—and Utley, at the end of his contract and about to become a free agent, to contending teams in 2015 once it became clear there would be no quick return to competitiveness for the franchise. In many ways, Chase Utley not finishing his career in Philadelphia—a city whose hard-core, no-excuse ethos he exemplified every day on the ballfield—was a disservice to his legacy as the second-best position player in Phillies franchise history, after Mike Schmidt.

# 11

# BASEBALL BACK IN WASHINGTON

"**I**t can't get any better than this! Remember where you are, so you'll remember where you were!" With those words shouted into the microphone, Washington Nationals' radio play-by-play broadcaster Charlie Slowes was setting the stage as Nationals Park rocked with anticipation for the raucous celebration that was sure to follow in a moment or two. With a 7–5 lead, a Cardinals runner on third, two outs, and the count 3-and-2 on Yadier Molina, the Nationals were a strike away from winning Game Five of their 2012 division series against St. Louis and having home-field advantage in the league championship series for the National League pennant. On the mound was closer Drew Storen, already with a save and a victory in the series.

It had been 79 years since the last time a team in the Nation's Capital won a pennant, although for 33 of those years, there was no team in Washington, DC. Except for the 10 years from 1924 to 1933, when the American League Washington Senators won three pennants and the 1924 World Series, the teams that called DC home were historically among the worst in major-league history. As one of the AL's original eight franchises, the Senators' record of persistent futility inspired the witticism "Washington—first in war, first in peace, and last in the American League." In 1961, the Senators abandoned their half-century-old decaying ballpark in a predominantly Black city—both major reasons why owner Calvin Griffith pulled up stakes—for Minnesota's Twin Cities (the Minneapolis–St. Paul metropolitan area). But with Major League Baseball feeling insecure about congressional hearings on whether antitrust statutes should apply to professional sports teams, Washington was quickly given one of the two new franchises in the American League's 1961 expansion. The new Senators were just as feckless as the old Senators. After eleven desultory seasons in which they finished with a winning record just once and failed to draw appreciable attendance even after moving into a new stadium built not far from Capitol Hill in 1969, the new Senators followed the old Senators out of town in 1972, relocating to the Dallas–Fort Worth metropolitan area to become the Texas Rangers.

It took a third of a century, but in 2005 baseball was back in Washington when Major League Baseball moved Montreal's failing Expos to DC even as negotiations continued with three groups of investors bidding to buy the franchise. (It would not be until May 2006 that the sale was finalized with a local ownership group led by real-estate magnate Ted Lerner.) Because DC is predominantly African American, there was some sentiment for naming Washington's new team the "Grays" in honor of the great Negro League team of the 1940s that played in the Nation's Capital, whose stars included slugging catcher Josh Gibson, first baseman Buck Leonard, and pitcher Ray Brown—all Hall of Famers. Controversy about cultural appropriation, particularly since the Grays' heyday was when Major League Baseball was for white ballplayers exclusively, contributed to the new team being called the "Nationals," to which the original American League Senators often answered. Renaming the transplanted Expos the "Senators" was a nonstarter for DC politicians, whose support in promised funding for a new stadium was essential to Washington winning the bid, because the Nation's Capital was not represented in the U.S. Senate.

The last manager of Washington's expansion-Senators before they moved to Texas in 1972 was Ted Williams, one of the greatest hitters in baseball history. The first manager of Washington's Nationals was Expos manager Frank Robinson, also one of the greatest hitters in baseball history. In 2005, their first year in Washington, the Nationals surprisingly led the NL East by 5½ games on July 3, exactly halfway through their schedule, then reverted to their Expos form by losing 50 of their remaining 81 games, finishing last with an 81–81 record. Still, it was a substantial improvement from 67–95 their last year in Montreal.

Except for 2007, when the Nats finished fourth in the NL's five-team Eastern Division, the slogan for Washington in their first seven years in DC could well have been "first in counterterrorism, first in governing dysfunction, and last in the National League East." The highlights those years were third baseman Ryan Zimmerman becoming the franchise cornerstone in his 2006 rookie season; the first game at brand-new Nationals Park, the defining feature of rehabilitated southeast DC in 2008, which the Nats won as the opening act of the new major-league season on a bottom-of-the-ninth walk-off home run by Zimmerman; and getting the first pick in baseball's annual amateur draft in both 2009 and 2010—their reward for all that losing. In 2009 they chose hard-throwing right-hander Stephen Strasburg, and in 2010 hard-hitting Bryce Harper. Both were considered the best in their amateur-draft class. Strasburg made his big-league debut at Nationals Park in June 2010, striking out 14 in seven innings. His rookie year came to a premature end in September when he went under the knife for Tommy John surgery. Strasburg had 92 strikeouts in the 68 innings of the 12 games he started. Harper's first major-league game came at Dodgers Stadium in late April 2012. He was 19 years old. Harper's debut was also Strasburg's 5th start of the year, and only his 10th since returning to action in September 2011.

Veteran manager Davey Johnson, hired in late June the previous year specifically to turn the Nationals into a winning team, did exactly that in 2012. Washington won their division with the best record in the major leagues. Their 98 wins were one short of the Washington record set by the 1933 Senators. They were the first team in franchise history, including when they were Montreal's Expos, to win a division title. Mostly batting second ahead of Zimmerman, Harper was an immediate star, hitting 22 home runs and winning Rookie of the Year honors. Veteran first baseman Adam LaRoche had the best year of his career with career highs in home runs and runs batted in. Ian Desmond, in his third year as the Nationals' shortstop, became an All-Star. Strasburg led a formidable starting rotation that included left-hander Gio Gonzalez, whose 21 wins led the league, and right-hander Jordan Zimmermann. Strasburg was shut down in early September with a 15–6 record in 28 starts and 197 strikeouts in 159⅓ innings because of a 160-innings limit imposed prior to the season to ensure he did not overwork his surgically repaired right arm.

The postseason may have been uncharted territory for the Nationals, but they expected to play in the World Series. They entered the postseason with a significant handicap, however; Strasburg's innings limit had come back to haunt them. Their ace would not be on the roster for any of Washington's postseason series. From the time Strasburg was shut down in September, there was a nasty debate about superagent Scott Boras being more concerned about cashing in on his client's free-agent future than the Nats' immediate championship quest; about Strasburg's commitment to the team; and about mismanagement of the entire situation by the front office. The decision to limit his innings was made in close consultation with Strasburg's surgeon and Boras, but rather than distribute those innings so that he would be available for the postseason, particularly when it was apparent by the All-Star break that the 2012 Nationals were legitimate contenders, the Nats continued to pitch Strasburg in turn until he reached his innings limit. Strasburg himself was portrayed as both wanting to pitch for a championship, innings limit be damned, and committed to following his doctor's orders so as not to risk his career future. Either way, Strasburg was a spectator—not a participant—as the Nationals went into postseason battle in 2012.

To reset: "It can't get any better than this! Remember where you are, so you'll remember where you were!" A raucous crowd was on its feet waiting to celebrate advancing to the NLCS. The Cardinals were down to their last strike, trailing by two runs with a runner on third. Closer Drew Storen delivered a 3–2 pitch to Yadier Molina—and walked him. The tying runs were now on base, but St. Louis still faced the reality of having just one out left. Storen also went to 3-and-2 on David Freese and walked him too. The bases loaded, the tying run on second base, and the stadium was still rocking—more with anxiety about getting that last out than anticipation. Light-hitting Daniel Descalso came to bat, toting a .227 batting average in 143 games during the season and six hits in the series, including a double and an eighth-inning home run in this game. Descalso singled up the middle on Storen's first pitch. The score was tied. Next up was Pete Kozma, 3-for-15 so far in the series, a rookie called up at the end of August when Cardinals shortstop Rafael Furcal was lost with a season-ending injury. Descalso stole second on the third pitch to Kozma, putting St. Louis runners on second and third. Two pitches later, Kozma singled to right field scoring both. The Cardinals had turned a 7–5 deficit into a 9–7 lead. The Nationals went down in order in their half of the ninth and then went home for the winter.

As disappointing as that was for Washington, there was a widespread assumption the Nationals would dominate the National League in the years ahead. They had Harper and Strasburg; Zimmerman, Desmond, and right fielder Jayson Werth, whose bottom-of-the-ninth home run in Game Four in their 2012 division series kept the Nationals alive for a fifth game; and strong starting pitching backed by a solid bullpen. To the extent the word still had meaning in an era where championship years for even the best teams was made more difficult because of the need to navigate three postseason rounds, Washington's Nationals looked to be a dynasty in the making. Their window, as the 2013 season began with great expectations, was understood to be six years—until 2018, after which Bryce Harper was expected to enter free agency. Already anointed at the age of 20 as likely to be one of the greatest players of his generation, it was assumed a player of his talent and charisma needed a bigger stage than the Nation's Capital; the Big Apple would certainly be that. It was further assumed Harper would be a prime target for the Yankees as soon as he became a free agent; Boras, his agent, always followed the most money for his clients. And it was known that the Nationals could never match whatever contract the Yankees might put on the table to outbid other franchises for his services.

The Nationals fell flat in 2013. Harper missed a month after injuring his knee in mid-May and was hobbled the rest of the year. The Nats were out of the running by the end of July. Davey Johnson was out as manager when it was over. In 2014, rookie manager Matt Williams guided the Nationals to 96 wins and the best record in the National League. It wasn't until after Harper returned from missing all of May and June with a hand injury that the Nationals took command of the division race. As in 2012, however, the Nationals failed to make it out of their division series, losing to San Francisco in four games. The series turned on an epic 18-inning Game Two played in Washington. Jordan Zimmermann, whose 19 wins led the league, was one out away from completing a 1–0 shutout to even the series when he walked the could-have-been Giants' 27th out. In came Drew Storen to secure the last out. He got it, but only after giving up a single and a double that tied the score. It stayed 1–1 till Brandon Belt homered to start the 18th. Washington did not score in their half of the inning. Harper went 0 for 7. Two games later, 'twas another winter come early for Washington's Nationals.

But it was a winter in which that "dynasty" word regained currency in Washington because, in January, the Nats signed free-agent right-hander Max Scherzer for seven years at $30 million per. Pitching for Detroit since 2010, Scherzer won a Cy Young Award with a 21–3 record in 2013 and led the AL in wins again in 2014. With a 39–8 record in 65 starts and 492 strikeouts in 434⅔ innings the two previous years, Scherzer was now just a half-step below Clayton Kershaw as baseball's best on the mound. The addition of Scherzer to a starting rotation that already included Strasburg, Zimmermann, and Gonzalez gave many in Washington visions of Atlanta's Maddux, Glavine, Smoltz, and Avery in 1993–1994. Contrary to expectations, however, the Nationals did not run away with the division. They settled for second, just four games over .500. Although he had a rough stretch of five starts in August, Scherzer pitched much better than his 14–12 record suggested. Strasburg (11–7) was bothered by shoulder and torso problems and made only 23 starts. Both Zimmermann (13–10) and Gonzalez (11–8) had disappointing years. Bryce Harper, however, affirmed his superstar status by crashing 44 homers, driving in 99 runs, batting .330, and reaching base in 46 percent of his plate appearances. He secured every first-place vote for the MVP Award.

Lack of a manager's foresight cost the Nationals dearly in 2015. Washington was in the driver's seat with a three-game lead over the second-place Mets when they arrived in New York for a three-game series at the end of July. A sweep of the Mets would have put the Nationals in virtually unassailable command, but Scherzer was not going to start any of those games because he had just pitched against the Miami Marlins—the team with the second-worst record in the National League. Instead Williams had Gonzalez, rookie right-hander Joe Ross, and Zimmermann lined up to start in New York. The Nats lost all three and now had to share the top spot with the Mets. Losing the next day to Arizona, Washington was never again first in the NL East. When the Mets came to DC for three games in early September holding a four-game lead, the Nats needed to win at least two of three to stay relevant. This time they had Scherzer, Zimmermann, and Strasburg lined up to face the Mets. New York again swept Washington, and the division race was over except for playing out the schedule.

Taking the fall for Washington's disappointing failure to repeat as division champs, Matt Williams was replaced in 2016 by managerial old-hand Dusty Baker, about to turn 67, whose 20 years of experience included winning five division titles and a wild card with three different teams. He did the same for Washington, managing the Nationals to division titles in both 2016 and 2017 with the second-best record in the National League both years. Both times, however, Baker's Nationals washed out in their division series, making it four times in six years they commanded the NL East only to lose in the first round of the postseason. In 2016, they held a two-games-to-one division series lead before losing both the fourth game in LA and the series finale in Washington by one run. In 2017, Baker brought Scherzer in from the bullpen to protect a one-run 4–3 lead in the fifth inning of the deciding Game Five in their division series against the Cubs. He was pitching on two days' rest after giving up one run in 6⅓ innings in his Game Three start. Baker was probably hoping for two, perhaps even three, innings of shutdown relief from his ace. After needing only six pitches to retire the first two batters, the Cubs manhandled Scherzer for four runs on three hits, abetted by two Nationals errors, to take a 7–4 lead in the game; they held on to win 9–7.

Once again, Washington's failure to get beyond the division series both years caused the Nationals to change managers. For 2018, they turned to another novice manager, Dave Martinez, as they had when Williams replaced Davey Johnson. The Nationals were still considered one of the best teams in baseball and certainly the favorite to win the NL East. They had Bryce Harper for at least another year before free agency. They had Stephen Strasburg, 15–4 in both 2016 and 2017, whom they gave a seven-year, $175 million contract in 2016 to head off his declaring for free agency in two years. And they had Max Scherzer fresh off back-to-back Cy Young Awards with a 20–7 record in 2016 and 16–6 the next year, striking out one-third of the batters he faced—552 in 429 innings.

If anything, the 2018 Nationals had their most impressive everyday lineup of the Harper era. Ryan Zimmerman, having moved from third base to first after being sidelined most of 2014 and 2015 with a bad throwing shoulder, had career highs in home runs (36) and runs batted in (108) in 2017. Second baseman Daniel Murphy, signed as a free agent in January 2016, led the league in doubles his first two years in Washington while crashing 48 home runs, driving in 197 runs, and batting .334, finishing second both years for the highest average. Third baseman Anthony Rendon, about to enter his sixth season, had become one of the National League's best position players. Shortstop Trea Turner, whose speed (33 steals) and .342 batting average earned him runner-up for Rookie of the Year in 2016, showcased as a potentially elite player; his 46 stolen bases in 2017 were third in the league (and the majors) even though a broken wrist limited him to just 98 games. And Harper, after a subpar year following his 2015 superstar performance, rebounded to 29 homers, 87

RBIs, and a .319 batting average in 2017 while playing in only 111 games because of another knee injury.

Baseball fans in the Nation's Capital were counting on the Nationals dominating the NL East and making it to the World Series in 2018. Many believed that without the Nationals making it that far, there was little chance Harper, bound for free agency at the end of the season, would stay in Washington. Turner, Rendon, and Scherzer, 18–7 with 300 strikeouts in 220⅔ innings, met expectations in Martinez's first year as manager. Nineteen-year-old prospect Juan Soto had an outstanding rookie season. But Strasburg missed more than two months with shoulder problems, and Harper, while slugging 34 homers, driving in 100 runs, and leading the league with 130 walks, did not get his batting average above .240 until mid-August. By then, the Nationals were has-beens in the division race after winning just 20 of their 50 games in June and July. It didn't help that Murphy was sidelined for two months at the beginning of the season and Zimmerman for two months during the summer with injuries. Washington ended up a noncompetitive second in the NL East with only 82 wins.

By season's end, the Nationals had also given up on being able to sign Harper to a new contract. The delta between the years and tens of millions of dollars that Washington was willing to offer and what Boras and Harper were willing to accept was too great to bridge. Moreover, rookie-sensation Soto and the pending arrival of 22-year-old Victor Robles, another of baseball's top prospects, both outfielders, contributed to the Nationals being less enthused about boosting their offer enough for Harper to accept. Bryce Harper did leave Washington after the 2018 season, going to division rival Philadelphia rather than, as had long been assumed, the Bronx. (The Yankees were relatively passive in the Harper sweepstakes.) In his first game in Washington for Philadelphia four games into the 2019 season, Harper went down on strikes in his first two at-bats against Scherzer, tagged him for a ringing double down the right field line in his third at-bat, singled in the sixth off a different pitcher to drive in a run, and finally blasted a mammoth two-run clout deep into the right-field stands of Nationals Park in the eighth inning to punctuate his new team's victory over his old team. It was quite the return.

When John Middleton, the Phillies' billionaire owner, told *USA Today* at the owners' winter meetings in November 2018 that "we're going . . . to spend money, and maybe even be a little bit stupid about it," there was some speculation as to whether he might make a bid for both of baseball's top two free agents on the market—Harper and Manny Machado. He was probably not going to do that—investing more than half a billion dollars over the next decade on just two players would have been more than a "little bit stupid"—but the owner was assuring his fan base that he intended to return Philadelphia to dynasty status. The Phillies had not had a winning season since their five-straight NL East titles, two pennants, and a World Series championship from 2007 to 2011, but in 2018 had taken advantage of the Nationals' and Mets' struggles to unexpectedly battle with the Braves for first place much of the summer before an 8–20 final month plunged them to 80–82 for the year. Third-year right-hander Aaron Nola competed for the Cy Young Award with a 17–6 record and 2.37 ERA. Left fielder Rhys Hoskins, in his second year, crashed 34 homers and drove in 96 runs.

If the Phillies were to challenge for the division title in 2019, they needed to do so by being aggressive on the trade and free-agent fronts, and since Middleton became controlling partner in November 2016, Philadelphia now had an owner willing to leverage his wealth to improve the club. In 2018, the Phillies had picked up free agent Jake Arrieta to be the ace of a promising young staff that included Nola, Nick Pivetta, and Zach Eflin. Signaling an intention to win their division in 2019 and compete to play in the World Series that very year, the Phillies' blockbuster moves in the off-season included trading top minor-league prospects for Seattle shortstop Jean Segura and Miami catcher J. T. Realmuto, two of the best at their positions; signing Yankees setup man David Robertson—averaging 1.3 strikeouts an inning in 657 innings over 11 seasons—as a free agent to be their closer; and giving Harper, though not Machado (they really couldn't afford to be *that* "stupid" to sign both), a record-setting 13-year free-agent contract.

After leading their division from late April to early June, losing 11 of their next 13 began Philadelphia's slide to the ranks of the also-ran. They ended fourth. Realmuto lived up to his billing, but all of the Phillies' principal starting pitchers regressed, as did Hoskins, and Robertson landed on the injured list on his way to season-ending Tommy John surgery after just seven games. While Harper slugged 35 homers and drove in a career-high 114 runs, he was not the dominating player Phillies fans expected.

Having taken advantage of the Nationals' faltering to win the division by eight games in 2018, and with Harper no longer in Washington, the Atlanta Braves had become the team to beat in the National League East. Their division title put an end to four losing seasons since their wild card in 2012 and winning the division in 2013. First baseman Freddie Freeman, their best player, and starting pitcher Julio Teheran were the only regulars on the 2013 Braves still in Atlanta in 2018. Along the way they parted with foundation players catcher Brian McCann, outfielder Jason Heyward, top-tier closer Craig Kimbrel, and stellar young shortstop Andrelton Simmons. All were in their mid-20s and approaching free agency. Rising from 90 losses to 90 wins in 2018, the Braves capitalized on Freeman's impactful consistency and a dazzling pair of very young fast-rising stars—outfielder Ronald Acuna Jr. and second baseman Ozzie Albies, Atlanta's answer to Washington's Soto and Robles. Twenty-year-old Acuna beat out 19-year-old Soto for Rookie of the Year honors in 2018, and Albies, a rookie the year before, also had a terrific year.

Even though their major-league track records were just 111 games for Acuna and 215 for Albies, the Braves bet on their futures before the 2019 season by signing both to long-term deals that would take them beyond their eligibility for free agency. Atlanta had already upped the ante on Washington by signing Josh Donaldson, a premier impact hitter, to a one-year, $23 million free-agent contract, a bargain price only because he was coming back from an injury-plagued season that limited him to only 52 games in 2018. The 2019 Braves won the NL East in a landslide. Acuna crushed 41 homers and led the league with 127 runs and 37 stolen bases. Albies, Donaldson, and Freeman all had outstanding years. And rookie right-hander Mike Soroka, 13–4 in 29 starts, and lefty Max Fried, 17–6 in 30 starts in his first full year in the majors, fortified a rotation that was considered the team's weak link—especially compared to Washington's—when the season began.

But it was wild-card Washington that won the World Series. The Nationals lost 31 of their first 50 games. Their bullpen was in shambles with an ERA of 7.05 in the first two months. After being swept four-straight by the Mets in New York in May, losing three of the four after taking a lead into the last of the eighth, the Nationals seemed finished for the year and the job security of second-year manager Dave Martinez seemed measured in days. He was not fired. Instead, from the day they left New York in shambles until the end of the season the Nationals tied the Dodgers for the best record in baseball. While their terrible start prevented them from catching Atlanta in the NL East, the Nationals took command of the wild-card race by winning 19 of 26 games in August. Anthony Rendon led the offensive charge in August with 9 homers, 29 RBIs, and a .394 batting average to thrust himself into the mix for NL batting champion.

More than making up for the departure of Bryce Harper, Rendon and Juan Soto were outstanding at the plate, both with 34 homers, more than 100 RBIs, on-base percentages over .400, and slugging percentages well over .500. Superior starting pitching, however, was the key to Washington's turnaround. Max Scherzer had one of the best stretches of his career in nine starts from late May to early July, going 7–0 while allowing only 6 runs and 40 hits in 64 innings while striking out 94 before landing on the injured list. Stephen Strasburg picked up the slack with a 7–1 record in 11 starts in July and August when Mad Max was hurt. (Scherzer was back in September for the stretch run and the postseason.) Strasburg finished at 18–6. Patrick Corbin, a top-tier free-agent pitcher signed in the off-season, lived up to the Nats' expectations with a 14–7 record of his own. Rendon and Strasburg leveraged their outstanding seasons for seven-year, $245 million contracts as 2019 free agents—Rendon signing with the Los Angeles Angels and Strasburg, opting out of the seven-year deal he had signed in 2017, back with Washington.

In the postseason, too, the Nationals kept coming back when their cause seemed lost. Trailing 3–1 in the eighth inning of the wild-card game and the Nats down to their could-have-been final four outs of the season against Brewers closer Josh Hader, who struck out 48 percent of the batters he faced in 61 regular-season games, Rendon walked to load the bases and Soto followed with a game-tying single, which was mis-played into an error that allowed the go-ahead run to score. Trailing the Dodgers after three games in their division series, Scherzer won Game Four to force a deciding fifth game in Los Angeles . . . which the Dodgers led 3–1 going into the 8th . . . until the dynamic duo of Rendon and Soto belted home runs on consecutive pitches to start the inning off Dodgers ace Clayton Kershaw, just called in for the save. In their fifth attempt— their first without Bryce Harper—Washington's Nationals finally made it past the division series, thanks to a 10th-inning grand slam by versatile role player Howie Kendrick. They went on to sweep St. Louis in the NLCS. Unheralded fourth-starter Anibal Sanchez came within four outs of a no-hitter in Game One, and Scherzer did not give up a hit until the first batter he faced in the seventh inning of Game Two. The Cardinals collected only 16 hits off Nationals pitchers in the four games.

"Finish the Fight" now their motto, the Nationals were in the World Series for the first time in franchise history against Houston's Astros, whose 107 wins were the most in the majors and whose starting pitching rivaled Washington's. Returning home after winning the first two games decisively in Houston, it looked like Washington would play host to the U.S. capital's first World Series championship since Walter Johnson and the old Senators in 1924. But the Astros won all three games in DC, limiting the Nats to one run in each, sending the series back to Houston with Washington again on the brink of elimination. It hardly helped that Scherzer was unable to make his scheduled start in the fifth game because of a neck and upper back strain that virtually immobilized him. Strasburg evened the series in Game Six. Scherzer took the mound for Game Seven against Zack Greinke, one of the Astros' aces. Mad Max gave up two runs in six innings; Greinke was nearly perfect through six, allowing just one hit and a walk.

Finishing the fight, Rendon homered with one out in the seventh to make the score 2–1 and Greinke walked Soto. With Kendrick coming to bat, the Astros went to their bullpen. Kendrick hit a two-run homer to put the Nationals in the lead. Not too long later, Charlie Slowes shouted over the airwaves: "And a World Series Game Seven–winning curly W is in the books! . . . Remember where you are so you'll remember where you are right now at 11:50 Eastern Time! Remember where you are on October 30, 2019, when the Washington Nationals finish the fight!"

# III

# Navigating the Competitive Landscape

# 12

# THE CARDINALS' LONGEVITY REBOOT

Tony La Russa, the highest-paid manager in baseball, left Oakland after the 1995 season to manage in St. Louis. The Cardinals, one of baseball's most successful franchises with 15 pennants and nine World Series championships in the books, had been adrift since winning the National League pennant in 1987. Eight years was hardly the longest stretch the Cardinals had gone without a pennant since winning their first in 1926, but they were in need of a makeover. They had had four winning and four losing seasons. Ozzie Smith, baseball's defensive wizard at shortstop and their marquee player, was 41 years old; had an injury-marred, unproductive year in 1995; and was no longer an everyday player.

Fortified by the trade for Royce Clayton to take over shortstop for the irreplaceable legend that was the Wizard Oz and the free-agent signings of outfielder Ron Gant and starting pitcher Andy Benes, La Russa managed the Cardinals to the 1996 NL Central Division title with a modest 88 wins in his first year as manager. Sweeping San Diego in their division series, St. Louis seemed destined for the World Series by taking a commanding three-games-to-one lead in the NLCS against Atlanta—until Smoltz, Maddux, and Glavine held the Cardinals to just one run in the final three games, while La Russa's staff was torched for 32 runs. The Cardinals were not players in the division race the next three years, but they did have the compelling story line of Mark McGwire aiming for 61 home runs after he came to St. Louis in July 1997 with 34 hit for Oakland (he finished the season with 58), his record-smashing 70 homers in 1998, and 65 more in 1999.

Turning from mediocrity to superiority as the centuries changed, from 2000 to 2011, La Russa's Cardinals won six division titles and the wild card twice. Their .560 winning percentage for those 12 years was the best in the National League. They had the best record in the major leagues with 105 wins in 2004 and 100 in 2005. The Yankees and Red Sox were the only teams to win more often than St. Louis. The Cardinals played in six league championship series and went to the World Series three times—swept by Boston in 2004, beating Detroit in five games in 2006 for their first World Series championship since 1982, and requiring all seven games to defeat Texas in 2011.

The mantle of St. Louis's starting ace in the first decade of the twenty-first century was handed from Matt Morris to Chris Carpenter to Adam Wainwright. Morris, 22–8 in 2001, was 10–1 in 12 starts in August and September to help St. Louis overcome an 8½-game deficit at the end of July to finish tied for first with Houston. A year after winning their division by 10 games in 2000, the Cardinals had to settle for the wild card because the Astros won their season series. Carpenter, signed as a free agent from Toronto in December 2002 even though he was still recovering from shoulder surgery, compiled a 51–18 record in 93 starts from 2004 to 2006 as the Cardinals won their division all three years and went to two World Series. His 21–5 record and 2.83 earned run average in 2005 secured a Cy Young trophy, and he was 15–8 in 2006 when the Cardinals won their division with a modest 83–78 record on their way to winning the World Series. Following Tommy John surgery that cost him the next two years, in both of which St. Louis missed the postseason, Carpenter returned in 2009 with a 17–4 record and 2.24 ERA as St. Louis returned to the top of the NL Central. Wainwright won 19 in 2009 to lead the league, followed by 20 the next year, and then had his own Tommy John operation in 2011.

The Cardinals prioritized going after high-impact position players in the amateur draft and in trades. In 1998 they signed outfielder J. D. Drew, one of the most coveted college players in baseball's amateur draft, with the fifth overall pick. A year after returning to college despite being the second pick in the 1997 draft, because he did not want to play in Philadelphia, Drew was happy to sign with St. Louis. Two years later, in the fourth round as the 113th overall pick, St. Louis drafted Yadier Molina, the youngest in a trio of brothers who were exceptional defensive catchers. Just before the 2000 season, the Cardinals traded for Angels star center fielder Jim Edmonds, and in July 2002 for Phillies third baseman Scott Rolen. Like Drew, Rolen wanted nothing to do with the City of Brotherly Love. Like Edmonds, Rolen was already an elite player when he came to St. Louis.

The left-handed-batting Drew was a star-crossed star in St. Louis. Often injured—he spent time on the injured list every year he played for the Cardinals—Drew's difficulty hitting southpaws caused La Russa to primarily platoon him in right field. His five years in St. Louis ended with his being traded to Atlanta after the 2003 season for, among others, Mr. Wainwright. If Drew was not quite as good as hoped, Edmonds was even better than expected. From 2000 to 2004, Edmonds was arguably the second-best outfielder in baseball after Barry Bonds, and without any taint of steroids to suggest his 181 homers, 501 runs batted in, .298 batting average, and 1.003 on-base plus slugging percentage were not legitimately earned. Rolen's 34 homers, 124 RBIs, .314 batting average, and exceptional 9.2 wins above replacement helped power the 2004 Cardinals toward their first World Series since 1987. In 2006, Molina belied his reputation for being a weak bat in the lineup—a .216 batting average and just six home runs that year—by hitting .348 with two homers and six RBIs in the Cardinals' NLCS triumph over the Mets; his seventh-game, ninth-inning two-run homer at Shea Stadium sent St. Louis to the World Series, wherein he batted .412.

In July 2009, in first place by only a game and a half at the time and having scored just 28 runs more than they allowed, the Cardinals acquired hard-hitting Colorado Rockies outfielder Matt Holliday to improve their chances for holding off their competition in the division race, even though he was due to become a free agent once the season ended. Holliday had won two-thirds of the Triple Crown—leading the league in batting average and runs batted in—two years earlier. As soon as he arrived in St. Louis, Holliday went on a hitting rampage, batting .375 with 9 homers and 36 RBIs in his first 36 games with the Cardinals, in which they went 27–9 to build an insurmountable 10-game lead going into the final month. The Cardinals rewarded him in free agency with the most expensive contract the club had ever extended. After failing to win the NL Central in 2010, St. Louis signed former Astros star Lance Berkman, despite his being 35 years old, to strengthen their hand for reclaiming the top spot. They didn't. But they did win the wild card, the pennant, and the

2011 World Series. Berkman's contribution was 31 home runs during the regular season and batting .423 (11 for 26) in the World Series.

Through all these years, St. Louis's indisputably best player was Albert Pujols—the perfect antidote to the steroids-use tragedy of Mark McGwire. He was the 402nd player chosen, a third baseman, in the 1999 amateur draft. He soared through the Cardinals' minor-league system in one year as a 20-year-old in 2000, earning an invitation to the major-league spring camp the next year. Batting sixth and playing left field, he was in La Russa's opening day lineup in Colorado. Pujols singled in his third at-bat. Four days later, in Arizona, he belted his first big-league home run with a runner on base. He ended his inaugural season with 37 homers, 130 RBIs, a .329 batting average, and the National League Rookie of the Year trophy. Pujols started 71 games in the outfield, 52 at third, and 31 at first base as part of La Russa's cover for McGwire when Big Mac, in his last season, was unable to play because of injury.

The next two years, Pujols was mostly an outfielder. He won a batting title with a .359 average in 2003 while also leading the league in runs (for the first of three straight years), hits (212), doubles (51), and extra-base hits (95), and his 43 home runs—the first of four 40-homer seasons in a row—gave him 114 total in his first three seasons. Pujols was 23 years old. In 2004, having just signed an eight-year, $111 million contract extension that would carry him four years beyond when he could first declare for free agency, Pujols was at first base to stay. He won his first MVP Award in 2005, powering the Cardinals to their second-straight 100-win season with 41 homers, 117 RBIs, and a .330 batting average. He won his second and third MVPs in 2008 (the Cardinals finished fourth) and 2009 (St. Louis back on top in the NL Central). He led the league in both runs scored and home runs in 2009 and 2010. The contract Pujols had signed after just three seasons paid him less than $15 million in 2010. Given that he was one of the very best—if not *the* best—player in baseball, it was a massive bargain for St. Louis.

Albert Pujols was now 30 years old and had played 10 seasons in the Big Time, hardly missing a game. He had 408 home runs to brag about. Forty-five percent of his 1,900 hits were for extra bases. He had 1,230 career runs batted in, never with less than 103 in any season. In 10 years, Albert Pujols had never failed to hit .300. Only once was his on-base percentage less than .400 (in 2002, his second year, he fell short by exactly some combination of four hits, walks, or being hit by a pitch). Since Mickey Mantle's on-base plus slugging percentage of 1.057 from 1955 to 1964, only Barry Bonds had an on-base percentage over any 10-year period that exceeded Pujols's 1.050, and in only the 2002 and 2007 seasons had Pujols been *below* 1.000. And, for a bona fide home run hitter, his career highs in strikeouts were 93 in his rookie season and 76 in his 10th year. Yet he was only the *third*-highest paid player on the Cardinals, after Chris Carpenter and Matt Holliday, even if by far the most valuable.

Pujols was already destined for the Hall of Fame, even more surely than the steroids-sullied Barry Bonds. He may have been born in the Dominican Republic but now embodied the American Dream. In addition to his prodigious baseball talents, Albert Pujols was a role model for civic virtue. In one of America's greatest baseball cities, where Cardinals fans are as passionate and knowledgeable as fans anywhere about the game's history and traditions and took justifiable pride in the depth of their team's history, Albert Pujols had become a civic treasure. He was perhaps not the greatest player to ever wear a Cardinals uniform—at least not yet, although a persuasive case could be made that he already was. And he was not the most beloved player to ever wear a Cardinals uniform. Stan Musial was that man—so far, the greatest and most beloved Cardinal.

It was conceivable for Pujols to become both the indisputably greatest and most beloved Cardinal in franchise history, *if* he finished his career in the city it began—St. Louis. But with his grossly undervalued contract set to expire at the end of the year, the 2011 season started amid considerable uncertainty about whether the franchise and its superstar would reach agreement on a new deal that would keep him in St. Louis rather than declaring for free agency. It was not going well. The team that gave a seven-year, $120 million deal in 2010 to 30-year-old Holliday was not willing to give more than $130 million and five years to Pujols, a far better player than his exactly one-day-older teammate. Pujols was clear in wanting to finish his career in St. Louis and was willing to give the Cardinals a discount for his excellent services. But he wasn't willing to be insulted. Stan the Man Musial had played 22 years in St. Louis before retiring at the age of 42. For all he had accomplished—his batting average after 10 years was the same as Musial's career .331 average, and he was certain to break Musial's Cardinals record of 475 home runs within just a few years—Pujols wanted to play at least another 10 years.

By the end of August, St. Louis was not only out of the running for the division title, which Milwaukee's Brewers had well in hand, they trailed Atlanta's Braves by 8½ games for the National League wild card with 136 games down and just 26 to go. Also, 66-year-old Tony La Russa had privately told the front office this would be his last season. Pujols had missed 14 games in June and July with a hand injury and was batting just .286, although he did have 32 home runs. Holliday had 19 homers and was batting .302. Then Pujols got hot, batting .355 with a team-leading 5 home runs and 20 RBIs in the final month, and so did the Cardinals.

They caught the Braves in the wild-card standings on the next-to-last day of the season, having won 17 of 25 since the beginning of September. In game 162, Pujols's first-inning single drove in the first of five runs in the inning that led to an 8–0 victory over the Astros. The Braves lost in 13 innings to the Phillies in their game 162, thus ending their season with the stigma of having blown an 8½-game wild-card lead by losing 18 of their final 27 games. Pujols batted .350 as St. Louis beat Philadelphia in their division series, then crushed two homers, drove in nine runs, and batted .478 in the Cardinals' six-game takedown of Milwaukee in the NLCS to propel his team to their third World Series in eight years.

The Texas Rangers were their Fall Classic opponent in 2011, back for the second year in a row after losing to the Giants in five games in 2010. The Rangers won three of the first five games and took a 7–4 lead into the 8th inning of Game Six in St. Louis. A home run by Allen Craig, a relatively unknown outfielder in just his second year and not an everyday regular, cut the lead by one in the 8th. Texas closer Neftali Feliz came in to get the last three outs for a Rangers championship. Pujols doubled with one out. Lance Berkman walked on four pitches. Craig whiffed. The Cardinals' last hope was David Freese, another relatively unknown second-year player. Three pitches later, Freese and the Cardinals were down to their last strike. Feliz delivered. Freese drove the pitch to the opposite field. Right fielder Nelson Cruz had difficulty gauging the flight of the ball. It carried to the wall for a game-tying triple. Texas scored two in the 10th. In their half of the 10th, St. Louis answered with two of their own. The score was tied again. Leading off the bottom of the 11th for the Cardinals was the aforementioned Mr. Freese. Freese ended the game with a walk-off home run. Then it was on to Game Seven.

The next day, the Rangers jumped on Cardinals ace Chris Carpenter for two runs in the first. With two outs in the bottom half, both Pujols and Berkman walked and Freese came through again—this time with a game-tying double. Texas did not score again. Craig's third-inning home run, his third in the series, broke the 2–2 tie. Six innings later, the St. Louis Cardinals had their 11th World Series championship. Only the Yankees with 27 have won more. It was the Cardinals' eighth that required all seven games to win, and the fifth time they won after trailing three-games-to-two, dating back to their first in 1926 against the Yankees. It was in keeping with the Cardinals' well-earned reputation, historically, for playing gritty, die-hard, we-ain't-gonna-lose baseball on the game's biggest stage.

It was a moment of unalloyed celebration—one, however, with an undertone of loss because of the uncertainty about whether Albert Pujols would return. Pujols had finished the year with 37 homers, still having never hit fewer than 32 in any season. But for the first time in his 11-year career, Pujols failed to drive in 100 runs or to bat .300; he had 99 RBIs and finished with a .299 batting average. Two days after the series ended, Pujols declared for free agency. Three days after that, La Russa announced he was stepping down after 16 years managing the Cardinals. He had begun his managerial career a third of a century before, in 1979 with the Chicago White Sox, and retired with 2,728 victories—just 35 fewer than second on the all-time list behind John McGraw.

Less than a month later, embittered by how he was treated by the front office, Albert Pujols left the Cardinals for the Los Angeles Angels with a 10-year, $240 million deal. The Cardinals reportedly had improved their offer to 10 years and $210 million, but it was too little—particularly since much of that was to be deferred salary—too late to keep him in the city that he loved and that loved him. A little more than two years later, Stan Musial, recently turned 92, also left St. Louis—for baseball's Mount Olympus of Immortals, where he will surely eventually be joined by Albert Pujols.

The absence of a manager who was already a certified genius by the time he got to St. Louis and a superstar who was the best first baseman in National League history with a reasonable claim to being the best current player in baseball (at least not one with a steroids asterisk attached to his achievements) did not prevent the St. Louis Cardinals from having the best record in baseball over the next four years. St. Louis interviewed widely respected veteran manager Terry Francona, whose tenure in Boston came to an end in 2011 after his team's controversy-filled September collapse. Instead they chose Mike Matheny, their widely respected former catcher. Unlike Francona, whose accomplishments were comparable to La Russa's when he became manager of the Cardinals, Matheny not only had no experience as a manager, even in the minor leagues, he had not even been a coach on any major-league team.

Matheny was a blank slate, and the Cardinals, one of the earliest clubs to follow the analytically minded Moneyball path blazed by Billy Beane and the Oakland A's, were okay with that. Respected for his clubhouse presence and leadership from his playing days, Matheny was recruited by the St. Louis front office after he retired as a player in 2007 to be a special assistant for player development, where he became intimately familiar with Cardinals prospects. Consistent with a growing trend in Major League Baseball, the Cardinals provided their new unseasoned manager extensive analytical support to guide his game preparation and in-game decisions. By the time La Russa retired, the Cardinals had put in place a comprehensive proprietary database on virtually everything there was to know about every player that became an exemplar for other franchises.

St. Louis was fortunate that 2012 was the year Major League Baseball added a second wild card to the postseason mix, since their 88–74 record was only fifth-best in the National League and six games behind Atlanta for the top wild-card slot. They beat the Braves in the wild-card game and required all five games to win their division series. Their deciding Game Five victory was a stunning (after falling behind 6–0 in the third), from-the-grave (trailing 7–5, with two on but down to their last out), ninth-inning takedown of Washington's Nationals, whose 98 wins were the most in the majors. That improbable mission accomplished, St. Louis could not capitalize on a three-games-to-one lead over San Francisco in the NLCS, scoring just one run while giving up 20 in the last three games of the series.

The Cardinals went on to win the next three Central Division titles, none by more than three games. In 2013, rookie right-hander Michael Wacha, making only his fifth start in a big-league uniform, evened the division series with a stellar one-hitter over 7⅓ innings over Pittsburgh to force a fifth game that sent St, Louis back to the NLCS; held the Dodgers without a run in two starts—including pennant-winning Game Six that sent the Cardinals back to the World Series; and ran his postseason string to 4–0 by winning the second game of the World Series, before losing the Game Six series finale to the Red Sox. In 2014, the Cardinals were knocked out in the NLCS. In 2015, their 100 wins were just two more than Pittsburgh's second-place Pirates and three more than Chicago's third-place Cubs. All three Central Division teams made the postseason. St. Louis lost to Chicago in their division series.

Yadier Molina replaced Pujols as the irrepressible heartbeat of the Cardinals. Renowned for his defensive prowess, Molina bolstered his case for a future home with baseball's Hall of Fame immortals by becoming a more dangerous hitter. Matt Carpenter, typically batting first or second and capable of playing any infield position, was also a cornerstone player for the Cardinals in their most recent division-winning seasons. Coincidentally, like Pujols ten years earlier, Carpenter was selected by St. Louis in the 13th round of the 2009 amateur draft. Former ace Chris Carpenter was forced into retirement in 2012 with shoulder problems, but Lance Lynn in his first full season as a starting pitcher picked up the slack with an 18–7 record; he was the Cardinals' most durable starter until Tommy John surgery forced him to miss the 2016 season. Adam Wainwright won 19 in 2013 and 20 the next year. When an ankle injury sidelined Wainwright for nearly all of 2015, Michael Wacha picked up the slack, leading 100-win St. Louis with a 17–7 record.

Then St. Louis faltered, unable to keep pace with Chicago and Milwaukee in the NL Central. In mid-July 2018, with the Cardinals a disappointing 47–46 for a team expected to contend for the division title, Matheny was replaced as manager by a virtual unknown—Mike Shildt, whose highest level attained as a player was in college. Realizing he was not good enough to have a professional playing career, Shildt coached high school and college teams, opened a baseball academy, went into scouting, was hired by the Cardinals, and by 2009 at the age of 40 was given charge of a rookie-league team. After eight years managing in the Cardinals' minor-league system, Shildt was promoted to be Matheny's bench coach in 2018, putting him in prime position to take over as "interim manager" when St. Louis failed to gain competitive traction. The job he did was so impressive that in the midst of the Cardinals' superb 22-6 month of August, Shildt's status was no longer "interim"—he was given a contract to manage in St. Louis for at least the next two years. The next year Shildt led the Cardinals to the 2019 division title—their 11th since the year 2000. It surely helped that before the season St. Louis traded for Arizona Diamondbacks power-hitting first baseman Adam Goldschmidt. The St. Louis Cardinals finally had the elite hitter they had been lacking since Albert Pujols left St. Louis after he helped them win the 2011 World Series.

# 13

# BREAKING THROUGH IN THE AL EAST

After the 1997 Yankees stumbled in defense of their 1996 World Series championship by finishing second in their division (but still winning the wild card), the standing rules of order in the AL East—perhaps we should say "the rules of *standing* order"—became something of a punchline: New York's Yankees first, Boston's Red Sox second, Toronto's Blue Jays third, Baltimore's Orioles fourth, and Tampa Bay's pathetic 1998-expansion Devil Rays dead last. That's the order they finished every year from 1998 to 2003, until a complete collapse of the Blue Jays in 2004 broke the pattern by allowing the Orioles to move up to third and the D-Rays to fourth.

Just 10 years earlier, the Blue Jays were trying for a three-peat after winning back-to-back World Series in 1992 and 1993—the first team to do so since the 1977–1978 Yankees. Toronto was not done in by the players' strike that prematurely ended the 1994 season but by their horrendous 18–34 record in May and June. And when baseball resumed in 1995, despite having the highest payroll in the majors, Toronto ended up tied with Oakland for the fewest wins of all 28 teams. They traded their best pitcher, David Cone, to the division-rival Yankees in July and did nothing to stop left-hander Al Leiter and second baseman Roberto Alomar, their best player, from leaving as free agents.

The Blue Jays did not exactly give up on competing. In December 1996, they outmaneuvered the Yankees to sign Red Sox ace Roger Clemens as a free agent to a three-year deal worth close to $25 million—*outmaneuvered*, not outbid, because Steinbrenner had put $32 million for four years on the table for Rocket Roger, who decided to bet on his future and take Toronto's three years instead of New York's four in order to get back on the free-agent market sooner. But it was also a gamble for Toronto because Clemens would soon be 34 years old and had won only 20 games the two previous years combined, although in 1996 he did strike out more than a batter an inning for the first time in eight years. Toronto's gamble paid off, as did Clemens's bet on himself. He went 21–7 and 20–6 in 1997 and 1998. He led the league in earned run average both years. He struck out 563 batters in 498⅔ innings. And Roger Clemens won the fourth and fifth Cy Young Awards of his career, eclipsing Greg Maddux's record of four.

Clemens's extraordinary rejuvenation, however, did not rejuvenate Toronto in the standings. The Blue Jays ended up last in the AL East in 1997 and were third in 1998. During spring training 1999, Steinbrenner finally got his man; Toronto traded Clemens to New York for David Wells, whose 18–4 record was the best in the league for the 114-win 1998 Yankees. Wells picked up Clemens's role as Toronto's ace until he was traded before his free-agency walk year in 2001, after leading the league with 20 wins in 2000.

By 2002 the Jays had a new ace—Roy Halladay, 19–7 that year, followed by a 22–7 record and the Cy Young Award in 2003. Halladay's winnings did nothing to keep Toronto from its predestined third-place in the AL East. What did was the throwing-shoulder injury that limited him to an ineffectual 8–8 record and 4.20 ERA in only 21 starts in 2004. The Jays were in last place to stay by mid-July. Besides being hamstrung with a team ERA close to 5.00, what had been the league's second-most prolific offense the previous year was undermined by injuries to slugging first baseman Carlos Delgado and All-Star center fielder Vernon Wells, each of whom was sidelined for a month. Delgado had averaged 36 homers and 116 runs batted as the cornerstone of Toronto's offense since 1996. Playing in only 128 games in 2004, Delgado still managed to hit 32 homers and drive in 99 runs, then left as a free agent.

Despite taking advantage of Toronto's 2004 troubles to move into third place after six-straight fourth-place endings, Baltimore's string of losing seasons extended to seven in a row. The Orioles' last winning season was 1997. In first place every day of the season, the O's beat out the Yankees by two games to win their division with an AL-best 98 wins. And in 1996, their first year under veteran manager Davey Johnson, the

O's were the American League's wild-card team. Mike Mussina, their ace, won 19 in 1996 and 15 in 1997. Center fielder Brady Anderson crushed 50 home runs in 1996; his previous career high was 21. First baseman Rafael Palmeiro hit 39 homers and drove in 142 runs in 1996 and had 38 home runs in 1997. Roberto Alomar, having left Toronto for Baltimore as a free agent in 1996, hit .330 over those two years. But the marquee name at Camden Yards was still the invincible Cal Ripken Jr. His consecutive games streak intact, Ripken reluctantly accepted being shifted from shortstop to third base in 1997 to accommodate his 36 years on Planet Earth. Baltimore made it as far as the league championship series both years.

Some might insist that the course of Baltimore's baseball destiny as the twentieth century headed toward the new millennium was changed by the 12-year-old kid who stuck his glove over the railing in right field in the opening game of the 1996 ALCS at Yankee Stadium to turn what might otherwise have been a catch by the Orioles' right fielder at the base of the wall on a long flyball into a game-tying, series-changing home run by Derek Jeter off closer Armando Benitez. The Yankees won that day and the series in five games. But the Orioles were back in the ALCS in 1997, this time against Cleveland. Trailing three-games-to-two with the series back in Baltimore, Mussina gave up just one hit and shut out the Indians through eight innings in Game Six. The Orioles, however, could not come up with a run, despite accruing nine hits of their own. The game was finally decided, 1–0, when the star-crossed Benitez surrendered an 11th-inning homer to Tony Fernandez. Soon after, Johnson resigned over irreconcilable differences—"your apparent lack of regard for my management skills," he wrote in his letter of resignation—with team owner Peter Angelos. Said Angelos in reply: "It would clearly be in the best interests of the Orioles organization for a change of field manager for 1998."

And with that began the Orioles' string of losing seasons. Ripken voluntarily ended his consecutive-games streak at 2,632 on September 20, 1998—Baltimore's last home game of the season. He retired in 2001. Alomar and Palmeiro both left as free agents in 1999. Mussina signed as a free agent with the Yankees in 2001. The Orioles' biggest strength when they finally moved out of fourth into third in 2004 was their infield, with Palmeiro back in Baltimore at first base, Brian Roberts at second, high-profile free agent Miguel Tejada at shortstop, and Melvin Mora at third. Tejada had the best year of his career with 34 homers and a league-leading 150 RBIs.

That the Devil Rays moved out of last place for the first time in their seven-year history in 2004 said more about the bad breaks and mediocre play of the Blue Jays than anything about the Tampa Bay ballclub. In its preseason preview on the valuation of major-league teams, *Forbes* business magazine was not shy about calling Tampa Bay "the most horrific baseball franchise of the modern era." The Devil Rays, however, did finally reach the 70-win threshold. In 2005, the AL East went back to the rules of standing order with Toronto, Baltimore, and Tampa Bay falling in line behind New York and Boston.

The Jays in 2006, with Vernon Wells and Roy Halladay both having terrific years, were the first team in eight years to break the Red Sox' stranglehold on second place. But leave it to Tampa Bay, of all teams, in 2008 to finally put an end to nobody but the Yankees and Red Sox (Boston, just once, in 2007) dominating the top spot in the American League's Eastern Division.

Dropping the "Devil" in their name in 2008, Tampa Bay's Rays, burdened by even smaller player payrolls than the A's, blazed their own trail off the Moneyball road to competitive success with an even more comprehensive data-driven analytical approach. That began when Stuart Sternberg bought into the franchise as majority owner in 2005. Like the Arizona Diamondbacks, the NL expansion team in 1998, the Devil Rays had started out by taking the road of trading for or signing well-paid veterans like Wade Boggs, Fred McGriff, Greg Vaughn, and Vinny Castilla to give the new franchise traction with fans on Florida's Gulf Coast. Unlike the D-backs, who won the World Series in 2001, the D-Rays had no success with that approach. By the time Sternberg bought the club, that tack had been largely abandoned and Tampa Bay had the lowest player payroll in the major leagues. But there was no plan on how to become competitive.

Sternberg, a Wall Street broker, had a plan. He brought two other highly successful financiers to run the D-Rays, one of whom—Andrew Friedman, with no baseball background whatsoever—was named general manager after the 2005 season. Applying data-based Wall Street investment strategies to building and sustaining a competitive baseball team, they developed data sets and proprietary analytical methodologies for analyzing not only Tampa Bay's needs but also those of other teams. And in November 2005 they hired soon-to-be-52 Joe Maddon as manager, whose major-league managerial experience was limited to two short stints as an *interim* manager for the Anaheim Angels, because Maddon was innovative in his approach and open to front-office data to help guide his decisions in the dugout.

Keeping to small budgets, Tampa Bay's strategy was to find efficiencies at the margins in both free-agent signings and their transactions with other teams. Friedman "bought low" by targeting players undervalued by other teams and "sold high" by trading Rays players whose performance attributes, while not necessarily what *they* needed, were highly prized by other teams. Perhaps their most consequential trade was sending outfielder Aubrey Huff, due to become a free agent at season's end, to Houston in July 2006 for middle-infielder Ben Zobrist, still in the low minors. The Astros were willing to part with their promising prospect for a proven power-hitter in hopes of reclaiming both the division title and National League pennant they had won the previous year. While Houston fell short of both goals, Zobrist went on to become one of baseball's best-ever multiposition regulars, playing all over the infield and outfield for Tampa Bay between 2009 and 2015.

Friedman also signed Tampa Bay's arbitration-eligible left fielder Carl Crawford, one of baseball's rising stars, to a six-year, $33.5 million contract in 2005. The deal simultaneously secured Crawford's financial future and was a bargain for the Rays by paying him average annual salaries less than $8 million, which were far below his market value in the back three years, after he would have been eligible for free agency. And Friedman gambled on rookie third baseman Evan Longoria likely emerging as a top-tier star just days into the start of his major-league career in 2008 by signing him to a six-year, $17.5 million contract.

In 2008—their first year as just the "Rays," a year after their 96 losses gave them the worst record in baseball, and with the least expensive player payroll in the American League (and second-lowest in the majors)—Tampa Bay won 97 games and the AL East by two games over Boston, whose players were paid nearly $90 million more than the Rays' $45 million payroll, then beat the defending-World Series champion Red Sox in the league championship series. (The Yankees, with their major-league high $212 million payroll—nearly $167 million more than Tampa Bay's—did not make the postseason at all.) It was the first time Tampa Bay had won more than 70. Tampa Bay won despite Crawford missing most of the last two months of the season on the injured list; he returned to bat .345 in the ALCS. Longoria was Rookie of the Year and went on to become one of baseball's best players the first six years of his career. Southpaw David Price, whose big-league career was just 14 innings over five games in September, got the save in Game Seven of the ALCS. Tampa Bay lost the World Series to Philadelphia.

With Price, Longoria, and Zobrist the constants, the Rays won the AL East again in 2010 and wild cards in 2011 and 2013, doing so with player payrolls consistently near the bottom of the league. They didn't make it past the division series any of those years. From 2008 to 2013, Tampa Bay qualified for the postseason exactly as many times as the powerhouse Yankees, whose average annual player payroll was three and a half times what the Rays paid their players. The Rays were celebrated as a small-market club that consistently overachieved for the talent they had, and that was as much about their manager as any player. Maddon's Rays became best known for using exaggerated infield shifts to great effect against opposing hitters. It was the beginning of a wave that revolutionized defenses, soon adapted by every major-league team.

The same as the A's, however, the Rays could not keep their core together for more than a few years on the budgets that defined their payrolls. Of their core regulars in 2008, the Rays traded lefty Scott Kazmir in August 2009, righty James Shields after the 2012 season, Price in July 2014, and Zobrist in 2015 shortly before they would have become free agents. Leaving as free agents were outfielders Crawford in 2011 and Melvin Upton Jr. (then known as B. J.) in 2013 left as free agents. Maddon departed Tampa Bay for Chicago and the Cubs once it became apparent that the low-budget Rays were building for far down the road rather than competing now. If for no other reason than being in the same division as two of baseball's biggest spenders—the Yankees and Red Sox—Tampa Bay's Rays were the franchise with the most competitive success while consistently in the bottom 20 percent in player salaries.

Baltimore winning the division in 2014 and Toronto in 2015 were the first consecutive years since the players' strike that neither New York nor Boston won the AL East. The Orioles' return to winning ways after 14 straight losing seasons began in 2012, when they won the wild card with 93 wins. They lost a tightly contested division series to the Yankees. Presiding over the Orioles' 2012 reboot was veteran manager Buck

Showalter, hired at the beginning of August 2010 to take over a team whose 32–73 record at the time was by far the worst in the majors. Baltimore swamped the competition in 2014, taking the division by 12 games ahead of the second-place Yankees (who did not make the wild card). This time, the Orioles were swept by the wild-card Kansas City Royals in the ALCS. And in 2016, tied with the Blue Jays for second in the AL East, which Boston won (New York finished fourth), the O's were a wild-card team again, losing the wild-card game to Toronto.

The years 2012 to 2016 were the best five-year run for the franchise since Baltimore went to six World Series, winning three, and won two additional division titles in 18 years between 1966 and 1983. Those were the days of Frank and Brooks Robinson, Jim Palmer and Eddie Murray, and their ever-feisty manager, Earl Weaver. Showalter's 2012–2016 Orioles' centerpiece players included center fielder Adam Jones, right fielder Nick Markakis, catcher Matt Wieters, first baseman Chris Davis, shortstop J. J. Hardy, and third baseman Manny Machado (promoted to Baltimore in August 2012). Machado quickly emerged as a budding superstar; Davis was rewarded by the Orioles as though he was one. Rewarding him for leading the league with 53 homers and 138 RBIs in 2013 and with 47 home runs in 2015, Baltimore gave Davis a contract extension worth $161 million over seven years. Starting pitching was Baltimore's biggest weakness. Except for 2014, the collective ERA for Orioles starters was among the worst in the league. Showalter, however, did have a strong corps of relievers—Darren O'Day, Brad Brach, and closer Zack Britton—to preserve late-inning leads.

Toronto's division title in 2015, their first since winning the World Series in 1993, could not have been anticipated as late as July 28. Their season nearly two-thirds over, the Blue Jays stood fourth in the AL East, eight games out, with a losing 50–51 record. The Jays were leading the majors in runs scored, but their pitching was letting them down. (Roy Halladay was long gone, traded after Toronto finished the 2009 season a distant fourth and determined, correctly, that competing for a postseason berth was best thought of as a long-term objective.) Mark Buehrle, their new ace, was 11–5 to this point, but knuckleball specialist R. A. Dickey, their other ace, was 4–10. Toronto's relievers had blown almost as many save-situation leads (15) as they had saves (16). And the Blue Jays had no shutdown closer.

The Blue Jays' turnaround came in August after 20-year-old rookie Roberto Osuna settled in as their closer and they traded for David Price, now with Detroit. Propelled by an 11-game winning streak at the beginning of August, the Blue Jays' 40–18 record the final two months of the season gave them the division title by six games over the Yankees. Osuna ran off 10 saves in a row in August. Price was excellent, going 9–1 in his 11 starts for Toronto; Buehrle finished with a 15–8 record; Dickey ended up even at 11–11; and the Blue Jays' starters ERA of 3.33 in August and September was one run lower than their earned run average the first four months of the season. The Jays' already formidable offense was even more productive in August and September. Third baseman Josh Donaldson, for whom the Jays traded prior to the season, finished the year with 41 home runs; right fielder Jose Bautista with 40; and DH Edwin Encarnacion hit 39. All three drove in more than 100 runs. Kevin Pillar, in his first full season, was superb defensively—often spectacular—in center field. Overcoming a two-games-to-none deficit to win their division series over Texas in five games, Toronto fell to Kansas City in six games in the ALCS.

The 2016 American League wild-card teams were division rivals Toronto and Baltimore. Both had power-hitting lineups. Baltimore led the majors with 253 homers, including a league-leading 47 by newcomer Mark Trumbo, picked up in a trade from Seattle. Toronto's 221 homers were third in the league. Encarnacion led the Jays with 42 homers and the league with 127 runs batted in. The Blue Jays' pitching was the stingiest in the league, even with Buehrle having retired and Price now pitching for Boston. Replacing them as frontline starters were free-agent veteran lefty J. A. Happ, 20–4 his first year in Toronto, and 23-year-old Aaron Sanchez, whose 15–2 record and 3.00 ERA led the league. The Orioles had the best bullpen in the American League. Zack Britton was all but untouchable during the season. He gave up only four earned runs in 67 innings for a 0.54 earned run average. His 47 saves led the league. He did not blow a save opportunity. That made him only the ninth pitcher in history to have a perfect season in save opportunities. All that prevented him from a perfect closer's season was the loss he suffered on April 30, in which he struck out the first two batters he faced, twisted his ankle trying to field a drag bunt single, and had to leave the game. 'Twas the pitcher relieving the wounded closer who gave up the game-winning hit, but Britton who took the loss.

The Blue Jays won the wild-card game on an 11th-inning walk-off three-run homer by Encarnacion that immediately raised questions about why the Orioles closer never got into the game. With the game tied at 2–2, Britton warmed up in every inning after the seventh but never got the call from his manager. With Toronto the home team, Showalter was keeping Britton in reserve for a save situation once Baltimore had the lead—a save situation that never came. Instead, Showalter went with lefty Brian Duensing to start the 11th, and after Duensing struck out the only batter he faced, brought in right-hander Ubaldo Jimenez, a starting pitcher with a 5.44 ERA for the season, to finish the inning against the right-handed Blue Jays batters due up next. The first two singled to bring up dangerous power-hitting Encarnacion. Showalter stuck with Jimenez rather than bring in the lefty Britton. Never mind that Britton had held right-handed batters to a .155 batting average against him and that Encarnacion was 0-for-2 with a strikeout against Britton during the regular season. Encarnacion drove the first pitch he saw from Jimenez over the fence, and Baltimore's season was over. Toronto then again lost the ALCS.

Toronto and Baltimore collapsed to fourth and fifth in the AL East the very next year, causing both to go into rebuilding mold. The Orioles' freefall was particularly traumatic because they were a much younger team than the Blue Jays in 2016 and had a strong bullpen, decent starting pitching, and one of the best players in the game in Manny Machado. Except for Machado, that all proved to be a chimera. The Orioles went from bad in 2017, to horrifically bad with 115 losses in 2018, to just very bad in 2019 with 108 losses. Along the way they parted with all their best players, including Britton and Machado during the 2018 season. The one player they couldn't part with was Chris Davis, whose expensive contract extension in 2016 turned almost immediately into a colossal mistake. In his four years in Baltimore before signing his big deal, from 2012 to 2015, Davis averaged 40 homers a season and batted .256 while striking out in 35 percent of his at-bats. In the first four years of his new contract, 2016 to 2019, Davis's home-run output declined every year to just 12 in 307 at-bats in 2019, while his strikeout rate soared to 41 percent in 323 fewer at-bats, and he batted just .198.

The Jays and O's sinking back into the depths of the AL East allowed the Tampa Bay Rays to reemerge as contenders. While both manager Joe Maddon and general manager Andrew Friedman had left in 2015, the

Rays resumed being able to excel with the lowest-salaried team in the major leagues. They also remained at the forefront of using data analytics to innovate the game on the field. In 2018, the Rays introduced the concept of the "bullpen game," in lieu of a fifth starter, in which an "opener" would pitch only the first or perhaps the first two innings and be followed by a succession of relievers. Other than reliever Ryne Stanek "opening" 29 games, the Rays' only pitcher with more than 20 official starts was left-hander Blake Snell, whose 21–5 record and league-leading 1.89 ERA in 31 starts earned him the Cy Young Award. They were back to 90 wins in 2018, won 96 and the second seed in the wild-card game in 2019, and went to the World Series in the pandemic-shortened 2020 season with the best record in the American League despite the second-lowest payroll in Major League Baseball.

# 14

# GIANTS AND RED SOX ROLLER-COASTER DYNASTIES

**N**o sooner did third baseman Pablo Sandoval squeeze the last out on a foul pop-up in Game Seven of the 2014 World Series than the word "dynasty" was being bandied about when considering this San Francisco Giants team's place in history. They had just won their third World Series in five years. "The San Francisco Giants are Now a Dynasty," proclaimed the data-based website *FiveThirtyEight*, using an algorithm developed by advanced-stats godfather Bill James. Reuters called the Giants "a different kind of Major League Baseball dynasty." And at the Giants' victory parade back in San Francisco, their ace Madison Bumgarner, winning both his starts and closing the series with a five-inning save to earn World Series MVP honors, intoned, "Like they've been saying, this is a dynasty."

But even before Game Six, with the Giants a game away from winning the series, *New York Times* national baseball columnist Tyler Kepner asked a provocative question: "Are they really a dynasty?" Before the beginning of two rounds of postseason series in 1995 to determine the World Series participants, the number of times finishing first—whether winning pennants outright with their league's best record until 1969 or division titles since then—as well as the number of World Series triumphs over any five-year period was a suitable baseline standard for beginning a discussion about "dynasties." Obvious additional factors for discriminating dynasties included not having a losing season in any of the intervening years and the extent to which a team dominates its league—

for example, some combination of number of seasons with 100 wins, winning pennant races by large margins, or run differential.

San Francisco's 2010 to 2014 Giants did not meet those standards, except the undeniably important one of winning three World Series. They won only two division titles on their way to three World Series; in 2014 they were the second of the National League's two wild-card teams. In neither year they won the NL West did the Giants have the best record in the league. They ran away with their division only once—in 2012, by eight games over the Dodgers. Their first division title, in 2010, was secured by defeating the second-place Padres on the last day of the season. They never approached 100 wins; the best they did was 94 wins in 2012, 92 in 2010, and 88 as a wild-card team in 2014. Their pitching staff did lead the league in earned run average in 2010—the only year they outscored their game opponents by more than 100 runs—but otherwise they were typically in the middle of the National League pack in runs scored and fewest allowed. And in the odd-numbered years between their World Series triumphs, the Giants were out of contention by the end of August in 2011 and by the All-Star break in 2013, when they ended up third with a losing 76–86 record. It was in fact an up-and-down roller-coaster ride for San Francisco.

For a team that was close to unbeatable in their three World Series–winning postseasons—the Giants won 34 of the 48 games they played for a .708 winning percentage—their regular-season winning percentage from 2010 to 2014 was a very pedestrian .538, the equivalent of an 87–75 record in a single season. They were not even close to as good, at least by their record, as a decade before, from 2000 to 2004 in the heyday of the Barry Bonds era, when the Giants had their winningest five-year stretch since moving to San Francisco in 1958, averaging 94 wins and never winning fewer than 90, while claiming two division titles and a wild card. Notwithstanding the force of nature (or perhaps steroids) that was Bonds those years (he won four-straight MVP Awards from 2001 to 2004), those Giants made it past the opening round of the postseason only once—as the NL wild card in 2002, when they advanced to the World Series. Including losing the 2002 World Series to Anaheim's Angels in seven games, those San Francisco Giants had a losing 12–13 record in the three postseasons they played, in part because Bonds was limited to just three hits in their 2000 division series and two hits in their 2003 division series losses.

Dynasties are also identifiable by the core group of players together for all or most of their run. Of recent dynasties, for example, there were the Braves of Maddux, Glavine, Smoltz, and Chipper and Andruw Jones, and the Yankees with their homegrown core of five—Jeter, Pettitte, Rivera, Posada, and Bernie Williams—not to mention long-serving imports O'Neill, Cone, and Tino Martinez. For the 2010 to 2014 Giants, they were starting pitchers Tim Lincecum, Matt Cain, and Madison Bumgarner; catcher Buster Posey; first baseman Brandon Belt; shortstop Brandon Crawford; and right fielder Hunter Pence and third baseman Pablo Sandoval, both of whose public images—Captain Underpants who rode a scooter to work (Pence) and cuddly Kung Fu Panda (Sandoval)—gave them a near-cult following. With the exception of Posey, the National League's Rookie of the Year in 2010 and Most Valuable Player in 2012, when his .336 batting average was the best in the majors, none of them were historically great players or players who were the best at their position for those years.

Like the Braves' Bobby Cox and the Yankees' Joe Torre, the Giants did have (probably) a future Hall of Fame manager. Bruce Bochy was already highly regarded as a manager when he left the Padres, whom he had just led to a division title, to take charge of the Giants in 2007, a team coming off two losing seasons since missing out on the 2004 division title by two games. Bochy inherited a team that was beginning its transition from the scandalized Barry Bonds with a cadre of young players just making it to the majors or soon to be there. Bochy's first year in San Francisco would be the last for Bonds in his career. On August 7, 2007, Bonds hit his 756th career home run in San Francisco to pass Hank Aaron.

The Giants finished last in the NL West in Bochy's first year as manager, and while the force of nature that was Bonds retired at the end of the season with his all-time record of 762 homers, a freak of nature was the new player sensation in San Francisco. "The Freak" (of nature) was 5-foot-11, whippet-thin Tim Lincecum, whose preternatural ability, given his size, to throw consistently in the upper-90s was all the more exaggerated by his unusually long stride for his height and late torso rotation that sent his long hair whipping across his neck. Predictions were that his pitching mechanics were so complex and intricate that he'd have great difficulty self-correcting if they began failing him and that the "violence" of his delivery was certain to blow out his hip or his arm or some other body part sooner than later.

In fact, it wouldn't be long before both those things came true, but after a 7–5 record in 24 starts as a rookie in 2007, Lincecum won back-to-back Cy Young Awards with a 15–5 record and 2.62 ERA in 2008 and a 15–7 record and 2.48 earned run average in 2009 while striking out 10.5 batters per nine innings in his 65 starts. Lincecum's dominance in 2009 overshadowed the year-younger Matt Cain's almost equally good 14–8 record and 2.89 earned run average and 45-year-old Randy Johnson's last season in the major leagues. Sitting on 295 career wins, Johnson signed with San Francisco as a free agent before the season. On June 4 in Washington, he became just the 24th pitcher in major-league history to win 300 games, to which he would add 3 victories. The Giants endured their fourth-straight losing season.

San Francisco improved from 90 losses to 88 wins in 2010. Playing from behind the Padres most of the summer, the Giants finally overtook Bochy's former team in the last three weeks on the schedule. Lincecum led the club with 16 wins and the league in strikeouts and strikeouts-per-nine-innings for the third-straight year, shut out the wild-card Braves in the opening game of their division series, beat Philadelphia in the opening game of the NLCS, and won both his starts against Texas in the World Series. The Freak gave up just one run on three hits in eight innings in the deciding Game Five. It was the Giants' first World Series championship since 1954, when they were still in New York, ending a 56-year championship drought.

The next time the Giants were in the World Series in 2012, Lincecum was no longer the front man in Bochy's rotation. Cain and 22-year-old southpaw Madison Bumgarner, both with 16 wins, were. After struggling through a 10–15 season with an unsightly 5.18 ERA, Lincecum was assigned the role of a middle-innings reliever for the postseason, and he made the most of it. In five relief appearances totaling 13 innings, Lincecum gave up just one earned run on three hits while striking out 15. He stymied the Tigers in the Giants' four-game sweep of the World Series, pitching 2⅓ innings in both Games One and Three without allowing a hit with eight strikeouts. Pablo Sandoval had a postseason to remember, batting .364 with six homers and 13 RBIs in San Francisco's 16 games—including home runs in his first three at-bats in the opening game of the World Series, the first two off Tigers ace Justin Verlander.

By the time the Giants made it back to the World Series in 2014, Lincecum's degenerative hip had put an end to his explosive fastball, and a chronically sore elbow was leading Cain rapidly to the end of his career. Neither pitcher started in the postseason. Bumgarner, 18–10 in 33 starts, was the Giants' new ace. Bumgarner threw a four-hit shutout to beat Pittsburgh in the single-elimination wild-card game; did not allow a run in 7⅔ innings to win the opening game of the NLCS against the Cardinals in St. Louis; pitched eight strong innings in the deciding fifth game of the NLCS that the Giants won on a walk-off three-run homer by reserve Travis Ishikawa; and then sealed his legacy as one of the best-ever pitchers in World Series history.

Bumgarner had not allowed a run in his two previous World Series starts—eight innings, giving up eight hits, against Texas in the 2010 World Series and seven innings, giving up two hits, to beat Detroit in 2012—when he took the mound in Kansas City for Game One of the 2014 Fall Classic. His string of World Series scoreless innings came to an end at 21⅔ when Royals catcher Salvador Perez homered off him with two outs in the seventh inning. It was only the third hit MadBum had given up in the game. With the Giants comfortably ahead, 7–1, Bochy let him finish the inning, then brought in relievers for the final two innings to preserve his ace for later games.

In the fifth inning of Game Seven in Kansas City, Bochy brought Bumgarner in to protect a 3–2 lead. MadBum was pitching on two days' rest after throwing 117 pitches in a complete-game shutout to win Game Five. Bochy's intent was for Bumgarner to get the game into the late innings for closer Sergio Romo to save the day. Fifty-two pitches later, Bumgarner had gotten the Giants through eight innings. With San Francisco still nursing a 3–2 lead, Bochy stayed with his starting ace rather than bring in his closer. Retiring the first two batters, Bumgarner had now thrown 60 pitches. The Royals down to their last out, Alex Gordon dumped a single into center field that the center fielder let skip by to the wall and that the left fielder had trouble picking up. At the direction of the third-base coach, Gordon put on the brakes as he raced into third. It remains debated to this day whether Gordon should have tried to score. The left fielder's failure to pick up the ball cleanly at the wall would have given him a good chance. It would have been close. It would have required a perfect relay throw to the plate. But Gordon held third . . . where he stayed as Bumgarner got Perez to pop out to Sandoval off the third base line. Kung Fu Panda fell to the grass after catching the baseball. The Giants were now World Series champions for the third time in five years and the seventh time in franchise history.

No pitcher who has thrown more than 27 innings in World Series competition has been stingier than Madison Bumgarner. In 36⅓ innings in 24 World Series relief appearances for the Yankees, Mariano Rivera has an earned run average of 0.99. Christy Mathewson, who threw three complete-game shutouts in the 1905 World Series, has an ERA of 0.97 in 101⅔ innings over 11 starts in four series; Sandy Koufax, a 0.95 earned run average in eight starts and 57 innings in four series; and Babe Ruth in 31 innings in two Fall Classics, an ERA of 0.87. In four World Series starts totaling 31 innings and his superb five-inning save in 2014, Mad-Bum has an ERA of 0.25. The Salvador Perez homer in Game One of the 2014 Series is the only run Bumgarner has given up in 36 World Series innings pitched.

Two years later, after another odd-numbered year in which the Giants *did not* qualify for the postseason—that became a "thing" in San Francisco—Bumgarner was again a postseason hero. San Francisco, second in the NL West, met the Mets in the wild-card game in New York. The game was scoreless until third baseman Conor Gillaspie, mostly a reserve (like Ishikawa in 2014), hit a three-run homer off Mets' closer Jeurys Familia with one out in the ninth, and MadBum retired the Mets on a flyout to each outfield position in the bottom of the ninth to complete a four-hit shutout. This time, the Giants did not make it out of their division series against the Cubs. The only game they won was Game Three started by Bumgarner, who left after five innings, trailing 3–2.

San Francisco's Giants have not had a winning season since 2016. Lincecum, no longer able "to sustain the end of my motion when my foot hits" the mound on his delivery because of a degenerative hip, had been released after the 2015 season. Matt Cain retired in 2017. Bruce Bochy retired after the 2019 season, and Madison Bumgarner left as a free agent in 2020, signing with division rival Arizona. Buster Posey, first baseman Brandon Belt, Brandon Crawford, and Pablo Sandoval (in a return engagement after leaving as a free agent) were the only players remaining from their run of three World Series in five years from 2010 to 2014.

The only franchise to win more than the Giants' three World Series since 2000 is the Boston Red Sox with four. If the Giants' "dynasty" was short-lived and perhaps tarnished by their *not* being a dominant team in the National League when they were winning three in five years, the Red Sox had a more sustained record of excellence. From 1998 to 2011, they and the New York Yankees were the only teams to never have a losing season. But beginning in 2011 Boston got onto its own roller coaster of championship highs and even more extreme dips—collapses, really—than San Francisco endured.

When the Red Sox finally finished ahead of the Yankees in 2007 to win the AL East and then won their second World Series in four years, they were already a different team from the "idiots" that dared believe they would overcome a three-games-to-none deficit to the evil empire in the 2004 ALCS and went on to win their first World Series since Babe Ruth was an ace in their starting rotation. Gone were starters Pedro Martinez, Derek Lowe, and Bronson Arroyo, and Curt Schilling was in his 40s working through injuries. Gone also was Johnny Damon, the charismatic, long-haired center fielder who dubbed that team the idiots. Still there in 2007 were catcher Jason Varitek, the team's inspirational leader; sluggers David Ortiz and Manny Ramirez; and knuckleballer Tim Wakefield. New to the Red Sox were first baseman Kevin Youkilis, scrappy second baseman Dustin Pedroia, third baseman Mike Lowell, right fielder J. D. Drew, sensational late-season call-up Jacoby Ellsbury, starting pitchers Josh Beckett (20–7 in 2007) and Japanese import Daisuke Matsuzaka (15–12 in his first year in the majors), and closer Jonathan Papelbon (striking out 84 batters in 58⅓ innings while saving 37 of Boston's 96 wins).

But both manager Terry Francona and general manager Theo Epstein, who presided over Boston's savaging the Curse of the Bambino in 2004, worried that the dynamic was different. The Red Sox were veering back to that old refrain of 25 cabs for 25 players that was meant to characterize the toxic individualism, rather than a spirited team-oriented collective will to win, that seemed to define the teams on which Ted Williams and then Carl Yastrzemski and then Wade Boggs and Roger Clemens played. It didn't help that the Red Sox' owners, over Epstein's misgivings, emphasized signing high-priced free agents to keep their team competitive with Steinbrenner's Yankees rather than focusing on investing in a fruitful farm system to replenish the club with homegrown talent, which ironically is exactly what the Yankees did to build their 1996 to 2001 juggernaut around the likes of Derek Jeter and Mariano Rivera. Matsuzaka and Drew were both high-priced free agents. Before them, the Red Sox in

December 2004 committed a combined $65 million in multiyear contracts to right-hander Matt Clement and shortstop Edgar Renteria, neither of whom were still in Boston by 2007.

Following their 2007 championship, Boston finished second and won 95 games and the wild card each of the next two years. Having had enough of "Manny being Manny," the Red Sox traded Ramirez at the trade deadline in 2008. Matsuzaka went 18–3 in 2008 but struggled through an injury-marred 2009 season and would never regain his effectiveness. Looking to give depth to a starting rotation now headlined by Beckett and homegrown lefty Jon Lester, Boston signed free agent John Lackey to an $82 million deal covering five years less than two months after he had shut them out on four hits in 7⅓ innings in the opening game of the Angels' 2009 ALCS sweep of the Red Sox. Boston beat the Yankees on opening day in 2010, were never again in first place, and ended up a disappointing third in the division, despite 19 wins by Lester and 17 by righty Clay Buchholz, in his first full year in the majors. Beckett missed two months with a bad back. Lackey was 14–11 with a 4.40 earned run average his first year in Boston.

Determined to return to the top of the heap in 2011, Boston traded for San Diego's highly regarded power-hitting first baseman Adrian Gonzalez, *after* privately negotiating a seven-year, $154 million contract with his agent, and signed Tampa Bay's free-agent outfielder Carl Crawford for seven years and $142 million. The Red Sox blew through June and July, winning 36 of 51 games, to correct for a slow start to the 2011 season, but could not shake the Yankees. Still, Boston entered September with the best record in the American League, a 1½-game lead over New York, and (not that it mattered at the time) a nine-game edge over third-place Tampa Bay. Beckett had a 12–5 record, and Lester was 14–6. Lackey and Crawford were struggling, but Gonzalez was leading the league with a .341 batting average. They lost their first two games in the final month to drop half a game back of the Yankees—and then . . . disaster.

Boston lost 20 of 27 games in September. Six of their losses were to Tampa Bay, meaning that by September 18, with just 12 games to play, the Red Sox were not only 4½ back of the Yankees but just two ahead of the Rays. After 160 games, with just two on the schedule for all teams, the Rays and Red Sox were tied for the wild card, both eight games back of the Yankees. Boston was in Baltimore, last in the AL East, and Tampa

Bay was hosting New York, whose only concern was the postseason just ahead. In their 161st games, the Rays came from behind to beat the Yankees, while the Red Sox allowed an 8–4 lead in the eighth to become 8–7 before Papelbon finally got the last out. In game 162, the Red Sox led 3–2 going into the bottom of the ninth. Papelbon struck out the first two batters he faced, gave up a double, and then gave up another double that tied the score. A looping single landing in front of Crawford in left field gave Baltimore the victory. Meanwhile, the Rays overcame a 7–0 Yankees' lead in the eighth to beat them in 12 innings. It was Tampa Bay finishing second to win the wild card by one game over Boston.

A *Boston Globe* exposé after the fact was damning toward the lack of commitment to winning in the clubhouse. Team leaders like David Ortiz, Dustin Pedroia and newcomer Adrian Gonzalez did not hold their slacking teammates, some of whom were obsessed by their own struggles, to account. Francona's voice lost its resonance, with some team sources suggesting his leadership and judgment were impaired by the pain medication he was taking for his surgically repaired knees. But perhaps most scathing was the reveal that Beckett, Lester, and Lackey were drinking beer and eating takeout fried chicken in the clubhouse during games rather than supporting their teammates from the dugout. All three put on body fat. None of the three pitched well down the stretch. In the 15 games they started in September, the trio won two, lost seven, and had a collective 6.45 ERA; Boston was 4–11 in those games.

The fallout from their September debacle was Boston's front office mimicking how the Yankees got rid of Joe Torre in 2007 by not committing to extend Francona's contract and implying it was up to him whether he wanted to stay as Red Sox manager. Torre had to ask the Yankees' brain trust, "Do you want me to manage?" Francona had to say, "If you don't want me, just tell me." "Sleep on it," he was told by team president Larry Lucchino, according to Francona and *Boston Globe* columnist Dan Shaughnessy in their book *Francona: The Red Sox Years*. "See how you feel." Rather than outright firing him, which risked a serious blowback from Red Sox Nation, they maneuvered Francona into resigning. Shortly thereafter, Theo Epstein left Boston's Sox to their clubhouse dysfunction for the challenge of trying to end the century-plus championship drought of Chicago's Cubs.

And like the Yankees choosing Joe Girardi to replace the mellow Torre, the Red Sox hired the complete opposite of Francona in the person of Bobby Valentine to take the helm at Fenway Park. Valentine had managed 15 years in the majors and, most recently, six years in Japan. Valentine's one year in Boston in 2012 was a disaster. Boston finished last in the division, winning only 16 of their 58 games after July. Gonzalez, Crawford, Beckett, and their expensive contracts were sent packing to the Dodgers in late August. Valentine was fired as soon as the season ended and replaced by John Farrell, who had left Francona's coaching staff in 2011 to manage in Toronto.

In an eerie parallel to Boston's 1967 Red Sox rising from 90 losses and 26 games behind the previous year to 90 wins and playing in the World Series, Boston's 2013 Red Sox rose from 93 losses—their most since 1965—and 26 games behind to reclaim the AL East with 97 wins and sweep through the postseason. The 2013 Red Sox were not dreaming the Impossible Dream of the 1967 Red Sox, however, because many of their core players—Ortiz, Pedroia, Ellsbury, and Lester—had been on Boston's 2007 championship team. Moreover, for the talent they had, the Red Sox had underachieved the two previous years, whereas the '67 Red Sox came out of nowhere to win the pennant. While Boston lost to St. Louis in the 1967 World Series, it was the other way around in 2013. David Ortiz nearly single-handedly demolished the Cardinals with 11 hits, including 2 homers, in 16 at-bats (a .688 batting average).

And then came another Red Sox dive to last in the AL East the very next year. They were last again in 2015. They achieved a rebound in 2016 for the first of three consecutive years atop their division with all the makings of a dynasty that would last into the 2020s. The Red Sox had not finished first in back-to-back seasons since 1915 and 1916. But while those two years a century earlier automatically meant the pennant, in both 2016 and 2017 Boston was eliminated in the division-series round. The second time cost Farrell his job. Once again, the manager was let go following a season of indiscipline in the clubhouse and sniping among players. It didn't help that they were one of only two clubs with a $200 million player payroll and that the other team was the Dodgers, *not* their archrivals in New York or the Houston team that felled them in their division series. Under rookie manager Alex Cora, the 2018 Red Sox set a franchise-record 108 wins, allowing them to finish comfortably ahead of the 100-win Yankees, whom they polished off in four games in their division series on their way to beating the Astros in the ALCS in five games and the Dodgers in the World Series in five games.

There had been an almost-complete turnover in core players in the five years since their last championship. After the Red Sox won the 2013 World Series, center fielder Jacoby Ellsbury followed in the footsteps of his top-of-the-order predecessor, Johnny Damon, by defecting to the Yankees as a free agent in 2014. David Ortiz, beloved by Red Sox fans as Big Papi, retired after leading the league in doubles and RBIs and hitting 38 homers while batting .315 in 2016. Of his 541 career home runs, 483 were hit in his 14 years in Boston. His absence was said to have contributed to the resumption of clubhouse dysfunction in 2017. Scrappy second baseman Dustin Pedroia, underrated because of his size but one of the best players of his generation, played only three games in 2018 because of knee surgery, putting a quick end to his career.

Boston's new stars were shortstop Xander Bogaerts and right fielder Mookie Betts, both 25 and in their fifth year in 2018. Betts led the league in runs, batting average (.346), and slugging percentage (.640); hit 32 homers; drove in 80 runs; and stole 30 bases in 36 attempts to solidify his superstar stature. Signing 30-year-old free agent J. D. Martinez to be their designated hitter in 2018, filling the hole left by Ortiz's retirement, proved a masterstroke. Martinez belted 43 homers, led the league with 130 runs batted in, and batted .330.

The pitching staff had also turned over, from Beckett, Lester, and Lackey to lefties Chris Sale and David Price and right-hander Rick Porcello atop the starting rotation. Hard-throwing Craig Kimbrel was now the closer. Porcello came from Detroit in a trade in 2015 and won the Cy Young Award with a 22–4 record for the Red Sox in 2016; Price was 17–9 and led the league in starts and innings pitched in 2016, his first year in Boston after signing as a free agent; and Sale was the best pitcher in the American League when the Red Sox traded with the White Sox to get him before the 2017 season. Sale's strikeout ratio of 10.9 per nine innings was the highest of any major-league pitcher in history for the first nine years of his career, and he had not had a significant injury . . . until he got to Boston. Beset by shoulder problems most of the second half of the 2018 season, Sale was 12–4 in 27 starts. Still, his 13.5 K/9 ratio would have been a single-season record had he pitched just four more innings. Porcello was 17–7 and Price 16–7 in 2018.

Notwithstanding that the Red Sox committed $217 million over seven years to put Price in their starting rotation with the expectation he would not only carry Boston to multiple postseasons but through them as well,

Red Sox Nation did not feel reassured when he was called to start against Astros ace Justin Verlander in Game Five of the 2018 ALCS—which, if Boston won, would send them to the World Series. For all his regular-season excellence, David Price seemed cursed in the postseason. In his 11 prior postseason starts for Tampa Bay, Detroit, and Boston, Price had lost nine without a single win. That included his only start in Boston's 2018 division series against the Yankees—he gave up three runs in 1⅔ innings. And in his Game Two start in the ALCS against Houston he surrendered four runs in 4⅔ innings of a game the Red Sox went on to win. Price's ERA in his 11 postseason starts was 6.16. But he came through with six shutout innings for the win in his fifth-game matchup against Verlander; gave up just two runs in six innings to beat the Dodgers in Game Two of the World Series; and, after giving up a home run to the first batter he faced in Game Five, did not allow another run before being relieved in the eighth inning. With Boston leading 5–1 in the ninth, the stage was set for closer Craig Kimbrel to secure the final three outs of the series.

Kimbrel came to Boston from San Diego in 2016 as one of baseball's elite closers after six National League seasons—five with Atlanta—in which he led the league in saves four years in a row, had a career earned run average of 1.63, held opponents to a .158 batting average, and averaged 14.5 strikeouts per nine innings. In 2018, he saved 42 of Boston's 108 wins, held opponents to a .146 batting average, and blew away 96 batters in 62⅓ innings. But, a year after being at his stingiest ever in giving up walks, the 2018 Kimbrel averaged a troubling 4.5 walks per nine innings. The Red Sox closer's command was especially wobbly in the postseason. Pitching nine times in Boston's 14 games on their way to the championship, Kimbrel's eight walks and nine hits allowed—including two homers—in 10⅔ innings had all of Red Sox Nation chomping on their fingernails with him on the mound.

So rather than his closer, it was Chris Sale whom manager Alex Cora called to get the last three outs of the World Series. Sale's shoulder problems had limited his starting assignments since mid-summer and hampered his efficiency in his opening-game starts in each of Boston's postseason series. In 13⅓ total innings in his three starts, Sale threw 270 pitches to the 58 batters he faced, walking eight. In his Game One start against the Dodgers, he lasted one batter into the fifth before leaving the game with 91 pitches thrown. But in his first relief appearance in any game since 2012, Sale needed 15 pitches to strike out the side and give

Boston its fourth World Series championship since 2004. After Boston celebrated, Kimbrel became a free agent the Red Sox had no interest in signing for the price he was asking.

As dominating a year as it had been for the Red Sox, they were just one of four superpower teams in Major League Baseball—the others being the Yankees, Astros, and Dodgers—all three massacred by Boston in five games or less in the 2018 postseason. Playing in their same division, the Yankees were their most formidable adversary, and they were back trying to reclaim their status as the "forever" dynasty. To keep ahead of the Yankees and give themselves an enduring pitching advantage, the Red Sox in spring training 2019 gave Chris Sale a five-year, $145 million contract extension beginning in 2020. Bothered by a sore elbow, Sale struggled through the season with a 6–11 record and 4.40 ERA before the Red Sox shut him down for the year in August, shortly after Price was shelved with an injured wrist. By then, the Red Sox had no hope of catching the Yankees in the AL East and were trailing three other teams in the wild-card race. Boston ended up 19 games back of the Yankees and eight games short of a wild card.

Having paid a premium for being far above baseball's competitive-balance tax threshold in 2019 with no postseason to show for their $243 million opening-day roster, the Red Sox determined they could not afford to keep Betts and wanted to be rid of the remaining three years and $96 million on Price's multiyear deal. While they could not say to Red Sox Nation that they were giving up on competing with the Yankees in 2020, the franchise was in fact deciding to cut payroll to get below the luxury tax as a prelude to rebuilding. Ironically, Boston trading superstar Mookie Betts came 100 years after they sold Babe Ruth to the Yankees. Their latest World Series championship in 2018 was 100 after they won the World Series in 1918. It took the Red Sox 86 years from then before they won another. History almost certainly won't repeat itself, but . . . just sayin'.

# 15

# METS MELTDOWNS

## The Superheroes' Hubris Episodes

**B**lockbusters featuring comic-book superheroes dominated the entertainment industry. So too in the mid-2010s did the New York Mets take on some of the same personas. In the movies, there were the Dark Knight, better known as Batman, and Thor, based on the mythological Norse God of Thunder, introduced to the comic-reading world in 1962 and, 50 years later, to the movie world as one of *The Avengers*. On the Mets, there was also a Dark Knight and a Thor, introduced to the baseball world in 2015. In the movies, Thor was played by hunky Australian actor Chris Hemsworth. On the Mets, the Thor persona belonged to the hunky 6-foot-6 Noah Syndergaard, himself of Danish ancestry with gorgeous flowing locks of blond hair whose hammer was a devastating fastball in the neighborhood of 100 miles an hour. In the movies, the Dark Knight—Batman—was played by English-born actor Christian Bale, who portrayed the Caped Crusader as a complicated brooding protagonist with issues, rather than the ever-cheerful crime-fighter of the campy mid-'60s TV show of my youth. On the Mets, the Dark Knight persona was adopted by hard-throwing right-hander Matt Harvey, himself a complicated protagonist determined to vanquish the villainous foes of "Gotham City" and its National League baseball team.

The rock star Jim Croce cautioned in his first megahit, "You Don't Mess Around with Jim," that "you don't tug on Superman's cape." Forty-three years later, the Mets' Dark Knight stepped on his. He was trying to demonstrate that you don't mess around with the Dark Knight—in Game Five of the 2015 World Series, with the Mets trailing the Kansas City Royals three-games-to-one. After winning 13 and losing 8 in a dramatic comeback from Tommy John surgery that cost him the entire 2014 season, for the expressed purpose of helping Gotham City's Mets win a championship, he cast caution aside. He had won the third game in the division series. His victory in the opening game of the league championship series set the Mets in motion to win the National League pennant. Harvey pitched six credible innings in the opening game of the World Series, leaving with the score tied. And in Game Five, at Citi Field in New York, in a must-win game, the Mets' Dark Knight seemed indomitable. He left the mound in the eighth with a 2–0 lead, having allowed just six base runners on four singles, a walk, and an error, never having faced more than four batters in any inning. He had nine strikeouts.

Harvey was also well beyond the number of innings he was supposed to pitch in his first year back from Tommy John surgery. Manager Terry Collins congratulated him on a game superbly pitched. Warming in the bullpen, set to save the day and send the Series back to Kansas City, was the Mets' outstanding closer, Jeurys Familia. But Matt Harvey was having none of that. He was the Dark Knight, after all, Gotham's go-to savior. He jawed with his manager and convinced Collins to keep him in the game. Needless to say, the Mets' heroic ace was cheered mightily as he took the mound in the ninth to complete the win. He faced two batters, walking one and giving up a run-scoring double to the other. Only then did Collins go with his original instinct—to bring in Familia to save the victory. Familia retired all three batters he faced, but the tying run scored anyway. Three innings later, the Royals scored five times and the World Series ended without having to make a return trip to Kansas City. Had it gone seven, Syndergaard—Thor—who had the Mets' only victory in the Series, would have taken the mound.

Late September meltdowns that cost them their lead and the NL Eastern Division title in both 2007 and 2008 set the Mets on a six-year odyssey of losing seasons. In 2009, the first of those years, the Mets moved into a new stadium, at the same site in Flushing, Queens, as their old. Named for the bank that purchased naming rights, one of its attractions was re-creating the famous rotunda that gave Brooklyn's Ebbets Field such character and therein remembering the ground-breaking career of Jackie Robinson. Attendance declined from 3.2 million their first year in Citi Field, when they finished fourth, to 2.1 million in 2014, when their 79–83 record was nonetheless good for second place. The last time the Mets drew so few fans was in 2003, when they were buried deep in last place. It didn't help that the new ballpark's original outfield dimensions and height of fences conspired against the power of star third baseman David Wright and outfielder Jason Bay, signed by the Mets as a free agent in 2010 precisely because he had averaged 30 home runs the six previous years.

And it certainly didn't help that Johan Santana, their ace, had suddenly become injury prone. After five straight years of hardly missing a start—the first four with Minnesota—Santana was sidelined in late August 2009 for the rest of the season for elbow surgery. In September the next year he underwent shoulder surgery that also cost him all of 2011. Back in the rotation in 2012, on June 1 Santana was allowed by manager Terry Collins to throw 134 pitches on his way to becoming the first pitcher in New York Mets history to throw a no-hitter. While he pitched decently the rest of the month, shoulder pain made him totally ineffective thereafter. He made only five more starts for the Mets—and in his career—losing all five while giving up 33 runs in 19 innings. There was much second-guessing even during the game, and certainly in retrospect, about Collins's decision to allow his ace with a known history of shoulder problems to keep pitching just for the sake of a historical Mets moment.

More damaging for the Mets than the karma of their 2007 and 2008 division-race meltdowns was the fallout from the late-2008 collapse of the "massive fraud" Ponzi scheme perpetrated by financier Bernie Madoff, with whom team owner Fred Wilpon had substantial investments that included Mets money. Now cash-strapped, the major-market Mets were forced to retrench on player salaries and reduce spending elsewhere as if they were a small-market team. By 2011, maintaining one of the National League's highest player payrolls dating back to their competitive 2006 to 2008 years had become unsustainable, particularly with the Mets having become irrelevant as a contender. In July 2011, the Mets traded away Francisco Rodriguez, their closer, in the final year of his expensive contract. Two weeks later, Carlos Beltran, whom they had signed for seven years and $119 million in 2005 and still arguably their best player, was next to go. As soon as the 2011 season ended, they let Jose Reyes leave as a free agent for a $106 million, six-year contract the Mets could not afford in their post-Madoff era of fiscal constraint, even though he had just become the first Met to win a batting title and was hugely popular in Queens. The next year they traded R. A. Dickey, a knuckleball pitcher who had just gone 20–6 and won the Cy Young Award, to Toronto for pitching prospect Noah Syndergaard.

The one player who was safe was David Wright, the face of the franchise. Realizing his credibility with Mets fans as franchise owner was at stake in the wake of the other departures, Wilpon approved an eight-year, $138 million contract extension for his star third baseman in November 2012. Shortly thereafter, following his starring role for the USA team in the March 2013 World Baseball Classic, Wright had his own superhero avatar—"Captain America," after the comic-book superhero who got his own movie in 2011. Unlike Harvey and Syndergaard, Wright inhabited "Captain America" modestly, preferring quiet leadership to preening. Ensuring Wright *could* remain a Met for the rest of his career did not silence demands Wilpon sell the team from a Mets' fanbase and much of the New York sports media incensed by his shedding the likes of Beltran, Reyes, and Dickey while doing nothing on the free-agent front to back up Wright since the Madoff scandal broke.

The Madoff affair finally behind them in 2015, the Mets engineered a dramatic turnaround by beating out the heavily favored Washington Nationals—division winners the year before, a whopping 17 games ahead of the second-place, 79-win Mets. This time the Mets did not blow a late September lead. Although they only won seven of their last 18 games, the 9½-game advantage they held in mid-September allowed them to coast to a final seven-game margin of victory.

Starring for the Mets were Matt Harvey, Jacob deGrom, and Noah Syndergaard. More promising futures were projected for them than had been for the much-hyped Pulsipher, Isringhausen, and Wilson two decades earlier before injuries ruined their careers. The Mets' new trio of aces were intimidating power-pitchers with an impressive array of pitches. But there were concerns about their durability. Harvey, in his third year, had missed the entire 2014 season after Tommy John surgery. DeGrom, in his second year after winning Rookie of the Year honors in 2013, had gone under the Tommy John knife soon after being selected by the Mets in the 2010 amateur draft. And the Mets kept a close watch on Syndergaard, whose big-league debut came in May, to ensure he did not throw out his arm. Consequently, all three were used judiciously to protect the valuable assets that were their right arms; none of the three completed any of their combined 83 starts. The Mets even had a fourth potentially imposing ace in the wings recovering from *his* Tommy John surgery—Zack Wheeler, the pitching prospect for whom the Mets traded Beltran to the Giants in July 2011.

As good as their starting pitching was, the Mets' offense left much to be desired. At the trade deadline on the last day of July, the Mets were just three games over .500 and trailed the Nationals by two games in the standings, mostly because they had scored the fewest runs of any team in the majors. They traded on that day for outfielder Yoenis Cespedes, having the best year of his career with 18 home runs, 51 RBIs, and a .293 batting average in 102 games for Detroit. Cespedes smacked 17 more homers and drove in 45 runs in the 57 games he played after joining the Mets. His new team won 36 of them and had the division well in hand by the end of August. Cespedes's impact was such there was even talk of him being voted the league's MVP despite playing only two months in the National League.

DeGrom and Harvey claimed all three wins in the Mets' five-game triumph over Los Angeles in their division series. And Harvey, Syndergaard, and deGrom won their starts in the 90-win Mets' four-game NLCS sweep of an imposing 97-win Chicago Cubs team looking to end a 107-year drought when it came to winning a World Series. But it was second baseman Daniel Murphy who dominated the headlines in the two series. Now in his seventh year with the Mets, Murphy was at best a competent role-player with a propensity for hitting doubles, not home runs. In 499 at-bats over 130 games during the 2015 season, Murphy had hit a career-high 14 homers, giving him a total of 62 in his career. But in nine postseason games against LA and Chicago, Murphy whacked 7 homers and drove in 11 runs. Against the Dodgers, Murphy hit two off left-handed ace Clayton Kershaw—the best pitcher in baseball—and a third off right-handed ace Zack Greinke that broke a 2–2 tie in the sixth and provided the one-run difference in winning Game Five. And against the Cubs, Murphy hit home runs in each of the four games to power the Mets into the World Series. There, they ran into Kansas City's Royals.

Beginning with the first game in Kansas City, the 2015 World Series did not go well for New York. Just as closer Armando Benitez failed to protect a one-run lead in the ninth inning of the opening game in the 2000 World Series against the Yankees, which the Mets lost in 12 innings, so

Mets closer Jeurys Familia, with 43 saves and 86 strikeouts in 78 innings during the season, failed to protect a one-run lead in the 9th inning of the series opener, which the Mets lost in the 14th inning. The same as in the 2000 World Series, the Mets lost in five games and their only victory came in Game Three in their home park. The fifth game was a particularly hard-to-swallow loss. Harvey and Familia could not hold a 2–0 lead in the 9th. The game went into extra innings. And after the Royals took a 3–2 lead with one out in the 12th, an error by Murphy opened the flood gates for six more runs before the inning mercifully ended. For Daniel Murphy, it was a bitter ending to a World Series in which he had just three hits in 20 at-bats, none for extra bases, after his extraordinary power-hitting display in the first two rounds of the postseason. The Royals played so much better that even a superhero couldn't save the Mets.

Fifty years before, in Game Five of the 1965 World Series, tied at two games apiece, Sandy Koufax pitched a four-hit complete-game shutout against the Minnesota Twins. No thought was given to him coming out of the game, no matter that the Dodgers had a comfortable 5–0 lead in the fifth and led 7–0 after seven. Three days later, Koufax surrendered just three hits in another complete-game shutout to win Game Seven and the World Series. This time the lead was just two runs, but despite pitching in near-exhaustion on two days' rest, manager Walt Alston gave no thought to bringing in Dodgers relief ace Ron Perranoski. But that was a different time. Top-tier starting pitchers were expected to finish what they started. By 2015, closers dominated the endgame, especially in endgames that are close, like 2–0, in the last inning.

That was the score when "the Dark Knight"—Matt Harvey—confronted manager Terry Collins in the dugout after eight superlative innings with an emphatic "No way!" after being told he had pitched brilliantly and Familia would close the game, just as he had done all year. Harvey had not completed a game all year. He had just one complete game in 65 major-league starts—a shutout in 2013. But there had been much controversy over his innings limit in his first year back from Tommy John surgery, just as there had been for Washington ace Stephen Strasburg three years before. Strasburg's 15–6 record helped the Nationals to the best record in baseball in 2012, but he was benched for the entire postseason because of an innings limit that had been decided upon before the season began. The Washington Nationals lost their division

series in five games, leaving many to complain they would have won—
and possibly gone all the way to the World Series—had the Nats relented
and allowed Strasburg to pitch, even if just one start in each series.

The controversy of Harvey's innings limits put him in the middle
between his agent, Scott Boras (also Strasburg's agent), who was ada-
mant about them, and the Mets' front office, which believed some flexibility was in order with a pennant at stake. Harvey's awkwardness in
addressing the issue during the summer came across as his being more
concerned about himself than his team, attributes hardly becoming of the
Dark Knight supposed to sweep away the Mets' baseball enemies. And so
there was "no way!"—possibly with an expletive for emphasis—Matt
Harvey wanted out of that game—no matter his surgically repaired arm,
no matter that he had thrown more than 100 pitches in the game, and no
matter that Familia was warmed up and ready to close out the Royals so
the Mets could get on their plane back to Kansas City.

With a slim lead in a game his team could not lose, it was time for
"Commissioner" Collins to tell his Dark Knight, Gotham City is enor-
mously grateful for your having drained the lifeblood from those Royal
jokers; they are not yet dead and buried, but Officer Familia can finish the
job, and besides, we may need to send out the bat-signal for you to save
the day on Wednesday—the day of the Final (Game Seven) Judgment—
to permanently vanquish these guys. Instead of being enamored of the
possibility to do his best Madison Bumgarner imitation in a seventh
game, which surely the Royals would not have wanted to see for a second
year in a row after being stymied by MadBum *out of the bullpen* over the
final five innings of Game Seven in the 2014 World Series, Harvey
insisted on finishing the job himself. Against his better judgment—"I let
my heart get in the way of my gut," his manager said afterward—"Commissioner" Collins yielded to the Dark Knight. Yielding to the macho
posturing of his ace rather than putting the priority of winning first,
Collins's decision to send Harvey back out to finish the game cost the
Mets the game . . . and the World Series.

Perhaps Collins, the Mets, and their fans should have considered
whether they bought too much into the Batman superhero persona that
Matt Harvey embraced and brought to the mound. They could now only
hope that the Dark Knight would survive the ugliness of his ninth inning
meltdown, that putting his Tommy John arm at risk didn't compromise
his future, and that he wouldn't be haunted by what happened. All that is

exactly what happened. It was clear from the beginning of the next season that Harvey was having trouble finding a consistent rhythm to his delivery, that he lacked command of his pitches, that his stuff was not so explosive. By mid-July he was out for the rest of 2016 with shoulder surgery. Harvey struggled to be effective upon his return the next year and was back under the knife in June for yet another shoulder surgery.

Meanwhile, the hardly humbled Dark Knight alienated team officials, teammates, and fans by serial episodes of violating team rules, including bogus reasons for why he didn't show up for a game. After having made just 35 starts in 2016 and 2017 with a 9–17 record and an unsightly 5.78 earned run average, Harvey pitched badly at the beginning of the 2018 season, violated more team rules, protested being sent to the bullpen, then refused a minor-league assignment to rediscover his talent, and finally was traded to Cincinnati. By 2019 his career was on life support.

With Harvey first pitching poorly and then sidelined in 2016, the Mets were unable to defend their division title against a superior Washington team, whose own strong rotation was headlined by Max Scherzer and Strasburg. And the Nationals also now had Daniel Murphy, who took his newfound hitting prowess from Queens to DC as a free agent. DeGrom was hampered by a bad elbow that limited him to 24 starts and just seven wins before requiring surgery near the end of the season; but Syndergaard had his breakout year with a 14–9 record, 2.60 ERA, and 10.7 K's per nine innings; and the endearing, rotund, 43-year-old Bartolo Colon led the team in wins with 15. The Mets claimed one of the NL's two wild cards but lost the wild-card game to San Francisco when Familia had another postseason meltdown, surrendering a three-run ninth-inning homer that broke up a scoreless game.

Perhaps Noah Syndergaard, like Matt Harvey, paid a price for embracing his superhero "Thor" avatar. Syndergaard certainly looked the part— tall, physically imposing, impressive hair—and already possessed a 100-mile fastball but decided nonetheless to spend the winter lifting weights so he would return to the mound in 2017 even stronger. He started the season allowing just two earned runs in 19 innings in his first three starts; was hardly Thor-like in his fourth start as he began experiencing some soreness in his biceps and shoulder; had his next start pushed back because of bicep discomfort; refused an MRI scan to determine if there was a problem that might need rehabilitation or surgical repair; was then torched by the Nationals for five runs in an inning and a third before leaving the game with considerable pain in his right side; and, it turned out, tore a muscle that cost him the rest of the season. The Mets' general manager raised the prospect that Syndergaard was trying "to show us he was fine" by throwing as hard as he could in the wake of questions about his ailing bicep, perhaps compensating in a way that resulted in his injury. Thor returned in 2018 to go 13–4 in 25 starts.

The Syndergaard episode was just the latest in a series of injuries in recent years that took a devastating toll on Mets players. When Thor went on the injured list in early 2017, Yoenis Cespedes was already there with a chronically bad hamstring—an injury that also cost him time in 2016 and would limit him to just 81 games in 2017 and 31 in 2018. Cespedes did not play at all in 2019 after breaking his foot stepping into a hole on his ranch while preparing for a hoped-for mid-summer return from previous surgeries. David Wright had not played since May 2016, his career prematurely ended by a degenerative bad back. While Wright's condition was likely congenital, about which there was little the team could have done, the rash of injuries to Cespedes and other Mets raised questions about the competency of the team's medical and training staff. That included not only shrugging off Syndergaard's decision not to have an MRI instead of ordering him to do so, but also not advising and monitoring Thor's weight-lifting regimen in the off-season that may (or may not) have contributed to his lost 2017 season.

Unlike Harvey and Syndergaard, Jacob deGrom did not have a superhero avatar. After going 15–10 while averaging 10.7 strikeouts per nine innings in 2017, however, deGrom may have tempted Samson's biblical fate when he cut the long hair that whipped across his face as he threw to the plate for the 2018 season. It turned out that, unlike Samson, whose prodigious strength was sapped when his locks were surreptitiously shorn, deGrom in 2018 had one of the best seasons ever by a pitcher. Although his win–lose record was an unimpressive 10–9, deGrom earned 29 of 30 first-place votes to win the Cy Young Award. He led the majors with a 1.70 earned run average, whiffed 269 batters in 217 innings, and walked only 46 while giving up just 152 hits. From April 16 until the end of the season, deGrom never gave up more than three runs in any of his 28 starts. In 17 of those starts he allowed one run or less, but because of poor run support he won only six of those games.

DeGrom's consecutive streak of games allowing no more than three runs reached 30 before coming to an end in his third start of the 2019 season. Struggling with his command, his earned run average zoomed to 4.85 after five starts in April. He didn't get his ERA below 3.00 until his 21st start in late July. But over the final three months, deGrom was back to the Jacob deGrom of 2018. In his 15 starts from the beginning of July to the end of the season, he gave up just 62 hits and 22 walks in 101 innings while striking out 127 batters. His ERA was 1.51. Once again, his 11–8 record was unimpressive for a would-be Cy Young candidate. For the second year in a row, he claimed the award with 29 of 30 first-place votes.

As for the 2019 Mets, they were effectively out of contention by the end of June. They finished third with a creditable 86 wins, 11 games out in their division and three games short of the second wild card. While their starters' ERA was fourth in the league, the Mets were betrayed by their bullpen's horrific 4.99 earned run average and 27 blown saves in 65 save opportunities. Most egregious was the meltdown of their newly acquired closer, Edwin Diaz, whose 57 saves for the Mariners the previous year led the majors. Diaz maintained his previous year's strikeout ratio of more than 15 per nine innings but gave up 15 home runs, compared to only 5 the year before, which contributed to his ERA ballooning from 1.96 his last year in Seattle to 5.59 in his first year in New York. The Mets, however, did showcase a new star—first baseman Pete Alonso, whose 53 home runs set a new rookie record.

# IV

# Paradigm Shifts

# 16

# CUBS' CLIMATE CHANGE IN CHICAGO; DROUGHTS CONTINUE ELSEWHERE

The 2016 World Series was destined to be a classic . . . if for no other reason than the two franchises that had gone the longest without winning baseball's ultimate championship faced off against each other . . . and one of them was the Chicago Cubs. The Cubs, famously and with a certain celebrity attached to the fact, had not won a World Series since 1908. Although they had played in seven since, equally famously the Cubs had not even been to one since 1945. The other team, the Cleveland Indians, had been to the World Series as recently as both 1995 and 1997 but had not won since 1948. That was only the second time in franchise history Cleveland played in the Fall Classic—they also won in 1920—and they would play in another in 1954, only to be swept by Willie Mays and the Giants, before going the next 41 years without even a division title to call their own.

The last time Cleveland came close to making the World Series was 2007, exactly halfway between their losing the ALCS in 1998 and winning the ALCS in 2016. Lefty ace CC Sabathia went 19–7, led the majors in innings pitched, and won the Cy Young Award. Right-hander Roberto Hernandez, then playing under the name Fausto Carmona, was 19–8 in his second big-league season. The Indians' key position players were center fielder and leadoff batter Grady Sizemore, switch-hitting catcher Victor Martinez, veteran DH Travis Hafner, and shortstop Jhonny (actual spelling) Peralta. The 2007 Indians beat the wild-card Yankees in their division series with an assist from midges invading the playing field in

Cleveland during the 8th inning of the second game, New York leading 1–0, which so distracted young Yankees phenom Joba Chamberlain, pitching in just his 20th major-league game, that he threw a wild pitch allowing the tying run to score in a game the Indians finally won in the 11th. In the ALCS, Cleveland defaulted on a three-games-to-one lead against Boston, managed by Terry Francona.

In 2013, Francona came to manage in Cleveland. The Indians had lost 94 the previous year and had not had a winning record since losing the 2007 ALCS. Sabathia was long gone, traded in July 2008 before Cleveland would have lost him to free agency. Also long gone was Cliff Lee, whose 22–3 record in 2008 earned him a Cy Young Award, traded in July 2009, a year before he would have been on the free-agent market. (Ironically, Cleveland's two former star lefties were on opposing sides—Sabathia with the Yankees, Lee with the Phillies—in the 2009 World Series.) Gone, too, was Sizemore, his career derailed by a series of injuries since 2009.

And the Detroit Tigers were the best team in the American League's Central Division, in the middle of winning four straight division titles from 2011 to 2014. Corner-infielder and hitter extraordinaire Miguel Cabrera, a rising star when acquired in 2008 from the Florida Marlins, became a superstar in Detroit. Cabrera won three straight batting titles from 2011 to 2013. In 2012, he won the Triple Crown—the first player to do that since Carl Yastrzemski in 1967—and the first of two consecutive MVP awards. The Tigers also capitalized on having a pair of right-handed aces—Justin Verlander, whose league-best 24–5 record and 2.40 earned run average in 2011 earned him both the Cy Young and Most Valuable Player Awards, and Max Scherzer, who captured his first Cy Young Award in 2013 with a league-best 21–3 record. Verlander's best four-year stretch was 2009 to 2012, when he went 78–31 in 135 starts, and Scherzer's was 70–24 in 130 starts in Detroit's four division-winning seasons. Ironically, the only one of the four years the Tigers went to the World Series was 2012, when their 88–74 record was good enough to win the AL Central but only seventh-best in the American League. They got there by sweeping the team with the best record—the 95-win Yankees—in the ALCS. The World Series was over almost before people realized there was one being played; Detroit was shut out twice and scored just six runs in San Francisco's four-game sweep.

In his first year in Cleveland, Francona guided the Indians to 92 wins, including a 10-game winning streak to end the season that secured home-field advantage in the wild-card game, which they lost to Tampa Bay. Falling back the next two years, Francona's Indians broke through as one of baseball's powerhouse teams in 2016, winning the division by a comfortable eight games over Detroit. Right-hander Corey Kluber, whose 18–9 record two years earlier made him a Cy Young winner, was 18–9 again. In addition to a strong starting rotation, Francona also had an exceptional bullpen—including closer Cody Allen and eighth-inning set-up man Bryan Shaw—that was made even stronger with the trade-deadline acquisition of hard-throwing lefty Andrew Miller from the Yankees. All three averaged more than a strikeout an inning. Jason Kipnis, in his sixth year, was a two-time All-Star at second base, and on the left side of the infield, the Indians had a pair of sensational young players in short-stop Francisco Lindor and third baseman Jose Ramirez, both switch-hitters.

Cleveland swept through their division and league championship series before meeting the Cubs in the World Series. Kluber for the first six innings, Miller for two, and Allen combined to shut out the Cubs in the opening game. Terry Francona, whose Red Sox had swept the Cardinals in 2004 and the Rockies in 2007, had now won the first nine games he managed in World Series play. Before Francona, the record for most consecutive wins by a manager to start his World Series résumé was four . . . by just four managers, none of whom ever managed in another World Series after the series they swept. Francona's undefeated World Series streak ended at nine when Chicago won the second game, but winning Games Three—by 1–0, with Miller, Shaw, and Allen pitching the last 4⅓ innings—and Four put the Indians one game away from their first World Series victory since 1948.

Still smarting from *how* they lost what seemed like a certain trip to the World Series in the 2003 NLCS, the Cubs turned to Theo Epstein as their new president of baseball operations in 2012 to put an end to their longer-than-a-century championship drought. Epstein, after all, had done precisely that with baseball's other historically star-crossed franchise, the Boston Red Sox, whose 86-year championship drought ended in just his second year as general manager. It would take longer in Chicago because the Cubs—having finished last in the NL Central in 2010 and 2011—

were in need of a wholesale makeover, whereas the Red Sox when Epstein took charge in 2002 were already a strong ballclub, just one that kept running into the Yankees' roadblock.

Epstein's strategy was to *not* worry about winning now. It was to deliberately accept being one of the worst teams in baseball in the near term for positioning in baseball's annual amateur draft to build for a competitive future. It was called "tanking." Perhaps a better term comes from chess—"sandbagging," defined as playing poorly to win more prize money (in baseball, a higher draft pick) in a lower-level tournament. The Cubs finished last each of Epstein's first three years as their commander-in-chief. Meanwhile, Epstein was counting on top-rated prospects being groomed in the Cubs' farm system to be the nuclear core of a championship-caliber team. They included not just Cubs' first-round picks like middle-infielder Javier Baez, third baseman Kris Bryant, catcher Kyle Schwarber, and outfielder Albert Almora, and international amateur free agents like middle-infielder Gleyber Torres, but also other teams' top prospects for whom Epstein traded—first baseman Anthony Rizzo from San Diego and shortstop Addison Russell, himself a first-round pick, from Oakland. The 22-year-old Rizzo, whom Epstein had originally drafted for Boston, was promoted to Wrigley in June 2012.

Despite the Cubs having won only 41 percent of their games in the first three years of Theo Epstein's era, by 2015 he was ready to push for higher in the standings in their rebuilding process. Epstein signed Jon Lester, his lefty ace in Boston, as a free agent to improve a starting rotation that had the third-highest earned run average in the league. Bryant and Russell were destined to be promoted to Chicago in April 2015—as opposed to opening day, a legerdemain for the purpose of delaying their eligibility for free agency by a year. But Epstein's most consequential move was to lure Joe Maddon from Tampa Bay to manage in Chicago. Maddon had become a cult figure of sorts as manager of the Rays for his success in turning them into a competitive ballclub on a limited budget, including by using data analytics to help inform his decisions, most notably in his team's infield shifts on any batter with a tendency to hit the ball a particular direction.

The payoff was the Cubs unexpectedly becoming not only an overnight sensation in making the postseason in 2015 but one of the majors' most dominant teams. A year after losing 89 games for the third-worst record in the National League, the Cubs' 97 wins in 2015 gave them the third-best record in the majors—all three of those teams in the NL's Central Division. Rizzo was the Cubs' best position player, leading the team in home runs, runs batted in, batting average, and on-base and slugging percentages; Bryant, right behind him in all those statistical categories, was Rookie of the Year; and right-hander Jake Arrieta, a *formerly* struggling pitcher for whom Epstein traded in 2013, was 22–6 with a 1.77 ERA to win the Cy Young Award. Arrieta ended the season with 11 straight wins, which he followed up by pitching a five-hit shutout to beat Pittsburgh's NL Central second-place, 98-win Pirates in the wild-card game. The Cubs followed up by sweeping St. Louis's 100-win Cardinals, first in the NL Central, in their division series. Being swept in turn by New York's Mets in the NLCS made it now 70 years since the Cubs played in a World Series.

Epstein's next off-season moves were to clear that hurdle. He signed the versatile Ben Zobrist, outfielder Jason Heyward, and right-hander John Lackey as free agents. Zobrist was perhaps Maddon's most indispensable player in Tampa Bay, and Heyward and Lackey were the Cardinals' two best players the previous year. Javier Baez, most of whose 2015 season was in the minors, was in Chicago to stay in 2016. Their first loss in 2016, after winning their first three games, was the only day of the season the Cubs were not in first place. Bryant, proving his defensive versatility by starting 31 games in left field in addition to playing third base, was the National League MVP. Baez was impressive playing all over the infield. Led by Lester (19–5) and Arrieta (18–8), the Cubs had by far the best starting pitching in baseball.

If the dominating Cubs had any weakness, it was the bullpen. Epstein addressed that in July by trading for Yankees closer Aroldis Chapman and his 100 miles an hour on any given pitch. Never mind that Chapman would be a free agent likely to leave once the season was over, Epstein was willing to part with Gleyber Torres, the Cubs' most prized minor-league prospect, to get him. Chapman averaging 15.7 strikeouts per nine innings as a closer since 2012 was reason enough for Epstein to sacrifice a top-five prospect because he assessed 2016 was Chicago's best chance of winning a World Series for the first time since 1908. It was a gamble that paid off. Chicago ended with 103 wins, eight more than any other team in either league. They won their division series. They won the NLCS. But after Cleveland's Game Four victory in the World Series, the Cubs had to win all three remaining games if they were to finally end their 108-year championship drought. Lester won Game Five at Wrigley, with Chapman getting a 42-pitch, 2⅔-innings save. Back in Cleveland, Arrieta beat the Indians in Game Six, 9–3.

The final game, played in Cleveland, was one for the ages. Chapman had blown a 6–3 Cubs lead after Maddon brought him in to save the game with two outs in the 8th and a runner on base by giving up a double and a two-run home run that tied the score. It was still 6–6 after 9 innings when the eternals on baseball's Mount Olympus intervened with a timely 17-minute rain delay. The Cubs retreated to their clubhouse. Heyward called a players-only meeting to rally his tired teammates. It worked. A single, a walk, and Zobrist's double in the 10th gave the Cubs a lead. A single by catcher Miguel Montero made it a two-run lead. That proved necessary when Cleveland scored with two outs in the bottom of the inning. Mike Montgomery, hardly a Cub with name recognition for whom Epstein traded a few days before his deal for Chapman, came in to get the final out. It may not have been at Wrigley Field, but Chicago's Cubs were World Series champions.

Both the Cubs and Indians were thought likely to be the teams to beat in their divisions for the rest of the decade. Both won their divisions handily in 2017. The Cubs had a dramatic come-from-behind victory in Game Five to beat Washington in their division series, scoring four times off Nationals' ace Max Scherzer, brought in as a reliever to protect a one-run lead in the fifth, after he retired Bryant and Rizzo—Chicago's two most dangerous hitters—to start the inning, but lost to Los Angeles in the NLCS in five games. The Indians, notwithstanding their league-leading 102 wins, including an AL record-setting 22-game winning streak from late August to mid-September, did not make it out of their division series. In Chicago, Chapman had indeed left as a free agent. To replace him, Epstein traded outfielder Jorge Soler, a top prospect, to the Royals for their closer, Wade Davis. In July he traded another top prospect, outfielder Eloy Jimenez, to the White Sox for lefty Jose Quintana to bolster a weaker-than-expected starting rotation. In Cleveland, Corey Kluber won his second Cy Young Award in four years with an 18–4 record, a league-leading 2.25 ERA, and a career-high 11.7 K's per nine innings. Shortstop Francisco Lindor and third baseman Jose Ramirez were the best at their positions in the American League.

Cleveland dominated the AL Central again in 2018. Kluber was a 20-game winner for the first time. In Chicago, Epstein traded with Texas for veteran southpaw Cole Hamels in July to strengthen a pitching staff undermined by a season-ending injury to expensive free-agent pickup Yu Darvish. The Cubs ended the season schedule tied for first in the NL Central with Milwaukee, both with a league-leading 95 wins, then lost to the Brewers in a playoff game to determine the division winner and had to settle for a wild card. Neither team went far in the postseason. Chicago lost the wild-card game, 2–1, in 13 innings to the Colorado Rockies. The Indians were swept in their division series.

Both Cleveland and Chicago were at a crossroads after unexpectedly *failing* to make the postseason in 2019. With 93 wins, the Indians were one of six teams to win 90 in the American League, but it was not enough to qualify for even a wild card. It didn't help that Kluber suffered a broken arm on a line drive back to the mound in only his seventh start of the season. With Lindor eligible for salary arbitration and Kluber a possible free agent after the 2020 season, Cleveland grappled with whether to trade them to rebuild for the future or try to return to the postseason in 2020. The Indians split the difference, signing Lindor to a one-year deal and trading Kluber.

The Cubs blew their chance at another division title or a wild card by losing 17 of their final 28 games. It didn't help that new closer Craig Kimbrel, signed as a free agent for three years and $33 million *in June* (because Kimbrel held out in hopes of a much better deal during the winter), pitched nothing like he had in his nine prior big-league seasons when he was arguably the best closer in baseball. While his strikeout ratio remained high at 13.1 per nine innings, Kimbrel lost four and had only 13 saves, and his ERA was 6.53 in 23 games. His career earned run average in 542 games coming into the season was 1.91.

Concerned even before the season that the Cubs didn't have "the same intensity, focus, hunger, ability to overcome adversity," Epstein warned that major changes might be in the offing if they regressed. The most prominent casualty of 2019's debacle was manager Joe Maddon being told his services were no longer required at Wrigley, notwithstanding his role in putting an end to the Cubs' 108 years of no championships. Although Kris Bryant and Anthony Rizzo, cornerstone players of their 2016 championship team, endured a winter of rumors that either or both would be traded elsewhere for a "bounty of prospects," Epstein made the calculated decision to try for another championship in 2020 with the core of players that changed the climate in Chicago in 2016.

On the south side of Chicago, the White Sox had their seventh-straight losing season in 2019. They had had just three winning seasons since winning the 2005 World Series—in 2008, when they won a playoff game 163 against the Twins to win the AL Central; 2010; and 2012. Left-hander Chris Sale was one of the best pitchers in baseball in the five years he was the White Sox ace from 2012 until being traded to the Red Sox for prospects in December 2016. The Chisox' best position players had been Cuban defectors Alexei Ramirez, their shortstop from 2008 to 2015, and first baseman Jose Abreu, the AL's 2014 Rookie of the Year. Abreu drove in more than 100 runs in five of his first six years in Chicago and likely would have in all six but for missing most of the final six weeks of the 2018 season.

But with an impressive group of young players—including shortstop Tim Anderson, whose .335 batting average led the league in 2019; left fielder Eloy Jimenez, whose 31 homers led AL rookies in 2019; third baseman Yoan Moncada, the star prospect they got in exchange for Sale; and right-hander Lucas Giolito, who nearly doubled his strikeout ratio from 6.5 per nine innings in 2018, his first full year in the starting rotation, to 11.5 in 2019—the White Sox had competitive aspirations for 2020. After three years in a row with the third-lowest player payroll in the American League, the White Sox went on a spending spree for top-flight veteran players, committing $178.5 million in salaries over four years to just three players—a contract extension for Abreu and free-agent deals for catcher Yasmani Grandal and lefty starter Dallas Keuchel. Signing the three veterans was a clear signal the White Sox intended to compete *now* with their young stars, and expand their window for winning, rather than grow them at the big-league level on a team mired in losing seasons. Compete now they did in 2020, only to lose seven of their last eight games after leading the AL Central by three games and having to settle for the first wild-card in the pandemic-shortened 60-game 2020 season.

The only team worse than the White Sox in 2019 was Detroit's Tigers, whose 114 losses put them in the conversation with the 119-loss 2003 Tigers as the worst team in franchise history. As Cleveland soared, Detroit's decline from four-straight division titles to mediocrity began in 2015 with Max Scherzer leaving as a free agent. The Tigers' fall from mediocrity to terrible was hastened by the huge eight-year, $248 million contract extension they gave Miguel Cabrera in 2016, followed by their decision the next year to drastically reduce player payroll and "tank" in anticipating of rebuilding for a more competitive future by the 2020s. By 2019 Detroit's player payroll was half of 2016, when theirs was one of the highest in the American League. After averaging 34 homers and 114 runs batted in with a .325 batting average his first nine years in Detroit from 2008 to 2016, Cabrera was no longer a force majeure. A string of injuries demolished his career. Justin Verlander was traded to Houston's runaway Astros in August 2017 as the Tigers were on their way to 98 losses and the worst record in the league.

The Texas Rangers, whose origins were as the 1961-expansion Washington Senators; the 1969-expansion San Diego Padres; the 1977-expansion Seattle Mariners; the 1993-expansion Colorado Rockies; and the 1998-expansion Tampa Bay Rays are the major leagues' only teams to have not won a World Series. After the Indians, currently at 72 years and counting since their 1948 championship, the Rangers have the current longest streak—59 years—of not winning a World Series, which they reached for the first time in 2010 and returned to in 2011.

After saying good-bye and good riddance in 2004 to Alex Rodriguez and the mind-boggling 10-year, $252 million contract they gave him three years earlier that resulted in three-straight last-place endings, the Rangers began systematically building toward a competitive ballclub that would win four division titles and a wild card in seven years between 2010 and 2016. The foundation for their future rested on a trio of home-grown stars—power-hitting first baseman Mark Teixeira, whose 43 homers and 144 RBIs in 2005 elevated him to the ranks of an elite player; second baseman Ian Kinsler; and versatile middle-infielder Michael Young, who moved over from second to replace A-Rod at shortstop in 2004. Teixeira's contribution was to be traded in July 2007, less than two years from free agency and with the Rangers sitting in the basement of the AL West, for a trio of young minor-league prospects—shortstop Elvis Andrus, a defensive gem whose rookie season would be 2009; Neftali Feliz, the AL's 2010 Rookie of the Year when he saved 40 of the Rangers' 90 wins on the way to their first division title in 11 years; and southpaw Matt Harrison, a rookie in 2008 whose breakout 14–9 record in 2011 helped Texas stay atop the AL West. In December 2007 Texas traded for Cincinnati center fielder Josh Hamilton, despite the red flag of his three years of minor-league suspensions for recreational substance abuse. And in January 2011, the Rangers signed veteran free-agent third baseman Adrian Beltre.

Hamilton, when healthy, was a superstar. He led the league with 130 runs batted in and hit 32 homers in 2008—his first year in Texas—and was overwhelmingly voted the AL's Most Valuable Player in 2010 for his 32 homers, 100 RBIs, and major-league best .359 batting average that powered the Rangers to their division title. He then demolished the Yankees in the ALCS with 4 homers and 7 RBIs to propel the Rangers to their first-ever World Series. In 2011, it was Beltre's 18 homers, 48 RBIs, and .367 batting average in the final two months that helped the Rangers break open a tight division race on their way to a return to the Fall Classic. The 2011 Rangers had the advantage of their five principal starters—lefties Harrison, C. J. Wilson (16–7), and Derek Holland (16–5) and righties Colby Lewis (14–10) and Alexei Ogando (13–8)—starting all but five of their games that year.

Stunned after twice being one out away in Game Six from winning the 2011 World Series—in the bottom of the 9th and the bottom of the 10th in St. Louis—only to lose both leads and the game, and then the series in seven games, the Rangers purchased the rights to sign hard-throwing Japanese ace Yu Darvish to help get them a championship. His five previous seasons in Japanese baseball, Darvish had a 76–28 record and 1.72 ERA. He went 16–9 in his "rookie" season, Harrison won 18, Hamilton smashed 43 homers and drove in 128, Beltre hit .321 with 36 home runs, but the Rangers had to settle for a wild card after leading the AL West every day from the fourth game of the 2012 season until losing game 162—and the division title—to Oakland. And then they lost the wild-card game.

The Rangers were not back in the postseason again until winning division titles in 2015 and 2016; then they fell back into rebuilding mode. Hamilton left as a free agent in 2013. Darvish missed the entire 2015 season with Tommy John surgery and was traded to the World Series–bound Dodgers in July 2017 as the long-since-out-of-contention Rangers were intent on dramatically reducing a player payroll that was the highest in the majors. Beltre retired after the 2018 season, his Hall of Fame credentials—including 3,166 careers hits, 477 homers, and exceptional defense at the hot corner—burnished by his eight years in Texas.

San Diego has had just three winning seasons since winning the NL West in Bruce Bochy's last year as manager in 2006. Until the pandemic-shortened 60-game 2020 season, the Padres' closest return to the postseason came the very next year under new manager Bud Black. Forced to play a game 163 against the Colorado Rockies for second place in the division and the wild card, their playoff was tied at 6–6 after 9 innings; the Padres scored twice in the top of the 13th to take the lead; and the Rockies scored three times in the bottom of the inning off Hall of Fame closer Trevor Hoffman to win the game. Padres ace Jake Peavy led the league with 19 wins and a 2.54 ERA and won the Cy Young Award. First baseman Adrian Gonzalez had the first of four 30-homer seasons in a row as the cornerstone slugger of the San Diego Padres.

In 2010, the Padres made another run at the postseason, leading their division for most of the summer into mid-September. They held a half-game division lead over the Giants and were also a half-game ahead in the wild-card race after 154 games, then lost five of their last eight to fumble both postseason options. Peavy was traded in 2009; Hoffman retired at the end of the season, his 601 career saves the most until Mariano Rivera passed him in 2013; and the Padres have had difficulty putting together a quality pitching staff. Gonzalez, two years away from free agency, was traded to Boston in 2011 for top-prospect Anthony Rizzo, who was in turn traded to the Cubs in 2012.

It wasn't until the end of the decade, in anticipation of the 2019 major-league debut of 20-year-old shortstop Fernando Tatis Jr., a top-10 prospect, that the Padres began a serious bid to become competitive in a division dominated by the Los Angeles Dodgers. Looking to a more glorious future, they gave third baseman Manny Machado—the best position player in the free-agent class of 2019—a contract for 10 years and $300 million that was, until a few days later, the most lucrative ever given a free agent. Tatis had an outstanding rookie year in 2019 before his season came to an end in August with a back injury. Machado did not play up to expectations his first year in San Diego, and the Padres suffered through a fourth-straight 90-loss season. Machado and Tatis were their two best players in 2020 when the Padres finished six games behind the Dodgers in the NL West, but with the second-best record in the National League.

Seattle's Mariners are the only one of Major League Baseball's 30 franchises to have never played in a World Series. They are also the team with the longest current postseason drought. Seattle has not been back since winning 116 games in 2001. The Mariners have not had back-to-back winning seasons since 2000 to 2003. The occasional years since then when there were bursts of optimism the Mariners were ready to contend again in the AL West all turned out to be disappointments, followed by losing seasons.

Ichiro Suzuki, the Mariners' best and most popular player since Ken Griffey Jr., was traded to the Yankees in 2012, less than 500 hits short of the major-league milestone of 3,000 hits. Counting his nine years in Japan, Suzuki already had 3,811 hits in his two-country big-league career. Seattle's next big star was Felix Hernandez, one of baseball's best and most durable pitchers from 2006 to 2015. Never starting fewer than 30 games in that 10-year stretch, "King Felix" led the league with a 19–5 record in 2009 and in earned run average in 2010 and 2014. His Cy Young Award in 2010, despite his middling 13–12 record for a team that lost 101 games, was noteworthy for being a triumph for the acceptance of player-value metrics; his 7.2 pitching wins above replacement was by far the best in the American League.

Raiding the Yankees to sign free-agent second baseman Robinson Cano, whose nine years in pinstripes had put him on a plausible fast track to Cooperstown, to a 10-year, $240 million deal in 2014 was seen as a Mariners' commitment to reverse their fortunes following four-straight losing seasons averaging 94 losses. It didn't work out that way. After three winning seasons in five years, the remaining $120 million on his contract was too much for the Mariners to handle, and Seattle traded him back to New York—to the Mets. It didn't help Cano's cause that he missed half of Seattle's 89-win 2018 season suspended for testing positive for steroids. Ichiro came back to Seattle to end his career in 2018, finishing with 3,089 major-league hits.

# 17

# HOUSTON'S CHEATSKATES

## A Dynasty's Self-Inflicted Wound

Following in the Cubs' 2016 championship footsteps validating the strategy of "tanking," where deliberately enduring losing seasons was a winning proposition over the longer term, were the Houston Astros. Just four years after losing 111 games—their third consecutive 100-loss season from 2011 to 2013—the Astros, whose National League Central Division affiliation was switched to the Western Division in the American League in 2013 (when Major League Baseball equalized both leagues at 15 teams), won 101 games and the AL West by a 21-game margin in 2017, took down the Yankees in the ALCS, then beat the Dodgers in seven games for the first World Series championship in franchise history. It was the first of three consecutive 100-win seasons, with escalating win totals of 103 in 2018 and 107 in 2019. Houston's was only the fifth team in major-league history to do that. It became impossible to set a record four-straight 100-win seasons in 2020 because the coronavirus pandemic limited the schedule to just 60 games.

Even more so than Chicago's Cubs, Houston's Astros became the model for building and sustaining a championship-caliber roster. The Astros leveraged their order-of-selection positioning from being among the worst teams in baseball to sign some of the best prospects in the first round of Major League Baseball's annual June draft: outfielder George Springer in 2011; shortstop Carlos Correa, the number one pick overall, in 2012; right-hander Lance McCullers Jr., selected later in the first round in 2012; third baseman Alex Bregman, chosen with the number two pick in 2015. By 2017 they had joined with 5-foot-6 Venezuelan-born second baseman Jose Altuve, signed as an international amateur free agent at the age of 17 in 2007, to anchor the nucleus of Houston's emergent dynasty. Altuve was the veteran, called up to the Astros in the midst of their 106-loss 2011 season. He quickly became an elite star, leading the league with at least 200 hits every year from 2014 to 2017, three times leading the league in batting average, and twice in stolen bases.

And like the Cubs, the Astros made astute trades to bolster their growing homegrown cadre of young stars on their major-league roster with other teams' undervalued players, including minor leaguers. Most notable among them were Marwin Gonzalez, whose ability to play virtually any infield or outfield position made him an indispensable multiposition regular on the 2017 and 2018 Astros, and outfielder Jake Marisnick, who became a valuable off-the-bench reserve in Houston's three-straight 100-win seasons. Following their disappointing third-place 2016 season after unexpectedly rising from 92 losses to 86 wins to win the second American League wild card in 2015, the Astros traded for 33-year-old catcher Brian McCann and signed free-agent outfielders Josh Reddick and about-to-turn-40 Carlos Beltran, whose extraordinary postseason exploits in the half-season he previously played for Houston in 2004 were still a vivid memory for Astros fans, to provide more veteran leadership. Used mostly as a DH, Beltran's would prove to be problematic leadership that came back to haunt Houston, calling into question the credibility of all that the 2017 Astros accomplished.

An 11-game winning streak gave Houston a decisive 14-game division lead by early June. Despite an unassailable 11½-game lead on August 31, the Astros went for the postseason jugular by trading prospects for Tigers ace Justin Verlander. Houston already had a strong starting rotation fronted by lefty Dallas Keuchel, whose victory over the Yankees in New York in the AL's 2015 wild card game earned him a place forever in Astros lore, but Verlander was a savvy veteran and an elite pitcher. Moreover, Keuchel's 5.35 earned run average in seven starts since returning from two months on the injured list in late July was a cause for concern. Verlander won all five of his September starts for the Astros with an outstanding 1.06 ERA.

After easily getting by Boston in their division series, with Verlander pitching 2⅔ innings of relief to get the win in the deciding fourth game, the Astros barely survived a scintillating ALCS against the Yankees. They won the first two games in Houston by identical 2–1 scores; lost the next three at Yankee Stadium, outscored by 19 to 5; and won the last two back home by 7–1 and 4–0 scores. Verlander pitched seven shutout innings to even the series in Game Six. But it was the tandem of veteran right-hander Charlie Morton, signed as a free agent before the season and 14–7 in his first year in Houston, and Lance McCullers Jr., 7–4 for the year in 22 starts at the bottom of the rotation, that returned the Astros to their first World Series since 2005. Morton shut out the Yankees on two hits through five innings in Game Seven, followed by McCullers finishing up with four sterling innings in which he allowed but one hit. Their roles were reversed in Game Seven of the World Series against the Dodgers in Los Angeles. McCullers pitched into the third inning; three other pitchers worked through the fifth, by which time the Astros led 5–0; and Morton pitched the last four innings to secure the World Series win.

Less than three months after winning the 2017 World Series, Houston traded for Pirates ace Gerrit Cole to join Verlander and Keuchel atop the rotation. The 2018 Astros had the best starting pitching in baseball. Their starters won two-thirds of their decisions, had the lowest ERA in the majors, and their 10.4 strikeouts per nine innings was the highest by any starting staff in history. Verlander was 16–9, Cole 15–5, Morton 15–3, Keuchel 13–12, and McCullers was 10–6. The 103-win Astros did not make it back to the World Series. After beating 108-win Boston in the first game of the ALCS, Houston lost the next four. Keuchel and Morton both became free agents after the season.

Except for the part about *not* winning the World Series, the Houston Astros were baseball's most dominant team in 2019. They won 107 games for the best record in the majors despite Altuve missing about a quarter and Correa more than half the season with injuries. They won their division by 10 games. Bregman solidified his superstar status by hitting 41 homers and driving in 112 runs. Springer belted 39 homers with 96 RBIs. And Verlander and Cole were virtually unbeatable and close to unhittable. They were the major leagues' only 20-game winners in 2019. Verlander, 21–6 with 300 strikeouts in 223 innings, narrowly beat out his teammate for the Cy Young Award. Cole, 20–5 and leading the league with a 2.50 ERA and 326 strikeouts (in 212⅓ innings), finished the season with 16 consecutive wins. As if Cole and Verlander's pitching dominance was not enough, and notwithstanding Houston having the second-most wins in the majors behind the Dodgers at the July 31 trade deadline, the Astros traded for Arizona Diamondbacks ace Zack Greinke, giving them three top-tier aces to throw at their postseason rivals. Greinke, 10–4 for the D-backs when he was traded, was 8–1 in 10 starts for the Astros.

The Astros' 2019 postseason was a struggle from the beginning. They beat Tampa Bay's wild-card Rays in the first two games *at home* (italics intended for reasons soon to be obvious) in their division series but lost the next two in Tampa Bay before returning to Houston to win the deciding fifth game. They took down the Yankees in six games in the ALCS on a bottom-of-the-ninth two-run homer by Altuve off elite closer Aroldis Chapman, *at home*. And then, in one of the most unusual World Series ever played—the first in which the *road team* won all seven games—the Astros fell *at home* to the Washington Nationals. Game Seven came unraveled with the Astros nursing a 2–0 lead into the seventh inning when Greinke gave up a home run and was relieved after walking a batter to put the tying run on base. In came Will Harris, who gave up just 10 earned runs in 68 relief appearances during the season, to pitch to Howie Kendrick. Five pitches later, Kendrick's two-run homer gave the Nationals a lead they would not relinquish.

Before losing to the Nationals in the opening game of the World Series, Gerrit Cole continued his mastery into the postseason by winning his first three starts—two in the division series and one in the ALCS—while allowing just one run in 22⅔ innings. Unofficially, because postseason games do not count toward regular-season records, Cole's 19 wins tied Rube Marquard for the most consecutive wins in a single year, although Marquard's 19-straight for the Giants in 1912, one of which was in relief, were all in the regular season.

Less than two weeks after the Astros lost the 2019 World Series, the legitimacy of their 2017 World Series championship was called into question by the revelation that Houston players that year, looking for every possible advantage, devised a system in their home ballpark to steal opposing catchers' signs and tip off Astros batters to the pitch using real-time, closed-circuit, high-definition television feeds. Former Houston starter Mike Fiers, whose 5.22 ERA in 28 starts in 2017 caused the Astros to leave him off the postseason roster and not re-sign him after the season, told *The Athletic* about the scheme. Fiers's revelation, which *The*

*Athletic* said was affirmed by three other sources, caused Major League Baseball to mount an investigation.

Even before *The Athletic* broke the story, there was a widespread perception among teams playing the Astros that they were nefariously stealing signs using advanced technology. Manager Bob Melvin of division rival Oakland said that playing in Minute Maid Park was "like you're going into the Pentagon or Langley." (Langley, Virginia, is the location of CIA headquarters.) Both the Yankees, whose 2019 World Series hopes came to a sudden end in Game Six in Houston when Altuve crushed his bottom-of-the-ninth, game-winning, two-run homer off Chapman to send the Astros to their second World Series in three years, and the Nationals, their World Series opponents, assumed the Astros were cheating and provided their pitchers and catchers with multiple sign sequences to protect against the possibility. While Fiers's revelation only concerned 2017, the Astros—had they not lost to Washington by dropping, ironically, all four games in Houston—would have had a second championship season tarnished, whether or not they actually cheated in 2019.

In January 2020, Commissioner Rob Manfred confirmed both the allegations and the particulars of the scheme. Astros players originated the video sign-stealing at the beginning of the 2017 season, relaying the information from the replay-review room to the dugout. "Approximately two months into the 2017 season," the investigation found, they progressed to a more direct approach by having an Astros player "bang a nearby trash can with a bat to communicate the upcoming pitch type to the batter." It was a Paul Revere–type signal—one bang if one kind of breaking ball or change-up, two bangs if another. If there was no bang, 'twas a fastball deciphered by the Astros. According to Manfred, "some Astros players" said "they did not believe the sign-stealing scheme was effective, and it was more distracting than useful to hitters"—an assertion the commissioner said could not be evaluated one way or the other.

Perhaps not, but the 2017 Astros dramatically improved in all facets of their offense compared to 2016. Except for home runs, Houston had been *below* the major-league average in all major statistical batting categories the previous year. The most telling improvement was in their batting-strikeout totals. In 2016 Houston batters struck out 1,452 times in 26 percent of their at-bats. The major-league average was 1,299 that year, and only three teams whiffed more often. In 2017, however, Houston batters struck out only 1,087 times—the fewest in the majors. That's 6.8 K's per nine innings when the major-league average was 8.3. Furthermore, Astros batters averaged a full strikeout less in home games than on the road—6.2 to 7.2—while the major-league per-game average was a much narrower 8 K's at home versus 8.5 on the road. After the banging scheme came into effect "approximately two months into the 2017 season," Astros batting strikeouts per game decreased at Minute Maid Park from 6.5 in the 30 home games they played in April and May to 6 in their remaining 51 games beginning in June. Carlos Correa, who admitted, "Yes, I used the trash cans," may have benefited the most from the scheme, based on his striking out in over a quarter of his at-bats in road games compared to only 17 percent of his at-bats in Houston.

The video-feed spying continued into the postseason, according to the commissioner's investigation. The first two games in their division series against the Red Sox were in Houston. The Astros scored 16 runs, 8 in each game, winning them both. They blasted four homers in the opener, two off Red Sox ace Chris Sale. Altuve hit three home runs in the game, something he had never done before, nor has he done since. In the ALCS against the Yankees, in which the home team won every game, 'twas a single by Altuve and a double by Correa (who earlier had hit a home run) off Aroldis Chapman that beat the Yankees, 2–1, in the bottom of the ninth of Game Two. Altuve, one of three Astros players Correa said "didn't use it [the trash can] at all," drove in three runs and hit a homer to beat the Yankees in a must-win Game Six in Houston to even the series and another the next day to help the Astros finish off the Yankees.

The 2017 World Series between the Dodgers, whose 104 wins gave them home-field advantage, and the Astros was a slugfest. The two teams combined for 25 home runs—15 by Houston, 8 of which were in the middle three games at Minute Maid Park. Game Five was a back-and-forth classic. Yuli Gurriel blasted a three-run homer off Dodgers ace Clayton Kershaw to tie the game at 4–4 in the 4th. After the Dodgers replied with a three-run homer of their own to take a 7–4 lead in the 5th, Altuve did the same in the bottom of the inning to tie the score again. LA went ahead, 8–7, in the top of the 7th, to which George Springer answered on the first pitch thrown by new reliever Brandon Morrow in the bottom of the inning with a game-tying home run—his fifth of the series, equaling the World Series record held by Reggie Jackson and Chase Utley. Alex Bregman followed with a single, Altuve doubled to give the

Astros the lead, and Correa homered to make the score 11–8. Brian McCann's homer in the 8th made it a 12–9 game, but the Dodgers tied the score at 12–12 in their half of the 9th. 'Twas Bregman's single off Dodgers closer Kenley Jansen in the bottom of the 10th with two runners on that won the game and sent the series back to Dodger Stadium with the Astros ahead, three games to two. After losing Game Six, Houston scored five times in the first two innings of Game Seven to finish off LA in the game and the series.

The commissioner refused to say in his report whether Houston's bang-the-can scheme helped the Astros win any games, including in the postseason. He did say the whole cheating enterprise was "player-driven." It was "a group of players, including Carlos Beltran," that devised the plan to "improve on decoding opposing teams' signs and communicating the signs to the batter," and Astros' bench coach Alex Cora who helped implement it by arranging "for a video room technician to install a monitor displaying the center field camera feed immediately outside of the Astros' dugout." Manfred concluded, however, that neither manager AJ Hinch nor general manager Jeff Luhnow authorized or approved of the scheme. Hinch was certainly aware and had twice sabotaged the monitor being used but did not tell them to stop. Luhnow was sent two e-mails about the scheme, but there was "no evidence to indicate" he was actually aware of it.

The only punishments the commissioner imposed were a large fine on the Astros, stripping them of a selection in the first two rounds of the upcoming amateur draft, and year-long suspensions for both Hinch and Luhnow as the responsible leaders who did nothing about it. Both were immediately fired by the Astros. So was Boston manager Cora, who had left Houston after the 2017 season to take over the Red Sox and led them to a World Series championship in 2018, and the Mets' new manager, Carlos Beltran, who never got to manage a game.

None of Houston's players, including Beltran, was fined or suspended by the commissioner or the Astros for their role. There was no punishment for them at all. But that did not mean they got off unscathed. When spring training got under way in February 2020, players from other teams turned harshly on the Astros. It was an unprecedented break from precedent about not speaking ill of their fellows in the players' fraternity, as might be expected in a sport that honored the precept that what happens in the clubhouse stays in the clubhouse. The 2017 Astros got no such benefit. Yankees outfielder Aaron Judge, runner-up to Altuve for the 2017 MVP Award, was one of the most outspoken in condemning what the Astros did. "You did not earn it," said Judge. "It wasn't earned playing the game right." The Yankees as a team, all four of their losses in the seven-game 2017 ALCS coming in Houston, were left to wonder whether the outcome would have been different had the Astros not cheated—perhaps especially in their 2–1 loss in Game Two that Houston won on Altuve's single and Correa's double off Chapman in the bottom of the ninth. And even though baseball's damning investigation was about 2017 and not 2019, the Yankees felt once again cheated out of a World Series by Houston.

The tragic irony of their tarnished legacy was that Houston's 2017–2019 Astros were in fact an outstanding team. Often accompanying greatness, however, is hubris. Besides outstanding pitching, especially the starters, the Astros had a potent offense. They not only hit for power but, in an era of record strikeouts, struck out by far the fewest of any major-league team. Although they may have been closer to the major-league average of batters striking out in 25 percent of their at-bats those three years than the 21 percent they actually did, the Astros would still have been substantially below the league average even without their sign-stealing scheme.

The Astros had established themselves as so dominant in the American League's Western Division that it did not seem possible for any other team to compete against them. They emerged from their competitive funk called "tanking" just when the Los Angeles Angels seemed poised to return to prominence following four desultory seasons since finishing first in the AL West five times in six years from 2004 to 2009. The Angels in 2014 won their division handily with 98 wins and the best record in baseball, only to be swept in their division series by Kansas City's wild-card Royals. Jered Weaver, their ace, was 18–9. Second baseman Howie Kendrick and shortstop Erick Aybar gave the Angels one of the best middle-infield pairings in baseball. The Angels had one aging superstar—first baseman Albert Pujols, in the third year of the 10-year, $240 million contract for which he left St. Louis in December 2011—and a phenomenal young superstar, name of Mike Trout. After batting .328 in his 11 years with the Cardinals, including six years in which he hit more than 40 homers, Pujols would never hit .300 as an Angel and reached 40 homers just once, in 2015. But Trout was already proving a super-talented, once-in-a-generation player on the order of Pujols in his Cardinals years or even Barry Bonds.

In retrospect, it seems unbelievable that 24 teams passed on Trout before he was selected by the Angels in the 2009 amateur draft. Hitting for power and average, with speed on the bases, and an excellent defensive center fielder besides, Mike Trout quickly became the best player in baseball. In his first eight major-league seasons from 2012 to 2019, Trout averaged nine wins above replacement—better than an MVP level of performance—winning three MVP awards and finishing second four times. The only year he was not in the MVP running was in 2017; a thumb injury limited him to just 114 games. Just before the start of the 2019 season, the Angels rewarded Trout with a 12-year contract extension worth $430 million intended to keep him in Anaheim through the 2031 season, when he'd turn 40. For the Angels, that was a bargain.

Trout's excellence aside, the *Los Angeles* (without the *"of Anaheim"*) Angels, whose name change in 2016 was their third in 30 years, have had just one winning season since finishing first in 2014. Mike Scioscia, the Angels manager since 2000, left after the 2018 season. But franchise owner Arturo Moreno was willing to spend big to build a winning team around Trout. In December 2015, Moreno took on the five years and $54 million remaining on Andrelton Simmons's contract when he traded Aybar to Atlanta to get the best all-around shortstop in baseball. In December 2019, Moreno gave free agent Anthony Rendon, arguably the best all-around third baseman in the game, $245 million to play in Anaheim for the next seven years. And to improve his team's most glaring weakness, Moreno also offered lucrative multiyear contracts to the best pitchers on the 2019 free-agent market, only to be outbid by the Yankees for Gerrit Cole and the Nationals for Stephen Strasburg.

The small-market Oakland Athletics, meanwhile, adhering to financial constraints that kept them among the teams with the lowest player payroll, had gone through a "tanking" of their own—three consecutive last-place endings in the AL West from 2015 to 2017—before emerging as a top-tier team in whose way stood only the Houston Astros. The A's quick drop from contention after winning 93 games and the division in 2006 prompted Moneyball architect Billy Beane to concede contending in the near term to build for the future by trading many of his best players for prospects over the next five years. While the A's did not finish any of those years with a winning record, they also were never close to being the worst team in the American League. Beane traded for or signed other teams' undervalued players, like 2009 free-agent outfielder Coco Crisp and 2011 free-agent 39-year-old right-hander Bartolo Colon, to keep his team from nosediving to the depths the Astros would soon go.

The payoff was back-to-back division titles in 2012 and 2013 as one of the lowest player-salaried teams in the majors and a wild card in 2014. Oakland's best players in their return to competitiveness included right-hander Sonny Gray and left-handed reliever Sean Doolittle, both A's selections in the amateur draft; third baseman Josh Donaldson, a minor-league prospect acquired from the Cubs who burst forth on the superstar track in 2013; and outfielder Yoenis Cespedes, signed by Oakland to a four-year, $36 million deal in 2012 after he defected from Cuba. The Cespedes deal seemed to go against Beane's Moneyball principles. So did Oakland's player payroll having soared from $69 million in 2013 to $89 million in their 2014 bid to "bust the bank" for a championship and Beane trading Cespedes in July 2014 to acquire Red Sox ace Jon Lester to boost the A's chances for a third-straight division title (they had to settle for a wild card) and to advance beyond the division series in the postseason (they didn't, losing the wild-card game). Failing on both counts, it was back to austerity for the Oakland A's. Donaldson was traded in 2015, and Gray and Doolittle during the 2017 season.

But with a new cadre of young stars in place—first baseman Matt Olson and third baseman Matt Chapman, both selected by the A's in the amateur draft; shortstop Marcus Semien and slugging DH Khris Davis, both picked up in trades *before* they began to shine brightly—Oakland surged from 75 wins in 2017 to 97 in 2018 and again in 2019 with one of the lowest payrolls in the majors. Both years they lost the wild-card game. Entering the 2020 season, the A's were poised to possibly threaten Houston's three-year dominance of the AL West, perhaps with the competitive incentive that their small-payroll team of outstanding players still affordable for Oakland could take on a would-be dynasty of outstanding players in Houston that nonetheless felt it was necessary to cheat to be even better than they were. The coronavirus pandemic held up the season for four months and limited it to 60 games, but when it was over, 'twas the A's on top by seven games over the second-place Astros, enduring their first losing season since 2014.

The A's winningest pitcher in 2019 (with a 15–4 record) and 2020 (6-3), all for the modest two-year, $14 million deal he signed before the season? Right-hander Mike Fiers. Yes, that Mike Fiers, formerly with Houston's 2017 "cheatskate" Astros.

# 18

# "WAIT 'TIL NEXT YEAR" COMES TO LA

Popular in the 1950s, *Wait 'Til Next Year*, set in Brooklyn, was about a baseball team playing in a classic ballpark located in Flatbush that turned 40 in 1952 and wasn't aging particularly well. Played out over multiple seasons, it was the story of an excellent team—arguably the best in baseball at the time—that somehow was always the underdog because of an inability to win a World Series. *Wait 'Til Next Year* had an ensemble cast that included Jackie Robinson as the first Black man to play in the whites-exclusive major leagues, forced to endure all manner of verbal and even physical (being spiked and thrown at) abuse without fighting back, just to hang in there so that "no Blacks allowed" would never again be an obstacle to anyone entering the inner sanctum of a major-league baseball clubhouse; Pee Wee Reese, as the Southern gent who graciously put his arm around Jackie when he was being booed in Cincinnati for being Black while playing baseball; Edwin Snider as the Duke of Flatbush, vying with the Mick in the Bronx and the Say Hey Kid in Manhattan for New York's finest in center field; along with Roy Campanella and Don Newcombe, Gil Hodges and Carl "the Reading Rifle" Furillo.

The villain of the tale was a ball-playing gang in a neighboring borough—the Bronx. They called themselves the Yankees, also went by the nom-de-guerre "Bronx Bombers." And every time Brooklyn's Boys of Summer played them in the World Series—1941, 1947, 1949, 1952, and 1953—well, the gang from the Bronx beat up the heroes of the tale, leaving them and their community of besotted admirers with nothing except to say at the end of every postseason fight, "Wait 'til next year." It was a plaintive refrain, "wait 'til next year," whether said in resigned optimism or optimistic resignation—until, in 1955, the script was flipped so that "next year" finally came.

Some 60 years later came a reboot. This time the setting was in the shadow of glitzy Hollywood in Los Angeles. It was about the descendants of the Brooklyn Boys of Summer, playing in a spruced-up aging classic-modern ballpark, half-a-century old. Played out over multiple seasons, it was the story of an excellent team—arguably the best in baseball at the time—that dominated its division year after year but had yet to win a World Series. Unlike *Wait 'Til Next Year* set in Brooklyn, the twist to this rendering was that they never assumed the mantle of an underdog. And it began as the spin-off of a Hollywood reality show involving all sorts of corrupt financial shenanigans, a marriage gone bad, and a custody battle for the team itself. It, too, had a stellar ensemble cast—Clayton Kershaw as the brilliant ace who somehow failed in the brightest of spotlights; Yasiel Puig as an enigmatic slugging Cuban defector shadowed by the criminal thugs who helped him get to LA; Justin Turner, as the under-achieving role player in New York who became a Hollywood star; Cody Bellinger, a late arrival to the cast, as the young phenom; and a host of versatile actors like Max Muncy and Chris Taylor capable of playing multiple roles.

We speak, of course, of the Los Angeles Dodgers. Winning World Series, historically, is the defining characteristic of great teams. The additional round of postseason series once division series were added to the equation in 1995 made navigating the road to get to the World Series, let alone win it, much more difficult. By regular-season measures, the Dodgers winning seven consecutive division titles from 2013 to 2019, averaging 96 wins a year, put them in the mix of dominant dynasties. But they were an echo of Atlanta's dynasty after the Braves were moved from the NL West to the NL East in 1994. From 1995 to 2005, the Braves won 11 straight division titles but made it to just three World Series—none since 1999. The upshot was that the Braves' accomplishments in their reign as the National League's dominant team seem somehow diminished. The same was happening to the always-first in the NL West 2013 to 2019 Dodgers, for whom "wait 'til next year" to play in a World Series didn't come until 2017, and "wait 'til next year" to win a World Series didn't happen in 2018 either.

When last we left the Dodgers, 'twas 2003 and they had been put up for sale by Fox Entertainment, which had bought the franchise six years earlier so that its ballgames would be the centerpiece of a new Los Angeles regional sports network the media conglomerate was establishing. Mission quickly accomplished, and not enamored with the baseball business—perhaps especially not after maintaining a player payroll at or near the top of National League teams every year failed to yield a single season where the Fox-owned Dodgers made it to the postseason, even as a wild card—Fox unloaded the club to Frank McCourt, a big-time real-estate developer in Boston whose ambitions to buy the Red Sox and build a new stadium to replace Fenway Park came to nothing. This sale of the Dodgers led to nearly a full decade of financial turmoil because it was a dodgy deal to begin with. For all his real-estate renown, McCourt financed his $430 million purchase of the Dodgers entirely with borrowed money, contributing nothing of whatever personal fortune he had. Some of that money was from Fox itself.

Thus began a Hollywood reality show that might have been called *The McCourts and Dodger Blue*. If Commissioner Selig had any misgivings about the sale when Major League Baseball gave its approval in January 2004—misgivings, if any, that were assuaged by Fox's huge contract with Major League Baseball to broadcast national games and the postseason—he ultimately couldn't be rid of McCourt fast enough. Or, more precisely, the McCourts—Frank and his wife, Jamie. He was the owner. She was the team president. They used their equity in the rapidly escalating value of the Los Angeles Dodgers to finance a lavish West Coast lifestyle. Their marriage went on the rocks. Divorce proceedings got ugly. He insisted the Dodgers were all his. She insisted half the value of the franchise belonged to her. One of baseball's iconic historical franchises was in the middle of a custody fight. A California court ruled in favor of Jamie.

By 2011, the Dodgers were on the verge of bankruptcy "caused by Mr. McCourt's excessive debt," Selig said in a statement, "and his diversion of club assets for his own personal needs." By January 2012, the Dodgers owed more than half a billion dollars to McCourt's creditors. Selig ordered the Dodgers be put up for sale. In March, the franchise was sold to an ownership group led by Guggenheim Partners, a global investment firm, that included the Los Angeles Lakers' maestro of "Showtime!" in the 1980s, Magic Johnson. The purchase price? An out-of-sight $2 billion.

The baseball team, meanwhile, persevered, even as its player payroll dropped into the middle ranks among the major leagues' 30 teams while the McCourts accumulated luxuries. But the Dodgers did not do badly. In the eight years McCourt was the franchise owner, they won three division titles and a wild card. But they didn't get to the World Series. In 2004 and 2006, LA was eliminated in their division series. In 2008 and 2009, both times winning the NL West with Joe Torre as their new manager, the Dodgers swept through the first round before meeting their comeuppance in five games each time at the hands of Philadelphia's Phillies in the league championship series. Including all 12 years he managed the Yankees, Torre had now tied Bobby Cox's record of 14 straight years managing his team into the postseason. That streak came to an end in 2010 when his Dodgers finished fourth.

The big story for the 2008 Dodgers was Manny Ramirez's extraordinary 53 games in August and September after Boston traded him to LA on the last day of July to finally be rid of Manny being Manny. About to become a free agent at the end of the year, Ramirez made a compelling case for himself by belting 17 homers, batting .396, and driving in 53 runs in his 53 games with the Dodgers. He went on to hit 4 more homers, drive in 10 runs, and bat .520 in LA's eight postseason games. Left field at Dodger Stadium, where most of his homers went, was dubbed "Mannywood." The Dodgers signed him to a two-year, $45 million contract as a free agent, which, now having to put up with Manny being Manny, they soon came to regret. Failing a test for performance-enhancing drugs during spring training in 2009 got him suspended for 50 games beginning in early May. Ramirez was having an outstanding season at the time, batting .348, helping the Dodgers get off to a 20–7 start that put them comfortably ahead in the NL West. Manny was not so spectacular in the 77 games he played after he returned without the benefits of steroids, batting just .269 with 13 homers. Various injuries limited his playing time in 2010, causing the Dodgers to put him on waivers in August. Manny Ramirez's career was all but over. He ended up with 555 career homers and a .312 lifetime batting average.

Torre came to LA in 2008 after being told by the Yankees he was no longer wanted. With the McCourt custody fight over the team becoming ugly, Torre retired as a manager after the 2010 season. Replacing Torre, ironically, given that 11 of the 18 World Series the Dodgers had played in were against the Yankees, was 1980s Yankees icon Don Mattingly. Serving as Torre's bench coach on the 2007 Yankees, Mattingly followed his manager to LA with the implicit understanding that he'd be in line to manage the Dodgers after Torre left. Although his Dodgers finished third in 2011—Mattingly's first year managing at any level—he kept his job after Guggenheim took over in 2012. On August 25, trailing the Giants by three games with 36 games left to play, the Dodgers made a blockbuster trade with the Red Sox for first baseman Adrian Gonzalez, outfielder Carl Crawford (who was injured at the time), and right-hander Josh Beckett— all top-tier players, in both ability and salary. Still, the Dodgers could not keep pace with the Giants.

It looked like Mattingly's days on the job were counting down quickly when the Dodgers got off to a bad start in 2013, particularly since Los Angeles had the highest player payroll—$254 million to the Yankees' $246.5 million—in major league baseball. His was a team of high-priced talent built to win—now! In addition to the nearly $57 million they were paying Gonzalez, Crawford, and Beckett, right fielder Matt Kemp was in the second year of the eight-year, $160 million contract the Dodgers gave him after his superb 2011 season leading the league with 39 homers and 126 runs batted in while batting .324, and Clayton Kershaw was in the second year of a two-year, $19 million contract the Dodgers had signed him to in order to avoid arbitration after he won the 2011 Cy Young Award with a 21–5 record while leading the league in earned run average and strikeouts. And the Dodgers' starting rotation was strengthened immeasurably by their signing free agent Zack Greinke, one of the best at his craft, to a six-year, $147 million deal over the winter.

On June 21, Mattingly's Dodgers were last in the NL West with a 30–42 record, 9½ games out of first place. Kemp, Crawford, Beckett, Greinke, and shortstop Hanley Ramirez—another of their high-priced stars—had all been hurt. With nearly half the season gone, the Dodgers seemed done. And then they went on a tear, winning 42 of their next 50 games to take command of the NL West by 8½ games on August 17—a swing of 17 games in the standings in less than two months. The Dodgers went on to win their division by 11 games, making up 20½ games in the standings from where they started on June 21. You had to go back 99 years to the 1914 Boston Braves to witness the only comeback of greater magnitude, last to first from such a deep hole. Not for nothing was that team called the "Miracle" Braves, coming from 15 games behind to win the National League pennant by 10½ games—a swing of 25½ games. Mattingly's team may have peaked too soon, however. Up by 13½ games with 138 down and 24 to go, LA was 9–15 the rest of the schedule to finish atop their division with only the fourth-best record in the National League. The Dodgers breezed through their division series and lost the NLCS.

The Dodgers made it two division titles in a row in 2014. Moving into first place in their 10th game of the year and never letting go on their way to an eight-game margin of victory, they made it three straight in 2015. In neither year did they make it to the NLCS. Kershaw and Greinke were brilliant both years. In 2014, Kershaw's major-league-leading 21–3 record and 1.77 earned run average earned him both his third Cy Young Award in four years and the MVP trophy. It was the fourth-straight year Kershaw led the league in ERA. Greinke's 19–3 record and 1.66 earned run average topped the league in 2015.

An untimely meltdown on defense in their 2015 division series against the Mets cost the Dodgers a chance for the World Series and Mattingly his job. Leading 2–1 in the fourth inning of the deciding fifth game with Greinke on the mound, the Dodgers went into an extreme infield overshift with third baseman Justin Turner moving into short right field when left-handed pull-hitting Lucas Duda came to bat with Daniel Murphy on first. Shortstop Corey Seager, called up in September and playing in just his 32nd big-league game, was playing close to second base, leaving virtually the entire left side of the infield defenseless. The shift itself was not the problem. What was, was the failure of Seager to make any move toward covering third after Duda drew a walk. Murphy jogged to second and, seeing no Dodger infielder anywhere in the reachable vicinity of third base, sprinted for third. By the time the Dodgers woke up to that, it was too late. Murphy scored the tying run from third on a sacrifice fly, and it was Murphy's sixth-inning home run off Greinke that won the game and forced the Dodgers to "wait 'til next year" again.

*That* was not popular programming in LA, especially since this was the Dodgers' third straight year of *not* making the World Series. Managing a team with a player payroll of $265 million that was $51 million more than the Yankees were paid and the largest by far in major league baseball, his players appearing to be asleep on the field in a win-or-go-home-for-the-winter game was not a good look for Mattingly. There were no hard feelings in his departure from the Dodgers.

Dave Roberts—the same whose fourth-game, ninth-inning stolen base off Mariano Rivera in the 2004 ALCS kicked off the Red Sox' unprecedented comeback in a postseason series—succeeded Mattingly in 2016. Of the three high-priced players LA had traded for from Boston, Josh Beckett and Carl Crawford were both gone, having contributed little to the Dodgers in large part because of injuries, and Adrian Gonzalez was not quite the impact player the Dodgers expected for the $85 million he was paid his first four years in LA. Matt Kemp, whose superstar career arc following his outstanding 2011 season never materialized because of injury, had been traded after the 2014 season. Opting out of his six-year contract to declare as a free agent following his superb 2015 season, also gone was Zack Greinke, the right-handed complement (as Don Drysdale was to Sandy Koufax in the 1960s) to lefty Clayton Kershaw.

Besides Gonzalez, LA's starting infield in 2016 included rookie shortstop Corey Seager and third baseman Justin Turner, signed as a free agent in 2014 after three underappreciated years in New York with the Mets. Both became high-impact players in Los Angeles. Yasiel Puig, the Cuban defector signed by the Dodgers to a seven-year, $42 million contract as an international amateur in June 2012 less than a month after he made his escape from Cuba on a speedboat that traversed 350 miles of open sea to get to Mexico, was equal parts exciting and exasperating. Making his big-league debut in June 2013, Puig had a stellar rookie season with 19 homers and a .319 batting average in 104 games while thrilling fans with no-bounce rifle-shot throws from the warning track to gun down baserunners and aggressive base running. But he was also an undisciplined player who antagonized opponents and teammates alike *and* who was the target of extortion attempts that included death threats from the Mexican drug cartel-affiliated thugs who smuggled him out of Cuba—and wanted to keep collecting on his major-league stardom.

Roberts's first year as manager was handicapped by Puig, for the second year in a row, missing considerable time because of hamstring injuries and Kershaw, for the second time in three years, being sidelined with back problems. While Puig was hardly as dynamic a player as in his first two years with the Dodgers, Kershaw was superb in the 21 starts he did make when healthy, with a 12–4 record, 1.69 ERA, and 172 strikeouts in 149 innings. The Dodgers overcame an eight-game deficit to San Francisco in late June to win their fourth-straight division title in 2016. In the Dodgers' division-series victory over Washington's Nationals, Kershaw came out of the bullpen to get the final two outs and the save in the bottom of the ninth of Game Five with two runners on and one out, just two days after he pitched 6⅔ innings in the fourth game. He followed up with seven superb innings to beat the Cubs 1-0 in his Game Two start in the NLCS, but lost Game Six to Chicago's destiny-bound team, giving up five runs in five innings, as the Dodgers failed yet again to make it to the World Series.

Chicago had gone 71 years without the north-side Cubs playing in the World Series. LA's Dodgers had now gone 28 years. That ended in 2017. The next three years they would be one of baseball's two most dominant teams, the other being Houston's Astros. Joining the high-priced (best-paid in the major leagues) cast in the LA reboot of *Wait 'Til Next Year* in 2017 were first baseman-outfielder Cody Bellinger and play-anywhere Chris Taylor and, in 2018, infielder Max Muncy. Bellinger quickly became a superstar: Rookie of the Year in 2017 on the back of his 39 home runs and Most Valuable Player in 2019, hitting 47 homers, driving in 115 runs, and batting .305. The versatility of Muncy, who also crushed 35 home runs in both 2018 and 2019, and Taylor allowed Roberts the flexibility to pinch-hit liberally for other starting position players knowing he could move either from one position to another in any game as circumstances dictated. Too much of a headache to handle and never quite attaining the level of performance the Dodgers expected, Puig was finally traded away in 2019.

Even with Greinke gone and Kershaw missing at least a month every year with persistent back problems, the Dodgers had by far the best pitching in the National League every year from 2017 to 2019. Left-hander Alex Wood was 16–3 in 25 starts in 2017. Korean right-hander Hyun-Jin Ryu's 2.32 earned run average was ahead of all major-league pitchers in 2019. From the beginning of May until mid-August, Ryu's ERA was a miniscule 1.09. And Walker Buehler's 14–4 record in 2019, his second major-league season, was the best in the National League. Since 2012, the Dodgers also had one of baseball's most reliable closers—Kenley Jansen. In 2017, Jansen had the best year of his career with a 5–0 record, 41 saves, only 1 blown save, and a 1.32 ERA while averaging 14.4 strikeouts per nine innings.

In 2017, the Dodgers had the best record in the majors with 104 wins. They won their division by 11 games, swept their division series, and denied the Cubs the chance at back-to-back championships by beating them easily in the NLCS. And they lost to Houston in seven exciting games in the World Series. The fifth game in Houston was a particularly wild one, won by the Astros, 13–12, on Alex Bregman's 10th-inning walk-off single off Jansen. The World Series loss was a bitter coda to the best year in franchise history since Brooklyn's 1953 Dodgers won 105 games *but* lost the World Series in six games. The coda to the coda was that 2017 was the year for which the Astros were sanctioned for cheating by using electronic means to spy on catchers' signs in their home ball-park, raising legitimate questions about whether the Astros' repeated comebacks in that wild Game Five were legitimately earned.

The Dodgers were back in the World Series the very next year. They got there the hard way, having to win a single-game playoff against Colorado's Rockies for the 2018 division title and requiring all seven games to beat Milwaukee's Brewers in the NLCS. Overmatched in the World Series by Boston's Red Sox—whose 108 wins were 16 more than the LA's 92—the Dodgers lost in five games. The only game they won was an epic 18-inning, 3–2 duel in Game Three.

In 2019, the Dodgers won a franchise-record 106 games to run away with their division. Many looked forward to a World Series rematch with the 107-win Astros to settle bets on which was the best team in baseball. But while Houston got to the Fall Classic, the Dodgers were derailed in their first-round division series by Washington's wild-card Nationals. Kershaw was summoned as a reliever in the 8th inning of the fifth game to protect a 3–1 lead that would send the Dodgers to their fourth league championship series in a row. Instead, he gave up home runs on consecutive pitches to Anthony Rendon and Juan Soto, the first two—and only two—batters he faced. Washington won the game and the pennant in the 10th on a grand slam by Howie Kendrick, the Dodgers' second baseman just three years before, off reliever Joe Kelly—with Kenley Jansen still waiting in the bullpen. They may have been the best team in baseball, but after their unexpectedly early exit from the 2019 postseason, LA's Dodgers were still forced to "wait 'til next year."

When he walked out of Dodger Stadium that day, the great Clayton Kershaw carried with him the enigma of being a merely mortal pitcher in postseason games, which made for a compelling *Wait 'Til Next Year* subplot. In 344 regular-season starts for LA since his rookie year in 2008, Kershaw had a 169–74 record with a 2.45 earned run average while averaging 6⅔ innings and 7.1 strikeouts a start. But in 27 postseason starts, he was 9–11. In the 13 games he started that the Dodgers won, Kershaw was very good—a 2.23 ERA in 84⅔ innings. In the 14 games he started that they lost, he pitched poorly—a 7.35 earned run average in 63⅔ innings. And in the seven games he was called into as a reliever, Kershaw gave up five earned runs in 10 innings. His struggles were most pronounced in the NLCS—a 3–5 record and 4.61 ERA—and the World Series, where he was 1–2 with a 5.40 earned run average.

Back in Brooklyn, Kershaw's perplexing inability to rise to the occasion of being the great pitcher he was—the best of his generation—in the crucible of critical postseason games might have caused some of the very elderly who were kids back in the Boys of Summer days to recall the postseason struggles of Don Newcombe—one of the best pitchers of his generation—in Fall Classics more than 60 years earlier. Newcombe was brilliant in his first World Series start against the Yankees in the opening game of the 1949 World Series until he lost his shutout and the game, 1–0, on a lead-off, last-of-the-ninth homer by Tommy Henrich. In his four World Series starts after that, all against the Yankees, Newk gave up 20 runs in 14 innings. In the opening game of the 1955 World Series—the one Brooklyn finally won—Newcombe was battered for 6 runs in 5⅔ innings and did not pitch in any of the next six games. Clayton Kershaw, for his failures, was not savaged by fans and pundits the way Newcombe was, accused of choking in the biggest games. Part of that was personal against Newcombe at a time when false racist stereotypes of the inadequacy of Black players included their not being able to cope with pressure situations.

When Zack Greinke put himself back on the free-agent market in 2015, the Arizona Diamondbacks had won the NL West just twice in the 13 years since the power-pitching duo of Randy Johnson and Curt Schilling led them to back-to-back division titles in 2001 and 2002. Neither time— in 2007 and 2011—did they make it to the World Series. The most noteworthy D-backs those years were right-hander Brandon Webb, one of baseball's elite pitchers from his rookie year in 2003 to 2008; Stephen Drew, their shortstop from 2006 to 2011; and right fielder Justin Upton, their right fielder from his 19-year-old 2007 rookie season until he was traded in 2013 because he was becoming too expensive to afford. Drew and Upton were the younger brothers of J. D. and B. J. (who later became Melvin Upton Jr.) who preceded them to the majors with other teams. Webb won the Cy Young Award in 2006 with a 16–8 record and was second in the voting the next two years. After his terrific 22–7 season in 2008, however, Webb pitched just once more in the major leagues; on opening day in 2009, he pitched just four innings before leaving the game with a bad shoulder that several subsequent surgeries could not repair well enough to save his career.

Giving Greinke, a 33-year-old pitcher, a six-year, $206.5 million contract in December 2015 for the highest average annual salary ever paid a major-league player signaled the Arizona Diamondbacks' intention to compete with LA, which had just won its third-straight division title, for top of the heap in the NL West, or at least for position in the wild-card race. Although they had not had a winning season since 2011, the D-backs were probably looking to boost their odds for a championship in a perceived window of opportunity lasting only a few more years before their talented core of players in or entering their prime baseball years became too expensive to afford. Foremost among them were power-hitting first baseman Paul Goldschmidt and center fielder AJ Pollock, both eligible for free agency in 2019, and two promising lefties—Patrick Corbin and Robbie Ray—whom the Diamondbacks envisioned as being cornerstone starting pitchers in the years ahead. In addition to bolstering their own pitching staff, the trade had the D-back advantage of separating Greinke from Kershaw in the Dodgers' rotation.

Arizona slid backward in Greinke's first year, losing 93 while he won 13 of 20 decisions. In 2017, the D-backs rebounded to 93 wins, finishing a distant 11 games behind the Dodgers but 7 games ahead of the third-place Rockies to claim the first wild card in a division where the three top teams all made it to the postseason. Greinke won 17, and Ray, 15–5 with a 2.89 ERA and 218 strikeouts in 162 innings, emerged as a star in his own right. Perhaps exhausted from outlasting the Rockies, 11–8, in the wild-card game, the Diamondbacks went down without much trouble to the Dodgers in their division series. In 2018 it was Corbin's turn to shine, his 11–7 record and 246 K's in 200 innings making him the most coveted starting pitcher on the free-agent market once the season ended. For the D-backs, however, 2018 ended in third place with a pedestrian 82–80 record.

Corbin and Pollock both signing elsewhere as free agents in the wake of the 2018 season all but closed the competitive future the Diamondbacks perceived when they signed Greinke three years earlier. Taking stock, Arizona traded Goldschmidt to St. Louis for prospects before he too could leave as a free agent and allowed Pollock, whose career had become defined by injuries as much as achievement, to declare for free agency a year early. In his eight years in Arizona, Goldschmidt was nothing if not consistently very good, averaging 31 homers, 105 runs scored, and 106 driven in per 162 games, while always batting around .300. Pollock signed a four-year, $55 million contract with the Dodgers. At the 2019 July 31 trade deadline, with their record a game under .500, the Diamondbacks traded Greinke to the Astros for prospects. Despite speculation that Robbie Ray would also be traded, he was not. Arizona ended up in second place with 85 wins. That would be 21 games behind LA—now waiting for 2020 it would finally be "next year."

## 19

# NOT THE SAME STEINBRENNER

## The Yankees' Long Road Back to "Forever"

The post-Torre era did not begin with the 2008 Yankees winning the World Series, or getting there, or winning the division, or even making the postseason. The Yankees finished a noncompetitive third. They did, however, set an all-time attendance record of nearly 4.3 million in the House That Ruth Built because 2008 was the last year for the original Yankee Stadium that opened in 1923 and was given a major facelift in 1974–1975. It was also the last year for 39-year-old Mike Mussina, their ace, winning 20 for the first time in his career and then following through on his plans to retire.

The arguable highlight of their 2008 season was Alex Rodriguez still in pinstripes after stunning the baseball world by making public in the middle of Game Four of the Red Sox' World Series sweep in 2007 that he was opting out of the remaining three years of his 10-year, $252 million contract. Perhaps some in the Yankees hierarchy appreciated that A-Rod's announcement upstaged Boston's second World Series championship in four years—during which time, the New Yorkers had none—but they also hustled to bring him back into the fold. Rodriguez, after all, had just blasted 54 homers (giving him 518 for his career), scored 143 runs, and had 156 runs batted in and would soon be honored as the American League MVP for the third time in five years. A-Rod quickly concluded he made a big mistake and blamed his agent, Scott Boras, who then negotiated a new 10-year, $275 million deal so Rodriguez could stay in New York.

Joe Girardi was not fired for his failure to bring the Yankees a championship in his first year as manager. He may have been saved by the transition to the post-Boss era having begun that year because George Steinbrenner's declining health forced him to turn over the day-to-day operations of running baseball's greatest franchise to his sons, Hal and his elder brother, Hank. In November it became official; Hal Steinbrenner was named managing general partner. The Yankees had also been uncharacteristically quiet on the free-agent front in recent years. Other than re-signing some of their own core players who became free agents—most notably, Mariano Rivera and Jorge Posada after the 2007 season—the Yankees had not made a splash by signing another team's star as a free agent since they nabbed Boston's Johnny Damon in 2006. Hal Steinbrenner's inclination was to stay on that course, but failing to make the postseason in 2008 even with A-Rod having another outstanding season made that an impossibility.

And so the Yankees went on a winter spending spree, committing $423 million in multiyear deals to a trio of top-tier free agents—power-hitting first baseman Mark Teixeira, left-handed ace CC Sabathia, and right-hander A. J. Burnett. The attention their arrival for spring training in 2009 should have drawn was quickly overtaken by A-Rod being exposed as having tested positive for steroids in a 2003 test survey of major-league players when he was in the third year of his first megadeal with the Texas Rangers. Henceforth, the slugger, now with 553 homers, to whom the Yankees had lavished such a generous contract extension anticipating that within 10 years he, as a Bronx Bomber, would break Barry Bonds's career record of 762 home runs, tainted because of his dalliance with steroids, was himself tainted. A-Rod was now "A-Fraud." He was also getting older (he was 33), losing mobility in the field, and more prone to injury. He began the season on the disabled list with a hip injury that cost him more than a month of the season.

The Yankees' spending spree paid immediate dividends. Teixeira led the team with 39 homers and 122 RBIs; Sabathia led the league with 19 wins; Burnett won 13; after his return to action, Rodriguez hit 30 homers and drove in 100 runs. And representing the old guard dating back to the Yankees' 1996 championship season, 35-year-old Derek Jeter had his best year since the turn of the millennium, with his fourth 200-hit season in five years, 30 stolen bases in 35 attempts, .334 batting average, and .406 on-base percentage; 39-year-old Mariano Rivera saved 44 games; and 37-year-old Andy Pettitte won 14. The Yankees won their division by eight games over arch-rival Boston. Their 103 wins were seven more than any other team in the majors. And they won the 40th pennant and 27th World Series in franchise history, allowing Girardi to up his uniform number "27"—since that goal was met—for "28" to indicate that his next objective was winning a 28th World Series for the forever dynasty.

Girardi managed the Yankees for eight more years without ever getting to change his number to "29." That 28th championship has proved hard to come by. It wasn't that Girardi didn't have very good teams. The Yankees won 95, 97, and 95 games the next three years, earning the wild card in 2010 and winning the division each of the next two years. They made it to the league championship series in 2010 and 2012 before being given their exit papers by Texas and Detroit. In 2010 they improved their offense by trading for Tigers' center fielder Curtis Granderson. In 2011 they signed free-agent catcher Russell Martin as a defensive improvement over 39-year-old Posada, who did not take kindly to be relegated to designated hitter. And in 2012 they signed Dodgers free agent Hiroki Kuroda to fortify their starting rotation, despite his being 37 years old with 15 years of wear on his right arm, including 11 in Japan. Granderson had back-to-back 40-homer seasons in 2011 and 2012 and led the league in runs and RBIs in 2011.

The next four years, from 2013 to 2016, the Yankees did not once finish first in the AL East. In January 2013, Alex Rodriguez was again exposed for using performance-enhancing drugs. In August, just as he was making his way back from a debilitating hip injury that had sidelined him all year, he was handed a 162-game suspension, which he at first contested while playing out the season in August and September. The Yankees finished tied for third in the AL East. A-Rod missed the entire 2014 season after finally deciding to accept his yearlong suspension rather than continue a fool's errand by challenging his punishment. Seven other teams had better records in the American League than the second-place (in the East) Yankees. Back in uniform in 2015, but at 39 with a chronically debilitated hip no longer able to play third base, A-Rod led the Yankees with 33 homers and 86 RBIs as their DH. They lost the wild-card game to the upstart Houston Astros, then plummeted to fourth in the AL East in 2016, their worst finish in 23 years.

It wasn't that they were not competitive. They were just not good enough in a strong division. And they were old. Every year from 2011 through 2016, the Yankees had the highest average age of position players in the major leagues. And until 2015, the age of nearly all their core starters and relievers was above the major-league average. Posada retired after the 2011 season. Rivera, now 42, missed nearly all of 2012 after blowing out his knee shagging fly balls before a game in early May. Jeter was increasingly criticized for his diminishing defensive skills at shortstop and refusal to change positions, as did Hall of Fame shortstops Robin Yount, when he was 29, and Cal Ripken, when he was 36. After batting .316 with a league-leading 216 hits at the age of 38 in 2012, Jeter broke his ankle in the opening game of the ALCS and played only 17 games the next year. Rivera retired after his 44 saves in 2013 brought his career total to 652; 41-year-old Pettitte, who resuscitated his reputation after he too was exposed in December 2007 as having used performance-enhancing drugs by admitting it was true and apologizing, also retired after 2013, his 219 wins as a Yankee the third-most in franchise history; and Jeter, still unwilling to play anywhere on the field other than short-stop, retired with 3,465 career hits—sixth all-time in the major leagues— after batting .256 in 2014.

Posada, Pettitte, Rivera, and Jeter—the "Core Four"—were the last links to Joe Torre's 1996–2001 Yankees that went to five World Series in six years and won four. As cornerstone homegrown Yankees, they were a departure from George Steinbrenner's history of prioritizing signing or trading for established stars to headline the Yankees. But the Yankees had gone back to old ways after 2001. Since then, second baseman Robinson Cano, outfielder Brett Gardner, and hard-throwing relievers David Robertson and Dellin Betances were the only Yankees to rise through their farm system and have sustained success in the Bronx. Once Jeter retired, Gardner and Betances were the only core players in pinstripes signed by the Yankees and groomed in their minor-league system. Chris Headley had replaced A-Rod at third, Didi Gregorius took over for Jeter at short, and first Brian Roberts and then Stephen Drew replaced Cano at second after he left as a free agent in 2014. All came to the Yankees from other teams, as did Andrew Miller, who replaced departed free agent Robertson as closer in 2015, and 2016 closer Aroldis Chapman.

In 2007, the Yankees debuted a homegrown trio of young top-ranked pitching prospects—Joba Chamberlain, Phil Hughes, and Ian Kennedy, all right-handers—they were counting on to be the foundation for their starting rotation in the future. Bedeviled by injuries, none lived up to the Yankees' expectations. Hughes had the most success as a Yankee, winning 18 and making the All-Star team in 2010 and winning 16 games in 2012, before leaving as a free agent in 2014. Kennedy, who made only 12 starts for New York, had the most successful career, making 277 starts for teams other than the Yankees, including a 21–4 record for Arizona in 2011. Treated gingerly when called up in August 2007—Torre was ordered to pitch him out of the bullpen according to specified "Joba Rules" on how and when to use him—Chamberlain, appearing in 19 games and allowing just one earned run in 24 innings, became a cautionary tale of a young pitcher whose immediate success made him a fan favorite ill-equipped to deal with such adulation. Failing to make the grade as either a starter or reliever, and undermining his career by problem drinking and not staying in shape, the Yankees let him go in 2013.

Contrary to his dad's proclivity to be a spendthrift on expensive established players in pursuit of his annual mandate that the Yankees win the World Series, Hal Steinbrenner wanted to take the franchise in the direction of fiscal restraint. The Yankees led the American League in player salaries every year, and the majors nearly every year, from 1999 to 2015. They were the only franchise to consistently pay the "luxury tax" penalty for exceeding the player-payroll threshold of Major League Baseball's competitive balance tax, which the Yankees had done every year since 2003. And for all that, the Yankees had been to just two World Series—in 2003 and 2009—with just one championship to show for their extravagant payroll. The Yankees were looking forward to off-loading in 2016 and 2017 the hefty contracts given to Teixeira and Sabathia in 2009, and especially the albatross of the 10-year deal they gave A-Rod that would come to an end in 2017.

Indicative of the new direction Hal was taking the franchise, the Yankees were not willing to entertain a new 10-year deal worth over $300 million that Robinson Cano was insisting on to stay in New York after 2013, his free-agent walk year. Cano was the Yankees' best player from 2009 to 2013, virtually the equal of Miguel Cabrera in value for best player in the major leagues, based on wins above replacement. He was arguably the best at his position in Yankees history, whose second basemen included Hall of Famers Tony Lazzeri and Joe Gordon. But Cano was now 30, and even if he were to remain an elite player for another five years, Hal was not inclined to commit to an elite salary for him as he approached 40. The Yankees refused to get into a bidding war for Cano after he declared for free agency. Cano did not get $300 million. But he did get a 10-year deal for over $228 million from the Mariners, and so left New York for Seattle in 2014.

The Yankees not signing their own best player turned out to be more about the number of years Cano was demanding and addressing weaknesses elsewhere on the ballclub than an ironclad commitment to new-found austerity. Despite Hal Steinbrenner's reluctance, unlike his dad, to sign players to extravagant contracts—Russell Martin and Hiroki Kuroda had been their only significant free-agent acquisitions since Teixeira, Sabathia, and Burnett in 2009—the Yankees dived deep into the free-agent market once again after ending the 2013 season with their fewest wins in a full season (85) in 21 years. This time they committed $438 million in multiyear contracts to Red Sox star center fielder Jacoby Ellsbury, following in the footsteps of Johnny Damon by jumping Boston for New York; Japanese ace Masahiro Tanaka, who went undefeated in 24 decisions with a 1.27 earned run average in Japan in 2013; veteran Brian McCann to fill the hole at catcher after Martin left as a free agent in 2012; and veteran outfielder Carlos Beltran. These were the New York Yankees, after all, and while the Boss was now watching from an executive suite on baseball's Mount Olympus, the Yankees still approached every year with his mandate, "Win the World Series."

With the exception of Tanaka—13–5 in 20 starts—none lived up to expectations in 2014. The Yankees failed to make the postseason for a second straight year. Tanaka would be a stalwart in the Yankees' rotation for the rest of the decade despite assorted arm problems that raised persistent concerns he would need Tommy John surgery. And if the Yankees came to regret the A-Rod contract, they would soon come to rue the $153 million, seven-year deal they gave Ellsbury. Indisputably a dynamic player with the Red Sox, Ellsbury had a history of being oft-injured that continued with the Yankees. In 2015 it was a knee; in 2017 a concussion; in 2018 an oblique injury and hip surgery. He missed all of 2019 with a foot injury. Ellsbury played in only 520 of the Yankees' 972 regular-season games those years. Even when healthy, Ellsbury's level of performance was not close to what it was in Boston. The Yankees released

Ellsbury in November 2019, paying him the remaining $26.3 million on his contract to not play baseball.

The Yankees went into 2016 with Hal Steinbrenner wanting to rebuild a championship team through their farm system, as was done in the 1990s. Falling quickly out of contention, the Yankees traded their top two relievers—Miller and Chapman—to contending ballclubs in return for top-tier minor-league prospects. They also ramped up the pressure on Alex Rodriguez to gracefully retire. He missed three weeks in May. He had only eight home runs and was batting just .220 at the All-Star break. By the end of July, A-Rod was no longer the regular DH. In early August, Hal Steinbrenner informed him he would not play in any more games— either that year or the next. The Yankees paid him the remainder of his contract for 2016 and 2017 and allowed him the dignity of two last games in Boston and his career finale at Yankee Stadium on August 12. A-Rod went 1 for 4 in his last major-league game.

Alex Rodriguez retired with 696 home runs, fourth on the all-time list. He was 18 homers shy of Babe Ruth's 714. When Rodriguez and George Steinbrenner agreed to his 10-year, $275 million deal in 2007, it included a provision for $6 million bonuses for passing Mays (which he did with his seventh home run of 2015), Ruth, and Aaron, and $12 million for tying and passing Bonds. A-Rod and the Boss had every expectation he would do so amid much hoopla—and a commercial bonanza for the franchise—with each milestone. Even though Rodriguez wanted to go for 67 more homers and the all-time record, Hal Steinbrenner was no longer interested in any hoopla for A-Rod eclipsing Ruth. The Babe was a Yankee icon; Rodriguez's dalliances with steroids made him still, to many, A-Fraud.

As his team struggled through 2016, Hal was counting on young prospects like right-hander Luis Severino, catcher Gary Sanchez, and slugging outfielder Aaron Judge working their way through the Yankees' farm system to the Bronx. Severino had gone 5–3 with a 2.89 earned run average in 2015 after being called up in August, started the 2016 season in the starting rotation, was sent back to the minors in May after going 0–6 with a 7.46 ERA in his first six starts, and returned to the Bronx in late July. Sanchez, called up in early August, went on a home-run tear, hitting 20 in 48 games. Along the way he set a major-league record for the most home runs (19) in his first 50 games. Judge, brought to Yankee

Stadium in mid-August, had a less auspicious start to his career, striking out in half of his 84 at-bats while hitting four homers.

The next generation of homegrown Yankees did indeed lead the team back to contention in 2017. Weighing in at about 280 pounds of muscle, the 6-foot-7, solidly built Judge had a monster rookie year. Although he struck out 208 times in 542 at-bats, Judge hit 52 home runs to crush Mark McGwire's rookie-record of 49 set thirty years earlier. Sanchez belted 33 homers. Severino was 14–6 in 31 starts, striking out 10.7 batters per nine innings. Veterans Tanaka and Sabathia, whose 300 pounds on his 6-foot-6 frame were becoming too much for his plant leg to bear on his follow-through, stabilized the starting rotation. And, as part of the hybrid approach adopted by Hal Steinbrenner and general manager Brian Cashman to build from within but acquire an expensive impact player that could make an immediate difference in any given year, the Yankees brought free agent Aroldis Chapman back to be their closer. The five-year, $86 million contract they gave Chapman was the biggest ever given to a reliever.

Finishing two games behind Boston in the AL East, their 91 wins good enough for a wild-card berth, the 2017 Yankees came their closest to getting back to the World Series since 2009. They lost to the Astros in the ALCS in seven games, winning all three at Yankee Stadium but losing all four in Houston. That loss became particularly bitter two years later after Major League Baseball's investigation confirmed that the 2017 Astros had used video technology in their ballpark to steal opposing catchers' signs. Given that the Yankees came within a game of playing in the World Series in what was widely thought to be a rebuilding year, Cashman's decision to end Joe Girardi's tenure after 10 years managing the Yankees was a stunning development.

Girardi's managerial style was the problem. He was criticized for being overly rigid in his dugout decisions and too intense in his player relationships. There were also times Girardi seemed disengaged, including when he did *not* ask for a video review in the Yankees' Game Two loss in their division series to contest the plate umpire's call that a Cleveland batter had been hit by a pitch (when a review would have shown he was not), after which the next batter hit a grand slam. It didn't matter that Girardi admitted, "I screwed up," that the Yankees stormed back to win the division series and nearly upended the favored Astros in the ALCS. Girardi was told he had lost the players' allegiance. His was a failure to relate to the Yankees' rising young stars. If Girardi was originally hired as the anti-Torre, the Yankees were now looking for an anti-Girardi—someone less intense and more engaged with his players. That new manager would be Aaron Boone—the same whose walk-off, 11th-inning home run in Game Seven of the 2003 ALCS sent the Yankees to the World Series.

Boone had never managed or even coached at any level in professional baseball. After retiring as a player in 2010, he became a baseball analyst for ESPN. But in his first year as a manager, the Yankees won 100 games and were back in the postseason. They had to settle for the wild card, however, because division rival Boston, also led by a first-year manager, Alex Cora, was indisputably the best team in baseball with 108 wins. If the Yankees needed any reminder of that, 'twas the Red Sox that ousted them in their division series. The 2018 Yankees were fortified by another pair of hot-shot prospects having outstanding rookie years—second baseman Gleyber Torres, for whom they traded Chapman to the Cubs during the lost-cause 2016 season, and third baseman Miguel Andujar. Judge, sidelined with a broken wrist for all of August and half of September, was one of four Yankees to hit 27 home runs. A fifth—Giancarlo Stanton, whose 13-year, $325 million megadeal signed with the Marlins in 2015 still had $295 million remaining when the Yankees traded for him before the season—led the club with 38. Stanton was the 2018 Yankees' big impact-player acquisition to backstop their increasingly home-grown team.

There was widespread expectation that the Yankees, in their bid to get past Boston and Houston to be the American League team to beat, would dive deeply into the most anticipated free-agent market in years after the 2018 season. There was Nationals outfielder Bryce Harper—at 26, looking for a contract of at least 10 years and $400 million—a superstar in name and reputation since his rookie year in 2012, even if his career had not quite lived up to consistent superstar performance. Adding Harper to a lineup that already included Judge and Stanton would have given the Yankees a "Murderers' Row" of three elite power-hitters. And there was infielder Manny Machado, another 26-year-old superstar in name and performance, whom the Yankees knew well from his seven years with Baltimore in the AL East. Machado, a shortstop in 2018, was considered a particularly likely free agent for the Yankees to woo because Didi Gregorius, their shortstop, had just had Tommy John surgery. Moreover,

Machado's string of at least four straight years with 33 or more homers would fit right into the Yankees' power-driven offense. The free-agent market also included two top-tier pitchers—Arizona's Patrick Corbin and Houston's Dallas Keuchel, both southpaws—either of whom could have added quality depth to the Yankees' starting rotation, the weakest part of their game.

Contrary to the spirit of George Steinbrenner, Hal's Yankees did not sign any of them. The Yankees, their mandate of winning the World Series still the same, were exercising fiscal restraint. In 2018 they got below baseball's competitive-balance "luxury tax" threshold for the first time since 2002, and even though the Yankees were willing to cross back over the line in 2019, Hal Steinbrenner was determined they not pay a substantially higher "tax" rate by exceeding the salary-threshold of $206 million by more than 10 percent. Instead of high-profile impact players, the Yankees bolstered their club with cheaper alternatives. They brought back three of their own on the free-agent market—starting pitchers Sabathia and J. A. Happ and reliever Zack Britton; signed Rockies second baseman DJ LeMahieu and hard-throwing reliever Adam Ottavino as free agents; gave center fielder Aaron Hicks a seven-year contract extension and Luis Severino, 19–8 in 2018, a four-year extension, both for an undervalued $10 million per year; and traded for 30-year-old Seattle southpaw James Paxton, whose talent was undeniable but undermined by a history of injuries.

Not committing hundreds of millions to the top free agents of 2018 proved a wise noninvestment. The Yankees won their division by seven games over Tampa Bay and 19 over Boston. Their 103 wins were third in the majors behind the Astros' 107 and Dodgers' 106. And they did it despite a major-league-record 30 players spending extensive time on the injured list. Sanchez started in just 101 games. Hicks missed three months, and Judge was out for two. Stanton played only 18 games, third baseman Miguel Andujar just 12, and first baseman Greg Bird was out for the year less than three weeks into the season. Severino, sidelined by assorted injuries almost immediately after signing his new contract, made only three starts late in the season. Dellin Betances was out of action the entire season until mid-September, then injured his Achilles tendon in his first game back. Gleyber Torres, Brett Gardner, and LeMahieu, signed to be a player off the bench capable of playing anywhere in the infield on any given day, were the only core position players to avoid (for the most part) being sidelined by injury, and infield reserves Gio Urshela and Luke Voit proved indispensable filling in for Andujar and Bird.

Despite the long absences of Judge, Stanton, and Sanchez, the 2019 Yankees led the majors in scoring while rocketing 306 home runs—39 more than their record-setting 267 the year before, but one less than the 307 by Minnesota's 2019 Twins. Until losing 7–0 to Texas on September 2, the Yankees had gone 220 consecutive games (dating back to June 30, 2018) without being shut out—the longest stretch of scoring at least one run every game since the Ruth and Gehrig Yankees did so in 308 straight between 1931 and 1933. The Yankees' only weakness was their starting rotation—especially after Severino was lost for the year before the season even began. Their two best starters were Paxton, 15–6, and Domingo German, 18–4, before he was suspended for domestic violence late in the season and thus ineligible for the postseason. Both missed close to a month with injuries. Neither was counted among the best pitchers in the league based on pitching wins above replacement. Along with Tanaka, Happ, and Sabathia, they gave the Yankees a reliable, better-than-average starting rotation (at least in the American League). But they were no match for the elite starting rotation of Houston's Astros led by Justin Verlander and Gerrit Cole, which became even better when they added Zack Greinke at the trade deadline.

Rather than go after Patrick Corbin in the 2018 free-agent market to strengthen their rotation, the Yankees put their faith in assembling an intimidating, indomitable tag team of relievers—Tommy Kahnle, Chad Green, Ottavino, and Britton—to call upon as early as the sixth inning to shut down the opposition until it was Aroldis Chapman closing time. And that didn't include the injured Betances, whose strikeout ratio the two previous years was higher than Chapman's. Their implicit gamble that bullpen depth in power-relievers, whose price tags were less than top-tier starting pitchers, could substitute for a *good-enough* starting rotation paid off in the regular season, perhaps only because the Yankees had such a potent offense.

But most games in the regular season are not against elite starting pitchers. Not so in the postseason, and the Yankees' significantly weaker starting rotation proved a liability against the Astros in the ALCS. Not so much because they gave up more runs—the Yankees starters' ERA in their six-game series loss was marginally lower than Houston's terrific threesome—but because they didn't work as deep into games, forcing the

Yankees to go to their overworked bullpen earlier than they would have liked.

Lesson learned the hard way, arguably for the third year in a row that the Yankees' starting rotation was outclassed by their postseason opponents, the Yankees went all-out to sign the best starting pitcher on the 2019 free-agent market—none other than Houston ace Gerrit Cole. They gave the 29-year-old right-hander a nine-year deal worth $324 million. It was the largest contract ever given to a pitcher. For Hal Steinbrenner and the Yankees, it was all about being the best team in baseball in 2020— with the most potent offense, with the best bullpen, and now with an elite starting pitcher to lead an otherwise reputable rotation. It was about winning the 2020 World Series . . . and returning the Yankees back to being the "forever" dynasty.

# EPILOGUE

## Baseball in the Year of Coronavirus

**B**aseball's expected story lines for 2020 began with the question of whether Houston's Astros, just months after their video-based, bang-the-can, sign-stealing scheme during their 2017 championship season was exposed, might find redemption by remaining a dominant team without the cheating. Seventy-year-old veteran manager Dusty Baker, one of the most respected no-nonsense people in baseball, was recruited to restore credibility to the franchise while guiding a genuinely great team toward another chance at a World Series championship—one that would not have the stigma of having cheated to get there. Jose Altuve, Alex Bregman, Carlos Correa, and George Springer were, after all, legitimately outstanding players. Their starting-pitching depth, however, had been undermined by Gerrit Cole signing as a free agent with the Yankees, leaving the Astros with just two top-tier aces—Justin Verlander and Zack Greinke, both in their mid-30s—rather than three.

Besides signaling that the Yankees were back to their big-spending ways, signing Cole, the most coveted player on the 2019 free-agent market, was also presumed to have vaulted New York's Yankees ahead of Houston as the most likely American League team to play in the 2020 World Series. That the Yankees were not undisputed favorites to win the 2020 World Series was only because the Dodgers, having won seven division titles in a row, were considered by many to be the best all-around team in baseball. And they got even better by matching the Yankees' acquisition of Cole with a trade for Boston's superstar outfielder Mookie Betts to join a potent lineup that already included Cody Bellinger, Justin Turner, and Max Muncy and getting left-hander David Price, a top-tier starting pitcher, as part of the deal to bolster a rotation that already had Clayton Kershaw, Walker Buehler, and top-rookie prospect Dustin May.

As for the four other powerhouse teams since the mid-2010s, the Red Sox' chances for getting back ahead of the Yankees in 2020 had already been dealt successive blows by the Yankees' signing of Cole and manager Alex Cora having to step aside because of his role as bench coach in the Astros' sign-stealing scandal two years earlier. The minor-league prospects Boston got in return for trading the too-expensive-to-keep Betts and Price were not even the best in the Dodgers' farm system. The Indians and Cubs were thought likely to shed high-priced stars—in Cleveland, Francisco Lindor; in Chicago, Kris Bryant and Anthony Rizzo, both of whom would be free agents after the season—for top prospects if either club looked to be out of contention by the end-of-July trade deadline. And Washington, which won the 2019 World Series as a wild-card team, was a bit of a wild card looking ahead to 2020. Even with rising superstar Juan Soto and a premier starting rotation fronted by Max Scherzer, Stephen Strasburg, and Patrick Corbin, there was no certainty the Nationals were a better ballclub in their division than the Atlanta Braves, especially having lost Anthony Rendon, their best position player, as a free agent.

How those story lines would unfold, however, had to wait. All 30 major-league teams were to take the field on opening day. The date—March 26—would have been the earliest opening day in major league history. Instead, opening day would not be for another four months. The longest Major League Baseball had gone without scheduled games being played was three and a half months, including the lost postseason, because of the 1994–1995 strike; the two-month players' strike in 1981; and the final month of the 1918 season (with the World Series moved to the beginning of September) because of World War I. The reason in 2020 was contagion. Specifically, COVID-19, a virulent coronavirus pandemic sweeping the world that in early March became a health crisis in the United States.

On March 12, as spring training was winding down, Major League Baseball announced that the start of the season would be delayed. Because the pandemic had yet to spread far and wide across America, everyone hoped it would very quickly be brought under control by social distancing and an economic pause to reduce people's risk of exposure. That didn't happen. As the pandemic spread, COVID-19 cases soared, and the death toll rose exponentially, the start of the season was put on hold indefinitely. Baseball was not possible with COVID-19 running rampant throughout the country because the coronavirus fed off people being together. Containment—"flattening the curve," in epidemiological parlance—required people *not* be together, certainly not in any numbers at ballparks around the country. It quickly became obvious that televised games played without fans in the stands was the only way to salvage the season. Superagent Scott Boras, in a *New York Times* op-ed in May, wrote that "while initially the fans won't be there in person," televised games "can give fans a unifying feeling . . . something to live vicariously through and a reason to cheer."

Notwithstanding that sentiment, however, an agreement between Major League Baseball and the players union to "discuss in good faith the economic feasibility of playing games in the absence of spectators" became a point of contention. Claiming that 40 percent of Major League Baseball's revenues—estimated at about $11 billion in 2019—was from ballpark attendance, the owners insisted that the only way to play a season under COVID-19 circumstances was for players to accept a pay cut. By that, they did not mean prorating players' contractual salaries according to however many games were ultimately played in 2020. "The industry isn't very profitable, to be honest," said one owner. The players disputed that very premise on the grounds that teams would still reap substantial revenue from broadcast rights and even more from baseball's lucrative postseason television deals—especially if the postseason was expanded to include more teams, an option the players were willing to negotiate. The union asked Major League Baseball to substantiate its claims of financial duress with documentation. None was forthcoming.

All this was occurring against the backdrop of pending negotiations in 2021 for baseball's next collective-bargaining agreement. The fact that in the 2018–2019 offseason the free-agent market was slow to develop for even top-tier players—Bryce Harper, Manny Machado, and closer Craig Kimbrel were still unsigned at the start of spring training in 2019 despite their status as elite major-leaguers—and for the second year in a row other experienced veterans were forced to accept undervalued contracts or were not signed at all, convinced the players that teams were exploiting the terms of the existing agreement to suppress player salaries. It didn't matter that the top free agents in 2019, including Cole, Strasburg, and Rendon, didn't have to wait very long to be signed to high-priced contracts; the union was preparing for a nasty fight to get an agreement more to the players' liking. Even before the COVID-19 crisis, players were warning—as they had in 1993 and 1994—that they might go on strike during the 2021 season if Major League Baseball did not negotiate in good faith. They weren't bluffing then. And they were serious now that franchise owners not be allowed to use the pandemic to gain concessions from the union they could use as leverage in the 2021 negotiations.

Finally, on June 23, with the two sides still at an impasse about the money, the commissioner announced the season would begin on July 23, preceded by three weeks of a second spring training—in July—which quickly became called "summer camp." Teams would play a 60-game schedule, with players receiving prorated pay based on their contract. There would be no fans at the ballparks. Every team would play only within its division. Interleague games would be only between teams in corresponding divisions. Because the minor-league season was canceled, teams were allowed a pool of 60 "active" players to feed the major-league roster. An extensive set of health, player-practice, and game protocols was put in place to minimize the risk of exposure to the coronavirus. Players and staff were to be frequently tested for COVID-19.

Everyone understood the pandemic could lay waste to the best-laid plans. Coincidentally, not in a good way, Major League Baseball's announcement about playing an abbreviated schedule came just as COVID-19 cases, after having plateaued at a lower level for most of May and June, began skyrocketing to new record highs. Nearly three dozen players had tested positive for COVID-19 before even arriving at their team's "summer camp" on July 3. And a handful of players, most notable among them David Price and the Giants' Buster Posey, opted out of playing in 2020. "We're trying to bring baseball back during a pandemic that's killed 130,000 people," said Washington Nationals reliever Sean Doolittle, putting it into perspective for players, owners, and fans alike. "We're way worse off as a country than we were in March when we shut this thing down."

On the day the season began on July 23, 2020, Major League Baseball and the players union agreed to an expanded postseason that would include eight of the 15 clubs in each league—those finishing first and second in their division and the two other teams with the best record. There would be no single-elimination wild-card games. Instead, the post-season would begin with every postseason-qualifying team participating in a three-game "wild-card series," four in each league preceding the division-series round, with the better-seeded team being the home-team for all three games. The Dodgers also announced they had reached agree-ment with Mookie Betts on a 12-year $365 million contract extension beginning in 2021.

But for all the hosannas about baseball being played—in empty sta-diums, with an acoustical accompaniment of the buzz of the crowd and cheering, and a visual backdrop in many ballparks of cardboard cutouts of fans strategically placed in the stands—the coronavirus pandemic had not only not abated; it was getting worse. The Canadian government an-nounced that because the breadth and severity of the pandemic in the United States would require all teams coming from the United States to quarantine for 14 days, no major-league games could be played in Toron-to, leaving the Blue Jays to scramble for a non-Canada home, which turned out to be Buffalo. And before their matchup in the first game of the 2020 season, the Yankees announced that closer Aroldis Chapman and infielder DJ LeMahieu, and the Nationals that budding-superstar out-fielder Juan Soto would not be playing, at least at the beginning, because they had tested positive for COVID-19.

It got worse. Just four days later, half of the Miami Marlins' players had tested positive for the coronavirus during their opening series in Philadelphia. Neither team played the following week, their would-be opponents scrambling to play other teams. By the next weekend, players on the St. Louis Cardinals came down with COVID-19, putting them and the Milwaukee Brewers out of action. Even as the U.S. government's coordinator for the health crisis was warning about the pandemic being far more widespread than in the spring, Commissioner Rob Manfred insisted that, while "we have had to be fluid," the situation "is manage-able." David Price said that he had opted out of the season because players' health wasn't being put first; "I can see that hasn't changed." The 2020 major-league season was on life support, baseball taking it day by day.

It helped that Major League Baseball decided after the season finally got under way that both games in any doubleheaders were set for seven innings. When the Cardinals returned to the field on August 15 after not having played since July 29, they had played just five games while most teams had played at least 18 and 13 had already played one-third of their 60-game schedule. The Cardinals were faced with playing 53 games in the remaining 44 days of the season, including 11 doubleheaders with just two off days, to complete a season that, for them, would be 58 games instead of 60. In the end, a 2020 major-league season was played in defiance of the COVID-19 pandemic before zero fans in the stands; which was better than no fans in the stands with games *not* being played, which was what happened—because of the war over free agency—to the final 52 days of the scheduled 1994 season and the first three weeks of the scheduled 1995 season.

How did it end? With "Next Year" in the Hollywood sequel to Brooklyn's Boys of Summer finally coming to Los Angeles in 2020. Mookie Betts lived up to expectations; he was the best position player in baseball, according to the wins above replacement metric. With Betts batting mostly leadoff, not only did the Dodgers prove themselves indisputably the best team in baseball with a 43-17 record—eight major-league teams had a better record than the fifth-best Yankees in the American League, and disgraced Houston barely made the wild-card round with a losing record—but LA's .717 winning percentage had them on a pace over a full season to match the 116 wins of Chicago's 1906 Cubs and Seattle's 2001 Mariners for most in a full major-league season. Their longest losing streak of the season was two games, four times. Of course, because of COVID-19, they only played 37 percent of a full major-league season. That didn't matter to the Dodgers. They swept through their wild card and division series, overcame a three-games-to-one deficit to beat Atlanta in the NLCS, and finally, after 32 years, emerged as baseball's World Series champions. And for the record, COVID victims Soto and LeMahieu won their respective league's batting title.

# QUOTES AND NOTES

## CLEVELAND'S RUNAWAY CENTRAL TRAIN

Cleveland GM John Hart quote that signing promising young players early in their careers "is the only way a small-market club like ours can survive." (Peter Pascarelli, "Baseball Report," *The Sporting News*, April 26, 1993.) (p. 29)

## THE BOTTOM 25 PERCENT

Keeping his team "perennially competitive" was Mark Attanasio's cornerstone pledge when he bought Milwaukee's last-in-the-NL-Central Brewers from the Selig family in 2005. (Attanasio bio in Milwaukee Brewers' Front Office Directory, https://mlb.com/brewers, 2020.) (p. 58)

Attanasio complaint about the overwhelming financial advantages had by big-market teams. (Tyler Kepner, "Owner Goes All In on the Brewers," *New York Times*, September 30, 2011.) (p. 59)

"Smaller payroll teams are less disadvantaged in an evidence-based environment," said Minnesota's chief of baseball operations Derek Falvey. (Adam Platt, "Fifteen Years after 'Moneyball,' the Twins Are Finally Embracing Analytics—Their Way," https://www.minnpost.com/twin-cities-business/2018/04/fifteen-years-after-moneyball-twins-are-finally-embracing-analytics-the/, April 6, 2018.) (p. 62)

## WILD-CARD WORLD SERIES

"It's not by any means what you're looking forward to doing," their
general manager said. "But we have our marching orders." (Murray Chass, "Everybody Must Go! Marlins Are Liquidating," *New York Times*, November 12, 1997.) (p. 67)

Jack McKeon, described by Florida's GM as a "resurrection specialist" based on turning around losing clubs in his two previous managerial stints. (Charlie Nobles, "McKeon Replaces Torborg," *New York Times*, May 12, 2003.) (p. 72)

## YANKEES "APOCALYPSE NOW" BECOMES RED SOX RESURRECTION

Boston media called attention to Vaughn's 240 pounds and asserted
that star first baseman just wanted "Mo Money." (Howard Bryant, *Shut Out: A Story of Race and Baseball in Boston*, 2002.) (p. 98)

"I don't believe this whole injury aspect of it," Torre told his team.
(Joe Torre and Tom Verducci, *The Yankee Years*, 2009.) (p. 105)

Johnny Damon called himself and his teammates "idiots." But "we
have something to prove," he elaborated. ("Just Call Them the Boston Idiots," http://www.espn.com/espn/wire/_/section/mlb/id/1896493, October 6, 2004.) (pp. 107–108)

"Corporate Joe," some players called him derisively. (Bob Klapisch
and Paul Sulotaroff, *Inside the Empire: The True Power behind the New York Yankees*, 2019.) (p. 110)

Joe Girardi fired by the Marlins for not being "a good fit." (Clark
Spencer, "Beinfest: Girardi 'Was Not a Good Fit,'" *Miami Herald*, October 3, 2006.) (p. 110)

## METS MELTDOWNS

Saberhagen set off firecrackers and sprayed bleach at reporters in
separate incidents as a "practical joke," he said. (Brian Jaramillo, "Mets' Coleman Faces Felony over Explosion Near Fans," *Los Angeles Times*, August 4, 1993.) (p. 112)

Mets general manager Joe McIlvaine quoted later by *Newsday* as saying he had told "somebody" that "one of them is going to be really
good, one of them is going to get hurt, and one of them is going to
underachieve." (Steven Marcus, "Rise and Fall of Generation K a
Cautionary Tale for Mets' Talented Young Arms," *Newsday*, July
21, 2015.) (pp. 112–113)

The intensity of Mets fans' feelings about the Braves inflamed by
Atlanta closer John Rocker acting like "a one-man psycho circus"
at Shea Stadium. (Jeff Pearlman, "At Full Blast Shooting Outrageously from the Lip, Braves Closer John Rocker Bangs Away at
His Favorite Targets: The Mets, Their Fans, Their City, and Just
About Everyone in It," *Sports Illustrated*, December 27, 1999.) (p.
115)

## BASEBALL BACK IN WASHINGTON

John Middleton, the Phillies' billionaire owner, told *USA Today* in
November 2018 that "we're going . . . to spend money, and maybe
even be a little bit stupid about it." (Bob Nightengale, "Phillies
Will Spend Big Bucks in Free Agency," *USA Today*, November
16, 2018.) (p. 140)

## BREAKING THROUGH IN THE AL EAST

Davey Johnson resigned over irreconcilable differences—"your apparent lack of regard for my management skills," he wrote in his
letter of resignation—with team owner Peter Angelos. Said Angelos in reply: "It would clearly be in the best interests of the Orioles
organization for a change of field manager for 1998." (Murray
Chass, "Johnson, the AL Manager of the Year, Resigns from Orioles," *New York Times*, November 6, 1997.) (p. 159)

*Forbes* business magazine was not shy about calling Tampa Bay "the
most horrific baseball franchise of the modern era." ("MLB Valua-
tions," https://www.forbes.com/forbes/2004/0426/066tab_30.html,
April 26, 2004.) (p. 160)

## GIANTS AND RED SOX ROLLER-COASTER DYNASTIES

"The San Francisco Giants Are Now a Dynasty," proclaimed the data-based website *FiveThirtyEight*. (Chadwick Matlin, "World Series Game 7 Live Blog," https://fivethirtyeight.com/live-blog/world-series-game-7-live-blog/, October 29, 2014.) (p. 167)

Madison Bumgarner intoned, "Like they've been saying, this is a dynasty." ("World Series Dynasty," https://www.nytimes.com/2014/10/30/sports/baseball/madison-bumgarner-sf-giants-world-series-2014-rises-to-the-moment-and-jaws-drop.html, October 30, 2014.) (p. 167)

Tyler Kepner asked a provocative question: "Are they really a dynasty?" (Tyler Kepner, "Unconventional Dynasty in the Making," *New York Times*, October 29, 2014.) (p. 167)

Torre had to ask the Yankees' brain trust, "Do you want me to manage?" (Joe Torre and Tom Verducci, *The Yankee Years*, 2009.) (p. 175)

## METS MELTDOWNS: THE SUPERHEROES HUBRIS EPISODES

"I let my heart get in the way of my gut," his manager [Terry Collins] said afterward. (Scott Davis, "Mets Manager Terry Collins Explains His Decision to Leave Matt Harvey in the Ninth Inning of the World Series," *Business Insider*, November 2, 2015.) (p. 187)

The Mets' general manager [Sandy Alderson] raised the prospect that Syndergaard was trying "to show us he was fine" by throwing as hard as he could. (James Wagner, "Mets' Noah Syndergaard Out Indefinitely with Torn Muscle in Torso," *New York Times*, May 1, 2017.) (p. 189)

## CUBS' CLIMATE CHANGE IN CHICAGO; DROUGHTS CONTINUE ELSEWHERE

Theo Epstein's concern that the Cubs didn't have "the same intensity, focus, hunger, ability to overcome adversity." (Tyler Kepner, "The

Cubs Hope to Recapture the Magic of 2016," *New York Times*, March 1, 2020.) (p. 199)

Rumors that Bryant or Rizzo would be traded elsewhere for a "bounty of prospects." (Matthew Schmidt, "ESPN Analyst Predicts the Cubs Will Trade Anthony Rizzo," https://clutchpoints.com/cubs-news-espn-analyst-predicts-chicago-will-trade-anthony-rizzo/, December 20, 2019.) (p. 199)

## HOUSTON'S CHEATSKATES

Manager Bob Melvin of division-rival Oakland said that playing in Minute Maid Park was "like you're going into the Pentagon or Langley." (Tyler Kepner, "The Astros Got Caught. Can the A's Finally Catch Them?" *New York Times*, February 28, 2020.) (p. 209)

Carlos Correa admitted, "Yes, I used trash cans," but says Jose Altuve "didn't use it [the trash can] at all." (Chandler Rome, "Carlos Correa's Fiery Interview in Defense of Teammates," *Houston Chronicle*, February 15, 2020.) (p. 210)

"You did not earn it," said Judge. (Tyler Kepner, "Judge Has a Big Problem with Houston," *New York Times*, February 19, 2020.) (p. 212)

Oakland willing to "bust the bank" for a championship. (Tyler Kepner, "$36 Million Deal Puts Spin on Athletics' 'Moneyball,'" *New York Times*, February 13, 2012.) (p. 214)

## NOT THE SAME STEINBRENNER

It didn't matter that Girardi admitted, "I screwed up." (Billy Witz, "Joe Girardi, upon Review, Offers a Rare Mea Culpa: 'I Screwed Up,'" *New York Times*, October 7, 2017.) (p. 236)

## BASEBALL IN THE YEAR OF CORONAVIRUS

Superagent Scott Boras, in a *New York Times* op-ed ("We Have to Bring Baseball Back," May 5, 2020), wrote that "while initially the fans won't be there in person," televised games "can give fans a unifying feeling." (p. 243)

"The industry isn't very profitable, to be honest," said one owner [the Cardinals' Bill DeWitt Jr.]. (James Wagner, "Tell Us When and Where: A 50-Game Season Seems Certain," *New York Times*, June 15, 2020.) (p. 243)

"We're trying to bring baseball back during a pandemic that's killed 130,000 people," said Washington Nationals reliever Sean Doolittle. (James Dougherty, "Sean Doolittle Sees Sports as a Reward America Hasn't Earned Yet," *Washington Post*, July 5, 2020.) (p. 244)

Manfred insisted the situation "is manageable" [and] Price saying players' health wasn't being put first. (James Wagner, "Commissioner's Optimistic Tone Fails to Reassure the Players," *New York Times*, August 3, 2020.) (p. 245)

# BIBLIOGRAPHY

## STATISTICAL SOURCES

This book relies on the indispensable website https://www.baseball-reference.com for player and team statistics. The site includes multiple data aggregations, including batter and pitcher splits, game logs, complete play-by-play, player transactions and salaries, and teams' player payrolls. This book also uses the site's version of wins above replacement (WAR), an advanced metric that measures the totality of a player's contributions in terms of how many additional wins that player contributed to his team over what a replacement player from the highest minor-league level would have contributed instead.

## RECOMMENDED READING

### Documents

Levin, Richard C., George J. Mitchell, Paul A. Volcker, and George F. Will. *The Report of the Independent Members of the Commissioner's Blue Ribbon Panel on Baseball Economics.* July 2000. (http://roadsidephotos.sabr.org/baseball/2000blueribbonreport.pdf)

Major League Baseball. *Major League Baseball Update to the Report of the Independent Members of the Commissioner's Blue Ribbon Panel on Baseball Economics.* December 2001. (http://roadsidephotos.sabr.org/baseball/BRPanelupd.htm)

———. *Official Press Release Announcing 2020 Regular Season.* June 23, 2020. (https://www.mlb.com/press-release/press-release-mlb-announces-2020-regular-season?t=mlb-press-releases)

Manfred, Robert D., Jr. *Statement of the Commissioner (re Houston Astros Decision).* January 13, 2020. (https://img.mlbstatic.com/mlb-images/image/upload/mlb/cglrhmlrwwbkacty

2717.pdf)

## Books

Appel, Martin. *Pinstripe Empire: The New York Yankees from before the Babe to after the Boss*. New York: Bloomsbury, 2012.

Armour, Mark L., and Daniel R. Levitt. *In Pursuit of Pennants: Baseball Operations from Deadball to Moneyball*. Lincoln: University of Nebraska Press, 2018.

Bissinger, Buzz. *Three Nights in August: Strategy, Heartbreak, and Joy inside the Mind of a Manager*. New York: Houghton Mifflin, 2005.

Bradbury, J. C. *The Baseball Economist: The Real Game Exposed*. New York: Plume, 2007.

Bryant, Howard. *Juicing the Game: Drugs, Power, and the Fight for the Soul of Major League Baseball*. New York: Plume, 2006.

———. *Shut Out: A Story of Race and Baseball in Boston*. Boston: Beacon Press, 2002.

Canseco, Jose. *Juiced: Wild Times, Rampant 'Roids, Smash Hits, and How Baseball Got Big*. New York: Regan Books, 2005.

Fainaru-Wada, Mark, and Lance Williams. *Game of Shadows: Barry Bonds, BALCO, and the Steroids Scandal That Rocked Professional Sports*. New York: Gotham Books, 2006.

Feinstein, John. *Living on the Black: Two Pitchers, Two Teams, One Season*. New York: Back Bay Books, 2008.

Foster, George, Norm O'Reilly, and Antonio Davila. *Sports Business Management: Decision Making around the Globe*. New York: Routledge, 2016.

Francona, Terry, and Dan Shaughnessy. *Francona: The Red Sox Years*. New York: Mariner Books, 2014.

Jaffe, Chris. *Evaluating Baseball's Managers: A History and Analysis of Performance in the Major Leagues, 1876–2008*. Jefferson, NC: McFarland, 2010.

Keri, Jonah. *The Extra 2 Percent: How Wall Street Strategies Took a Major League Baseball Team from Worst to First*. New York: Ballantine Books, 2011.

———. *Up, Up, & Away: The Kid, The Hawk, Rock, Vladi, Pedro, Le Grand Orange, Youppi!, The Crazy Business of Baseball, & the Ill-Fated But Unforgettable Montreal Expos*. Toronto: Vintage Canada, 2014.

Klapisch, Bob, and Paul Sulotaroff. *Inside the Empire: The True Power behind the New York Yankees*. New York: Houghton Mifflin Harcourt, 2019.

Knight, Molly. *The Best Team Money Can Buy: The Los Angeles Dodgers' Wild Struggle to Build a Baseball Powerhouse*. New York: Simon & Schuster, 2015.

Lewis, Michael. *Moneyball: The Art of Winning an Unfair Game*. New York: W. W. Norton, 2003.

Madden, Bill. *Steinbrenner: The Last Lion of Baseball*. New York: Harper, 2010.

O'Connor, Ian. *The Captain: The Journey of Derek Jeter*. Boston: Mariner Books, 2012.

Olney, Buster. *The Last Night of the Yankee Dynasty: The Game, the Team, and the Cost of Greatness*. New York: Ecco, 2005.

Pessah, Jon. *The Game: Inside the Secret World of Major League Baseball's Power Brokers*. New York: Back Bay Books, 2015.

Schiavone, Michael. *The Dodgers: 60 Years in Los Angeles*. New York: Ports Publishing, 2018.

Torre, Joe, and Tom Verducci. *The Yankee Years*. New York: Anchor Books, 2009.

Verducci, Tom. *The Cubs Way: The Zen of Building the Best Team in Baseball and Breaking the Curse*. New York: Crown Archetype, 2017.

## Selected Publications Articles

*Forbes (https://www.forbes.com)*

Kaplan, Ari. "Chris Sale Seals Contract after Sealing World Series." March 25, 2019.
Solomon, Brian. "$2 Billion Dodgers Sale Tops List of Most Expensive Sports Team Purchases Ever." March 29, 2012.

*Sporting News (https://www.sportingnews.com)*

Fagan, Ryan. "What If: With Mark Prior and Kerry Wood, Cubs Fans Still Wonder What Might Have Been." May 25, 2019.
"High Hopes: The Mets Place Their Future in the Arms of Bill Pulsipher, Paul Wilson, and Jason Isringhausen." *The Sporting News 1996 Baseball Yearbook*, April 1996.
Rodgers, Joe. "Buck Showalter Explains Why Zach Britton Didn't Pitch in O's Wild Card Loss." October 5, 2016.

*Sports Illustrated (https://www.si.com)*

Chen, Albert. "The Colorado Rockies and Coors Field: A Tale of Struggles, Homers, and Acceptance." July 13, 2017.
Corcoran, Cliff. "Johan Santana's Career Threatened by Reoccurrence of Shoulder Tear." March 28, 2013.
Heyman, Jon. "Daniels' Strong Winter Pays Off as Rangers Get Back to ALCS." October 5, 2011.
Pearlman, Jeff. "A Nifty Pickup—Signing Free-Agent Rafael Palmeiro." July 19, 1999.
———. "At Full Blast Shooting Outrageously from the Lip, Braves Closer John Rocker Bangs Away at His Favorite Targets: The Mets, Their Fans, Their City, and Just About Everyone in It." December 27, 1999.
Tayler, Jon. "Derek Jeter's Reported Plan to Slash Payroll Is a Cruel Twist to Suffering Marlins Fans." September 4, 2017.
———. "John Farrell Ran Out of Time under the Current Red Sox Regime." October 11, 2017.
———. "Yankees Splurge for Aroldis Chapman in Deal That Carries Real Risk." December 8, 2016.
Taylor, Phil. "No-no Regrets: Johan Santana Would Not Alter a Thing. Terry Collins Might." June 1, 2015.
Verducci, Tom. "The Best Infield Ever? Four Amazing Mets." September 6, 1999.
———. "Careers That Began with Great Expectations Suddenly Turned Sour for Three Young Guns of the New York Mets—Jason Isringhausen, Bill Pulsipher and Paul Wilson." May 19, 1997.
———. "How Tiny Tim [Lincecum] Became a Pitching Giant." July 7, 2008.
———. "MLB to Mandate That Baseballs Are Stored in Air-Conditioned Room for 2018." February 23, 2018.
———. "Powerball: Alex Rodriguez Hit the Jackpot." December 18, 2000.
———. "Totally Juiced: Confessions of a Former MVP." June 3, 2002.

## Other Selected Articles

Dempsey, John. "Murdoch's Dodgers Sell for $400 Million." *Variety*, October 12, 2003.
Katz, Jesse. "Escape from Cuba: Yasiel Puig's Untold Journey to the Dodgers." *Los Angeles Magazine*, April 14, 2014.
Rosenthal, Ken, and Evan Drellich. "The Astros Stole Signs Electronically in 2017—Part of a Much Broader Issue for Major League Baseball." *The Athletic*, November 12, 2019.

Wojciechowski, Gene. "Kiss Him [Sammy Sosa] Goodbye." *ESPN the Magazine*, February 28, 2005.
Zimbalist, Andrew. "A Miami Fish Story." *New York Times Magazine*, October 18, 1998.

## Newspapers

The following newspapers were consulted in researching this book:

*Baltimore Sun* (https://www.baltimoresun.com)
*Boston Globe* (https://www.bostonglobe.com)
*Boston Herald* (https://www.bostonherald.com)
*Chicago Tribune* (https://www.chicagotribune.com)
*Dallas Morning News* (https://www.dallasnews.com)
*Houston Chronicle* (https://www.chron.com)
[Minneapolis] *Star Tribune* (https://www.startribune.com)
*Los Angeles Times* (https://www.latimes.com)
*New York Daily News* (https://www.nydailynews.com)
[New York] *Newsday* (https://www.newsday.com)
*New York Post* (https://www.nypost.com)
*New York Times* (https://www.nytimes.com)
*Philadelphia Inquirer* (https://www.inquirer.com)
*Pittsburgh Post-Gazette* (https://www.post-gazette.com)
*San Francisco Chronicle* (https://www.sfchronicle.com)
*Seattle Times* (https://www.seattletimes.com)
*South Florida Sun Sentinel* (https://www.sun-sentinel.com)
*St. Louis Post-Dispatch* (https://www.stltoday.com)
*USA Today* (https://www.usatadoy.com)
*Wall Street Journal* (https://www.wsj.com)
*Washington Post* (https://www.washingtonpost.com)

## Selected Newspaper Articles

### New York Daily News

Madden, Bill. "Yankees' Joba Chamberlain Only Has Himself to Blame for Potentially Career-Ending Injury." March 24, 2012.
O'Connor, Ian. "Clueless Joe: Torre Has No Idea What He's Getting Into." November 3, 1995.

### New York Times

Chass, Murray. "Big-Spending Marlins Lure Alou to Florida." December 13, 1996.
———. "A Family Circle Breaks: Murdoch Owns Dodgers." March 20, 1998.
Crouse, Karen. "No Surprise That Don Mattingly and Dodgers Parted Ways." October 22, 2015.
Curry, Jack. "Kent and Bonds: Close in the Order, but Always Distant." July 15, 2007.
———. "Steinbrenner's Money Can't Buy Clemens's Love." December 14, 1996.
Futterman, Matthew. "What's Behind the Recent Spate of Comebacks." May 31, 2020.
Kepner, Tyler. "$36 Million Deal Puts Spin on Athletics' 'Moneyball.'" February 13, 2012.
———. "After a Flurry of Deals, Zack Greinke Still Stands Alone." March 5, 2019.
———. "The Astros Got Caught. Can the A's Finally Catch Them?" February 28, 2020.
———. "The Astros Took a Long Strange Trip from Worst to First to Disgrace." January 19, 2020.

———. "Baseball's Nightmare: One Team, 14 Infections." July 28, 2020.
———. "Brewers New GM Looks to Change Story Line." September 26, 2015.
———. "Cardinals Morph into the Cardinals." September 11, 2018.
———. "Games Postponed after Two Cardinals Players Test Positive for Coronavirus." August 1, 2020.
———. "Judge Has a Big Problem with Houston." February 19, 2020.
———. "Milwaukee Brewers Emerge as a Contender, Ahead of Schedule." July 7, 2017.
———. "Owner Goes All in on the Brewers." September 30, 2011.
———. "Rays Win a Wild-Card Matchup of Overachievers." October 3, 2019.
———. "Uncertainty as Far as the Eye Can See." June 29, 2020.
———. "Unconventional Dynasty in the Making." October 29, 2014.
———. "What Could Stop the Season? For One Thing, Money." April 19, 2020.
Kepner, Tyler, and David Waldstein. "Yankees Chose Aaron Boone to Be Their Next Manager." December 1, 2017.
Kovaleski, Serge F., and David Waldstein. "Madoff Had Wide Role in Mets' Finances." February 1, 2011.
Powell, Michael. "Astros Crossed the Line from Quaint Con to High-Tech High Crime." January 15, 2020.
Sandomir, Richard, and Ken Belson. "Mets Agree to Settle Madoff Suit for $162 Million." March 19, 2012.
Schachter, Jim. "O'Malley to Murdoch to Chance." August 5, 2007.
Schmidt, Michael S., and David Waldstein. "Baseball Gave $25 Million Lifeline to Mets." February 25, 2011.
Wagner, James. "Alex Rodriguez to Retire and Join Yankees as an Adviser." August 7, 2016.
———. "Baseball Is Showing Some Early Optimism. How Long Can It Last?" July 5, 2020.
———. "The Boss's Son Preferred Horses to Players: 'Horses Don't Talk Back.'" April 15, 2020.
———. "Manfred Signals Tough Line on Cheating." November 20, 2019.
Waldstein, David. "Betts Deal Tests Plan, and Will of Fans." February 6, 2020.
Witz, Billy. "Joe Girardi, upon Review, Offers a Rare Mea Culpa: 'I Screwed Up.'" October 7, 2017.

## Washington Post

Boswell, Thomas. "Stephen Strasburg Shutdown Debate Masks the Washington Nationals' True Story." August 14, 2012.
Heath, Thomas. "Lerner Adds to Two Investors to Group." April 21, 2006.
Kilgore, Adam. "David Ortiz's Origin Story with the Red Sox." November 18, 2015.
———. "Stephen Strasburg Shut Down for the Season." September 8, 2012.

## Other Newspaper Articles

Fainaru-Wada, Mark, and Lance Williams. "What Bonds Told Grand Jury." *San Francisco Chronicle*, December 3, 2004.
Greenstein, Teddy. "Don't Be Fooled by the Sammy Sosa on Your TV Screen." *Chicago Tribune*, May 3, 2019.
Hohler, Bob. "Inside the Collapse of the 2011 Red Sox." *Boston Globe*, October 11, 2011.
Kosman, Josh. "Mets Owners Take $40M Loan." *New York Post*, December 13, 2011.
Kubatko, Roch. "Calling His Own Number, Ripken Ends the Streak." *Baltimore Sun*, September 21, 1998.
Lauber, Scott. "2008 World Series Game 5, and All the Rain That Delayed the Phillies' Reign: An Oral History." *Philadelphia Inquirer*, August 3, 2018.
Marcus, Steven. "Rise and Fall of Generation K a Cautionary Tale for Mets' Talented Young Arms." *Newsday*, July 21, 2015.

Mastrodonato, Jason. "Latest Chris Sale Injury Casts a Dark Cloud over Red Sox Future." *Boston Herald*, August 17, 2019.

Orwall, Bruce. "Murdoch Agrees to Sell Dodgers Baseball Team." *Wall Street Journal*, October 13, 2003.

Rome, Chandler. "Carlos Correa's Fiery Interview in Defense of Teammates." *Houston Chronicle*, February 15, 2020.

Strauss, Joe. "Pujols Signs with Angels: 10 Years, $254 Million." *St. Louis Post-Dispatch*, December 8, 2011.

## Blogs

### Bleacher Report (http://bleacherreport.com)

Chancey, Asher. "Joe Torre Steps Down from the Dodgers: 10 Reasons It All Fell Apart in 2010." September 17, 2010.

Levy, Dan. "Are the SF Giants a Dynasty? Only If We Redefine the Term." October 30, 2014.

Nielsen, Cody. "Got Young Pitching? Keep Them Away from Dusty Baker!" March 23, 2010.

Rymer, Zachary D. "Andrew Friedman's Baseball Genius, Dodgers Resources Are Dangerous MLB Marriage." October 14, 2014.

### Business Insider (https://www.businessinsider.com)

Gaines, Cork. "Carl Crawford's $142 Million Contract Has Been a Complete Disaster." March 8, 2016.

———. "The New York Mets May Finally Be Getting Out from under the Bernie Madoff Scandal." August 23, 2015.

### Fivethirtyeight (https://fivethirtyeight.com)

Paine, Neil. "Remember Those 2003 Tigers? This Year's Team Might Be Even Worse." August 23, 2019.

———. "There's a Dynasty at Stake for the Giants." October 29, 2014.

———. "The Strange Dynasty of the San Francisco Giants Is Over. (Yes, It Was a Dynasty)." May 21, 2019.

Silver, Nate. "Send Alex Gordon!" October 30, 2014.

## Other Blog Articles

Bodig, Chris. "Davey Johnson's Managerial Career and Cooperstown Credentials." Cooperstown Cred, December 2, 2018. https://www.cooperstowncred.com/davey-johnsons-managerial-career-and-cooperstown-credentials.

Borden, Craig. "Things Were Worse in 2004." Jays Journal, June 26, 2017. https://jaysjournal.com/2017/06/26/blue-jays-fan-notice-things-worse-2004.

Maahs, Adam. "An Analysis of Pitch Movement at Coors." FanGraphs, January 11, 2019. https://community.fangraphs.com/an-analysis-of-pitch-movement-at-coors-field.

Miller, Randy. "Yankees Paying Luxury Tax Again: How It Could Affect Hal Steinbrenner's Spending Moving Forward." nj.com, November 12, 2019. https://www.nj.com/yankees/2019/11/yankees-paying-luxury-tax-again-what-it-means.html.

Polinsky, Jay. "The 'What If?' Machine: The Bobby Abreu Trade." The Good Phight, January 26, 2015. https://www.thegoodphight.com/2015/1/26/7877313/the-what-if-machine-the-bobby-abreu-trade.

## Other Websites

https://www.ballparksofbaseball.com

https://baseball-almanac.com

https://www.baseball-reference.com (including the Society for American Baseball Research "Bio Project" and "Team Ownership Histories Project")

https://www.mlbplayers.com (website of Major League Baseball Players Association, including "MLBPA History")

https://www.mlbtraderumors.com (includes average annual salaries of free agents signed since 2014.)

# INDEX

# ABOUT THE AUTHOR

**Bryan Soderholm-Difatte** is the author of *The Golden Era of Major League Baseball: A Time of Transition and Integration* (2015), *America's Game: A History of Major League Baseball through World War II* (2018), *Tumultuous Times in America's Game: From Jackie Robinson's Breakthrough to the War over Free Agency* (2019), and *The Reshaping of America's Game: Major League Baseball since the Players' Strike* (2021).